HTML5 GAME DEVELOPMENT
from the Ground Up with
CONSTRUCT 2

HTML5 GAME DEVELOPMENT
from the Ground Up with
CONSTRUCT 2

Roberto Dillon

CRC Press
Taylor & Francis Group
Boca Raton London New York

CRC Press is an imprint of the
Taylor & Francis Group, an **informa** business

CRC Press
Taylor & Francis Group
6000 Broken Sound Parkway NW, Suite 300
Boca Raton, FL 33487-2742

© 2014 by Taylor & Francis Group, LLC
CRC Press is an imprint of Taylor & Francis Group, an Informa business

No claim to original U.S. Government works

Printed on acid-free paper
Version Date: 20131104

International Standard Book Number-13: 978-1-4822-1661-5 (Paperback)

Library of Congress Cataloging-in-Publication Data

Dillon, Roberto.
  HTML5 game development from the ground up with Construct 2 / Roberto Dillon.
    pages cm
  Includes bibliographical references and index.
  ISBN 978-1-4822-1661-5 (pbk.)
    1. Computer games--Programming. 2. HTML (Document markup language) 3. Internet games--Design. 4. Construct 2. I. Title.

  QA76.76.C672D534 2014
  794.8'1536--dc23   2013042302

Visit the Taylor & Francis Web site at
http://www.taylorandfrancis.com

and the CRC Press Web site at
http://www.crcpress.com

To my Students

Contents

Foreword

Scirra started out life several years ago as a loosely organized band of volunteer students working in our spare time around full-time courses. We were fairly casual and a little chaotic in getting the first (and rather flawed) iteration of our software, Construct Classic, off the ground. Sometimes there were periods of neglect when exams and other concerns came up, but we always returned to it. We really loved it solving the technical problems, working with the community, and slowly gaining recognition. Years later, through a complete ground-up rewrite and release of the successor, Construct 2, I find myself sitting in our office in the outskirts of London and making a living from it all! Passion and persistence can get you a long way, even from the most humble of beginnings.

I won't go into Construct 2 itself, since this book by Prof. Dillon will teach you a great deal about that. However, I will add a word about technology in general. I think technology is amazing. You can buy consumer graphics processors that have thousands of cores, using billions of individual transistors. Most of the computers in the world are connected together and can communicate in real time via the Internet. Phones are now computers with apps that you carry everywhere with you, and tablets are a whole new type of device. There are, of course, even more exciting technologies, and there are surely more innovations to come that we cannot even anticipate. When it comes though, as ever, software will be the glue that connects all of it together.

Traditionally software development has been a complicated endeavor requiring expertise to combine exciting technologies in interesting ways. One of our aims with Construct 2 is to help people get involved in this fascinating, fast-paced world. It's designed to considerably lower the barrier of entry, while remaining a productive and useful tool. We hope that even without much experience you can come up with something exciting that combines graphics processors, Internet communication, phones, tablets, and more—all made possible by a whole stack of technology, right down to the individual transistors.

If you are using Construct 2 and ever experience the delight of seeing something working the way you wanted it, or feel curious to find out how something works and are compelled to learn more, or just awe at how much is working together to make it all possible, then we have succeeded. If you are young, or have never really been involved in technology, and Construct 2 is your first inspiration on a longer path of involvement in technology (just as other technologies fascinated us when we were young), then it truly is a privilege to have provided that for you. Just remember that with your persistance and Construct 2, you can create great games!

Ashley Gullen
Director, Scirra Ltd.
London, September 2013

Preface

The exponential growth in sales of smart phones and tablets, together with more widespread and faster Internet connections worldwide, has made playing video games more popular than ever before. Internet-enabled personal computers and mobile device sales worldwide are fast approaching 1 billion units, and research data show that a significant portion of time spent online is dedicated to playing games. It's no wonder then that game development is attracting more and more attention, as a hobby as well as a possible career, where even small teams, relying exclusively on online platforms, can find success.

In an industry that was dominated until recently by big blockbusters sold at retail and developed by teams of 100+ professionals with budgets topping $100 million or even more, this may look like a dramatic and totally unexpected revolution. In reality, it can also be seen as a resurgence of the original spirit that characterized the early days of the gaming industry: in the 1980s, in fact, the relative simplicity of 8-bit computers allowed for the emergence of the so-called "bedroom coders," young students and teenagers who, through their passion and commitment, managed to find success in a market that started as a niche but soon expanded in ways that were truly unimaginable.

As the market became more demanding and complex, though, so did the underlying technology. Consequently, more resources, more time, and bigger teams were needed to develop successful titles. Today, instead, we are witnessing a new generation of technology that sidestepped raw power and complexity for convenience and ease of use. The new tools that are now available are so advanced and yet so intuitive that they enable anyone to develop commercially viable products. We can actually say that the time for the "bedroom coders" is back!

This book is written for this new generation of hobbyists and aspiring game developers who realized that exciting things can actually be done with the right tools and knowledge. Indeed, there's a plethora of new and very good manuals available already covering all possible game engines and middleware, but, still, the book you are currently holding aims at being a little different, and I'm very glad it found a place on your shelf.

Not only will it teach you how to use a modern tool, in this case Construct 2, an HTML5-based game engine that will enable you to develop and release polished two-dimensional games on a multitude of different platforms, but it will also cover a foundational knowledge of game analysis and design based on my personal research on the subject. This more theoretical part will be covered in the exact same way I have been successfully teaching it in specialized classes across different institutions, including DigiPen Institute of Technology and James Cook University.

It is my hope that the first part of this book will help you in understanding what really matters in games and contribute to making you a better game designer from the ground up, able to play any game critically and to express your ideas in a clear and concise format. The practical chapters that follow from Chapter 5 onward are structured through step-by-step tutorials. There, we will build an arcade-style game, a platformer integrating some physics elements, and then a more complex puzzle game, remaking my own game *Turky on the Run*, published on Apple App Store and on BlackBerry World.

Lastly, the book will discuss different ways to deploy and monetize games across several platforms, including Facebook, iOS, Android, web-based marketplaces, and more. A couple of appendices are also included to provide some additional resources you may want to investigate as you progress in your journey as an independent ("indie") game developer.

Get ready to work hard and play harder!

Roberto Dillon
Singapore
September 6, 2013

Acknowledgments

I'm grateful to all editorial staff at CRC Press for believing in this project, in particular to Mr. Rick Adams and Ms. Jennifer Ahringer, and to Ms. Carmen Tropeano for her invaluable feedback on the different tutorials. Special thanks also to my family for providing constant support and encouragement. Last but not least, I'm also very grateful to the guys at Scirra for making Construct 2 such a fantastic tool!

About the Author

Roberto Dillon was born in Genoa, Italy, and holds a Master's and a Ph.D. degree in Electrical and Computer Engineering from the University of Genoa.

Over the years he has worked in prestigious academic institutions across Europe and Asia, including the Kungliga Tekniska Högskolan (Royal Institute of Technology, KTH) in Stockholm, Nanyang Technical University (NTU) in Singapore, and the DigiPen Institute of Technology in Singapore.

While at DigiPen, he served as an Assistant Professor and Game Design Department Chair, teaching a variety of subjects like Game Mechanics and Game History, with his students gaining top honors at competitions like the Independent Games Festival (IGF) both in San Francisco and Shanghai.

He is now an Associate Professor at the Singapore campus of James Cook University, where he teaches game design and project management subjects to both undergraduate and graduate students.

As a game developer, Roberto has led high-profile research projects on innovative game mechanics and has designed indie games that were showcased by the international press and at events like Sense of Wonder Night in Tokyo, Electronic Language International Festival (FILE) Games in Rio de Janeiro, and the Indie Showcase at Casual Connect Asia.

Besides *HTML5 Game Development from the Ground Up with Construct 2*, Roberto wrote two other books: *On the Way to Fun* and *The Golden Age of Video Games*, published by A K Peters and CRC Press.

About the Book

This book covers game design and development in a manner suitable for beginners, hobbyists, and aspiring indie developers. No specific programming knowledge is required, although familiarity with very basic concepts (e.g., what is a variable, an array, or a function) is assumed.

The practical chapters are based on Construct 2, an HTML5-based game engine that runs under Windows. Note that Construct 2 is an ever-evolving engine with new versions being released very often. To make the book as "future proof" as possible, the tutorials have been carefully designed around stable and proven features that shouldn't change significantly in upcoming versions of the software. But remember that these were developed and tested up to the latest stable and beta releases available at the moment of writing, and specific implementations may have to be tweaked and modified in the future. The underlying game design concepts discussed here, though, will not be affected by any change in software and should help you in building a solid foundation in game design and development regardless of the actual tools used later in production.

Sample Construct 2 project files for the games designed in this book can be found on the author's website, http://programandplay.com.

CHAPTER 1

HTML5 and Construct 2

E VEN THOUGH HTML5 IS a relative newcomer to the world of game
development, it already managed to capture lots of interest among
both big companies and young startups alike, thanks to the promise of
delivering a straightforward experience common to all web-based devices.
In other words, HTML5 aims at building a new Internet where installing
plugins would be redundant and where relatively advanced multimedia
features would be natively supported by the browser itself.

For example, thanks to the new <canvas> tag, it is actually possible to
define an area where we can start drawing and manipulating images right
into the webpage on the fly through JavaScript. A simple script like the following would set up a canvas covering a 200 × 100 pixel area, frame it with
a 1 pixel wide black border, and then fill its upper half with a red rectangle.

```
<html><body>
<canvas id = "myCanvas" width = "200" height = "100" style =
"border:1px solid #000000;"> </canvas>
<script>
var c = document.getElementById("myCanvas");
var ctx = c.getContext("2d"); //getContext("2d") is an HTML5 object
with many predefined properties and methods for drawing rectangles,
circles, images, text, etc.
ctx.fillStyle = "#FF0000"; //we will fill our rectangle in red
ctx.fillRect(0,0,200,50); //drawing a filled rectangle. 0,0 is the
top right corner of the canvas
</script>
</body> </html>
```

Despite these ambitious and exciting premises, though, after an initial announcement in 2008 by the W3C,* actual development started only in 2011, and support by the different browsers wasn't as fast as many developers hoped. Indeed, performance across devices and browsers is not really consistent yet, and several features are supported only by specific browsers on specific platforms. Luckily, the situation is improving steadily on a daily basis (see Figure 1.1).

Today we can finally say that HTML5 is getting advanced enough to offer the kind of capabilities needed by the game industry, thanks also to an effective integration of the JavaScript-based Web graphics library (WebGL) application programming interface (API) to provide two- and three-dimensional graphics and effects.

As HTML5 matures, the reasons it could be a major revolution for online games become more and more apparent: games can be shared simply as links and can be run instantly without the need for any installation. Players don't need to download specific plugins, while developers don't have to wait for approval by the different app stores. In addition, when there is a new version, users won't need to explicitly update anything because the browser will automatically download the latest version. Offline support is also possible, making HTML5 an extremely flexible, and potentially very successful, approach to casual game development.

All that glitters is not gold, though, and actual game performance in browsers is often lacking, making complex HTML5 games in practice much less feasible and appealing than native games on most devices.

Wouldn't it be great, then, if we could have the flexibility of HTML5, the capability of converting our games to native apps when needed, and a very user-friendly environment, suitable even for nontechnical people? This is where Construct 2 by Scirra comes into the picture. Writing games in HTML5 involves dealing with HTML, CSS3, and JavaScript, but all these can be circumvented by using Scirra's tool, which adopts a very visual approach to game development. In addition, third-party tools are available to wrap the final HTML5 game that Construct builds to turn it into an iOS or Android game with performance close to that of a native app, for example. This is what we are going to explore in the rest of this book, so let's get acquainted with our tool of choice.

---

* The World Wide Web Consortium (W3C) is the main international standards organization for the World Wide Web.

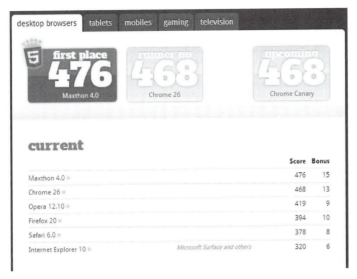

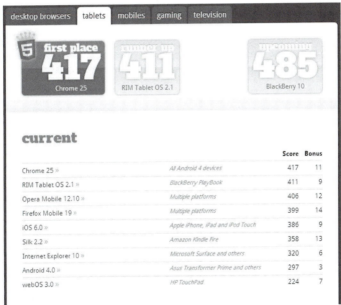

FIGURE 1.1 Pointing your browser to http://html5test.com/ will show exactly what HTML5 features it is supporting. Here we have the results for different desktop browsers, for tablets, for mobile devices, and also for a new possible gaming frontier: smart TVs. The maximum possible score, i.e., score for a browser where everything is supported, is 500. (*Continued*)

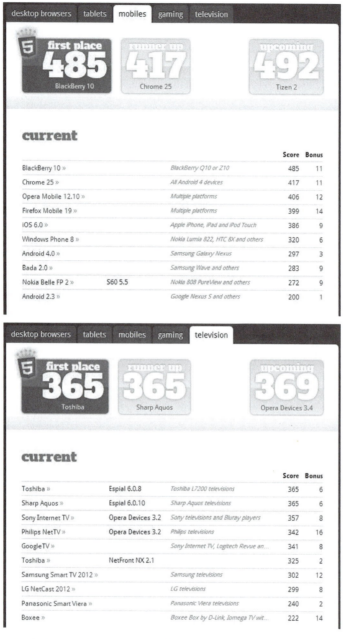

FIGURE 1.1 (*Continued*) Pointing your browser to http://html5test.com/ will show exactly what HTML5 features it is supporting. Here we have the results for different desktop browsers, for tablets, for mobile devices, and also for a new possible gaming frontier: smart TVs. The maximum possible score, i.e., score for a browser where everything is supported, is 500.

Construct 2 comes with three different licenses. First, a free license with no time limit is available. This is the first thing you should get if you haven't done so already. Go to www.scirra.com, click on "download," get the latest stable release, and install it.

The free version has some important limitations you should be aware of, though. Your projects are limited to 100 events,* and the ability to export to platforms such as iOS and Android is disabled, as well as other features. In order to enable these features, use over 100 events, and have the option of releasing projects commercially, you will need the "Personal Edition" license. This license is the perfect choice for indie and aspiring developers. If the revenue from Construct creations exceeds $5000 or you are buying licenses for a company, then you will need the "Business Edition" license.

Let's now have a first look at our game engine of choice. Once launched, it greets you with the screen shown in Figure 1.2.

Open one of the provided examples, like Space Blaster, and you will see a screen like Figure 1.3 in front of you.

The working area is divided into three main sections. Note that all tabs and windows can be dragged and moved around to a configuration that suits your working style, but throughout the book we will be using the standard layout configuration for simplicity's sake. The first thing that will likely capture our attention is the main window at the center of the screen. This is where we define a **layout** for our game (i.e., a level or playing area, a splash screen, etc.), and where we place and manipulate the different objects that will make up our game.

The column on the left instead is where we can check for specific properties of any object in the game as well as for the project itself. Try clicking on any sprite, for example, on one of the spaceships displayed on the left side of the layout, to select it (Figure 1.4): its properties will be displayed on the left side panel ready to be analyzed and eventually modified.

The section on the right instead shows the project files and structure, with an additional tab named **Layers** that we will discuss later (see Section 6.1 and Figure 6.5). There is also a list of all the objects available in the current layout (Figure 1.5).

---

* With the exception of the last, more complex, game, all examples in this book will be encapsulated within 100 events to allow you to experiment with the free version as much as possible. When specific features requiring the "Personal Edition" license are used, these will be pointed out clearly in the text.

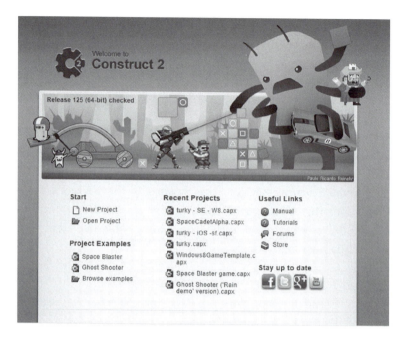

FIGURE 1.2   Launching Construct 2 provides us with options for loading recent projects, starting new ones, and checking the manual pages and other tutorials.

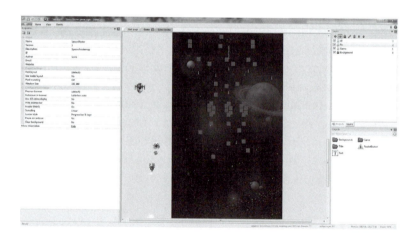

FIGURE 1.3   *Space Blaster*: a sample project we can use to familiarize ourselves with the development environment.

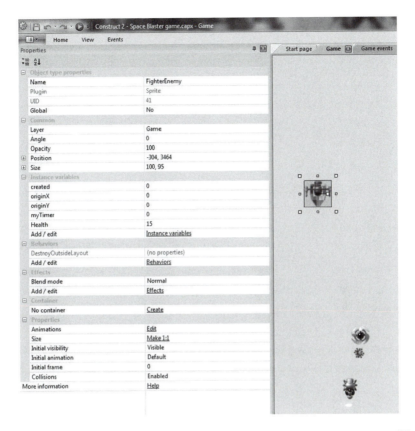

FIGURE 1.4 Select the player's sprite by clicking on it, and its properties will be displayed on the column on the left.

You may have also noticed that on top of the main layout view there are a few tabs: **Start page** (which brings us back to Figure 1.2), **Game** (the name of our current layout), and **Game events** (the programming sheet currently associated with the game layout).

Clicking on the latter changes the display to the **Game events** sheet (Figure 1.6).

All actual programming takes place in this tab, and Construct handles this phase of game development in a very visual and intuitive way through **events**. Events are created by selecting possible conditions and actions specific to the objects defined in the associated game layout. Through these, we can define what happens to them or what they do when specific conditions or triggers happen in the game.

While visual in nature, the logic behind this approach is the very same as in any programming language, and it will definitely help any beginner

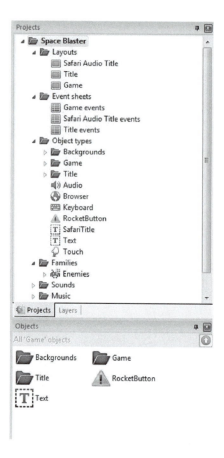

FIGURE 1.5 The **Projects** tab on the right side is where we can get a quick overview of all our files and import new objects into the game.

to learn how to think like a real programmer and to learn useful skills that are valid regardless of the development environment and tools used.

The last important feature we should check at this stage to have a proper overview of Construct 2 capabilities relates to the different options offered for actual distribution of our finished games. If we open the file menu and then click on **Export project**, as shown in Figure 1.7, we will see all available choices (Figure 1.8).

While actual choices are limited for the free trial, by registering Construct many opportunities and platforms become easily accessible, ranging from online platforms, desktop units, and mobile devices, which will surely excite your imagination. A word of caution, though: Construct

FIGURE 1.6   The **Game events** sheet. It is here that we program our game's logic. For example, we can see here that we are triggering an event at the start of the associated layout (near the bottom of the screen, the **System** icon is followed by **On start of layout**) where we can initialize objects and variables, start playing audio files, etc.

2 is an extensible platform, and many useful plugins are released by third parties, exporters included. This means that not all possible features you may like to use in your games will actually be supported on each platform, and you may have to check on a case-by-case basis when working with non-Scirra plugins. On the bright side, all these tools are being developed and tested by a very smart and active community: their functionalities, as well as their cross compatibility, are constantly being improved, opening up new possibilities and expanding on existing functionalities.

All these aspects we just introduced will be discussed in much more detail in the upcoming tutorials and chapters. For now, feel free to experiment a little bit, look around, and try out the game demo in your browser simply by clicking on the **Run Layout** icon shown in Figure 1.9.

FIGURE 1.7   Opening the main menu and selecting the **Export project** option.

FIGURE 1.8   Some among the several exporting options at our disposal, from HTML5 games running in a browser to mobile applications. We will discuss many of these later in the book.

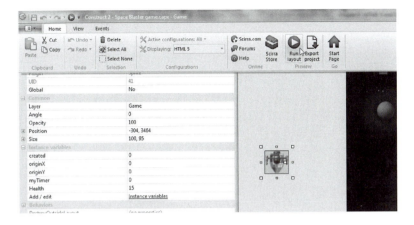

FIGURE 1.9   Click on the **Run layout** icon to preview your current project in any of your installed browsers. If the bar is not visible, click on the **Home** tab first.

TAKE AWAY

In this chapter we learned a little about what HTML5 is and its pros and cons, and then we had a first look at our game engine of choice for developing multiplatform two-dimensional games: Construct 2.

CHAPTER 2

Understanding How Games Work

"A method is needed in order to reason accurately."

—**René Descartes**

THOUGH IT IS TEMPTING to jump right into practical game development exercises, in my experience from years of teaching, the quality and effectiveness of your work will benefit greatly from starting out with a thorough understanding of the main theoretical principles behind the field.

So what are these "principles"? How can we uncover them to gain a better understanding of what makes games tick and turns them into something engaging, and ultimately fun, for so many people?

As the French philosopher and mathematician René Descartes (1596–1650) once said, "A method is needed in order to reason accurately."* Unfortunately this is an area where games have always been struggling: game designers, in fact, still lack a common jargon. They often refer to different concepts using the same words or define the same concepts using completely different words, making idea sharing and definitions of possible methods challenging to say the least.

Despite the difficulties, a first real attempt to define uniform terms was made a few years ago by three game designers named Robin Hunicke, Marc LeBlanc, and Robert Zubek, whose approach, called the MDA framework, was to understand games by dividing them into the three main layers:

---

* *Regulae ad directionem ingenii (Rules for the Direction of the Mind)*, unfinished treatise, 1628.

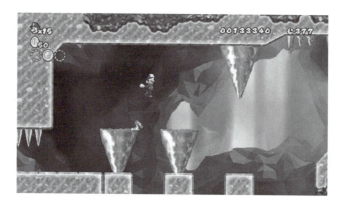

FIGURE 2.1   Jumping is a typical action characteristic of most platform games: here, *Super Mario Bros. Wii.* (© 2009 Nintendo.)

mechanics, dynamics, and aesthetics.* Their groundbreaking work also served as an inspiration for different methodologies, including one that has been successfully used both by myself in my own work and by my students, the AGE framework (standing for actions, gameplay, and experience), which I will present in this chapter.

As with the MDA, the main idea behind the AGE model is to offer a reliable approach to understanding how games work by breaking them down into different levels of abstraction and then analyze how they relate and integrate with each other.

In the case of the AGE framework, the levels we focus on are as follows:

- **Actions:** The core, atomic actions that a player can perform in a game, which can usually be described in terms of verbs: for example, moving, jumping, kicking a ball, punching, shooting, taking cover, shifting tiles, etc. (see Figure 2.1).

- **Gameplay:** The result that players achieve by using and combining the available actions, which can be described either in terms of verbs or higher-level concepts: for example, fighting, race to an end, territorial acquisition, etc. (see Figure 2.2).

- **Experience:** The emotional experience that engages players during the game.

---

* The interested reader can check their original paper, "MDA: A Formal Approach to Game Design and Game Research," available online at http://www.cs.northwestern.edu/~hunicke/MDA.pdf.

FIGURE 2.2 Race to end is a typical and straightforward example of gameplay we can find in countless games. In *Super Mario Bros. Wii*, for example, our running and jumping are finalized to reaching a flagpole, allowing us to proceed to the next level.

These concepts do not work in isolation, but they can be related to each other for describing a game in all its complexities by realizing that players apply the predefined rules to give a purpose to the available actions, producing the resulting gameplay. This then is used to overcome different challenges and goals, which serve to link the gameplay to the experience by providing players with a reason to immerse themselves in the gaming world and then get emotionally engaged in what they are doing (see the AGE model in Figure 2.3).

Now, while describing actions and gameplay can be relatively straightforward, how can we effectively describe the emotional experience of players in a way suitable for relating it back to the gameplay?

To answer this question, the AGE framework adopts another model, the "6-11 Framework."[*]

The idea behind this model is that games can be so engaging at a subconscious level because they successfully rely on a subset of six basic emotions and eleven instincts that are well known in psychology and deeply rooted in all of us, regardless of our cultural background or ethnicity.

---

[*] First introduced in *On the Way to Fun: An Emotion-Based Approach to Successful Game Design*, A K Peters, 2010.

Game

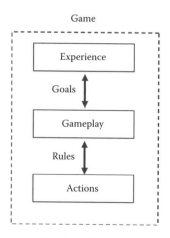

FIGURE 2.3 A game seen under the schematic representation of the actions, gameplay, and experience (AGE) model: Players perform some specific action that, in accordance with the game's own rules, allows for the emergence of one or more types of gameplay. Through gameplay, players aim to overcome a series of challenges or reach a goal, and, in doing so, they can get emotionally engaged and immersed in the virtual world.

In particular, the following six emotions seem to be the most relevant to games:

- **Fear:** This is one of the most common emotions in games today. Thanks to the newest technologies, it is now possible to represent realistic environments and situations where fear can easily be triggered: think of all the recent survival horror games or dungeon explorations in role playing games for plenty of examples (see Figure 2.4).

FIGURE 2.4 Fear is at the center of our emotional experience in *Silent Hill: Shattered Memories*. (© 2010 Konami.)

FIGURE 2.5 Even cute and cartoonish games like *Angry Birds* rely on anger to motivate players to take a side and get into the game. (© 2009 Rovio.)

- **Anger:** This is a powerful emotion that is often used as a motivational factor to play again or to advance in the story to correct any wrongs that some evil character has committed (see Figure 2.5).

- **Pride:** Rewarding players (and thus making them feel good) for their achievements and successes is an important motivational factor for pushing them to improve further and advance in the game to face even more difficult challenges (see Figure 2.6).

- **Joy/happiness:** Arguably, this is the most relevant emotion for having a fun gaming experience. Usually this is a consequence of the

FIGURE 2.6 Getting a top score and unlocking an achievement are reasons for pride for many gamers: here, getting a high score in a level of Rovio's *Angry Birds*. (© 2009 Rovio.)

FIGURE 2.7   Expressing joy can even become a mini game by itself, like in *FIFA Soccer 11*. (© 2010 Electronic Arts.)

player succeeding in some task and being rewarded by means of power-ups, story advancements, and so on (see Figure 2.7).

- **Sadness:** Though this emotion doesn't seem to match with the concept of "fun," game designers have always been attracted by sadness as a way to reach new artistic heights and touch more complex and mature themes (see Figure 2.8).

- **Excitement:** This is an emotion achieved by players at some point during most games worth playing, and it should happen naturally as a consequence of successfully triggering other emotions and/or instincts (see Figure 2.9).

The eleven core instincts we take into consideration instead are the following:

- **Survival (fight or flight):** This most fundamental and primordial of all instincts is triggered when we, like any other living being, are faced with a life threat. According to the situation, we will have to decide whether we should face the threat and fight for our life or try to avoid it by finding a possible way to escape. This is widely used in many modern video games, especially first-person shooter (FPS) and survival horror games (see Figure 2.10).

FIGURE 2.8 Despite being only a text adventure and having no graphics, *Planetfall* was the first game that succeeded in defining a memorable experience by making its players cry. How? Throughout the adventure the player established a bond with Floyd, a nonplayer character (NPC) robot that becomes the player's only companion. Floyd then sacrifices itself to save the player toward the end of the game, bringing a very emotionally charged and engaging moment that made players feel like they were losing a real friend. (© 1983 Infocom.)

- **Self-identification:** People tend to admire successful individuals or smart fictional characters and naturally start to imagine being like their models (see Figure 2.11).

- **Collecting:** A very strong instinct that motivates players is the formation of patterns of objects by completing sets with a common theme. This also relates to our hunting instinct and has been widely used in games since the early days of the medium (see Figure 2.12).

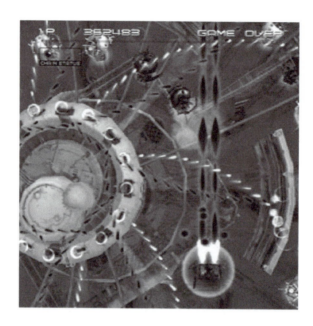

FIGURE 2.9 Hectic shoot 'em up action where we have to exercise sharp reflexes and make quick decisions to avoid being overwhelmed is a perfect setting for making players excited and focused on the game: here, *Ikaruga*. (© 2002 ESP.)

FIGURE 2.10 Putting players in a deadly setting will make them committed and resourceful: here, playing as Heather Mason in *Silent Hill 3*. (© 2003 Konami.)

FIGURE 2.11   We all dream of being in the hero's shoes. Sometimes things can even get out of hand and go beyond fantasy: in 2009 in Venice several witnesses reported seeing a blade-equipped hooded figure roaming the streets like Ezio Auditore, the main character in *Assassin's Creed II*. (© 2009 Ubisoft.)

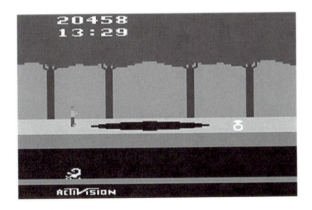

FIGURE 2.12   Relying on our collective instinct for finding and recovering all the treasure is enough to make for compelling gameplay in *Pitfall!* (© 1982 Activision.)

FIGURE 2.13 As *Nintendogs* and other virtual pet games show, taking care of a virtual puppy can easily commit players to focus on the game 100%. (© 2005 Nintendo.)

- **Protection/care/nurture:** This is arguably the "best" instinct of all—the one that pushes every parent to love their children and every person to care about and help those in need despite the possible dangers, including countless princesses in distress and kidnapped girlfriends (see Figure 2.13).

- **Aggressiveness:** The other side of the coin, this usually leads to violence when coupled with greed or anger. It is exploited in countless games (see Figure 2.14).

FIGURE 2.14 There's a reason that fighting games have always been an important and successful genre; whether we like it or not, violence has always played an important role in human evolution: here, *Street Fighter IV*. (© 2009 Capcom.)

FIGURE 2.15   Manage your game studio and get rich: a simple and very attractive proposition in *Game Dev Story*. (© 2010 Kairosoft.)

- **Greed:** Often we are prone to go beyond a simple "collection" and start to amass much more than actually needed. This is another typical human behavior that is responsible for the addictive qualities of many games: even when we are just talking about the virtual coins and resources that we need to build our fantasy empire in a strategy game, a greedy instinct is likely to surface very early in many players' gaming habits (see Figure 2.15).

- **Revenge:** This is another powerful instinct that can act as a motivational force and is often used in games to advance the storyline or justify why we need to annihilate some alien or enemy (see Figure 2.16).

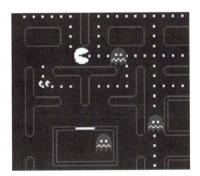

FIGURE 2.16   Having the opportunity to chase back the ghosts in *Pac-Man* is actually one of the most satisfying and rewarding moments in the game. We simply love getting revenge! (© 1980 Namco.)

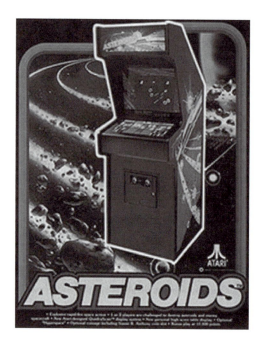

FIGURE 2.17 By adding a leaderboard for players to sign, *Asteroids* managed to push players' competitive instincts as no games ever did before. (© 1979 Atari.)

- **Competition:** Deeply linked with the social aspects of our psyche, this is one of the most important instincts in relation to gaming, e.g., leaderboards. Without competition, games would lose much of their appeal (see Figure 2.17).

- **Communication:** The need for expressing ideas, thoughts, or just gossip was very influential for human evolution. It can be used to great effect in games too, while seeking information by talking to a nonplaying character (NPC) or while sharing experiences with other players in chat rooms and forums (see Figure 2.18).

- **Exploration/curiosity:** All human discoveries, whether of a scientific or geographical nature, have been made thanks to this instinct. Exploration always pushes us toward the unknown (see Figure 2.19).

- **Color appreciation:** Scenes and environments full of vibrant colors naturally attract us, whether it is an abstract or a photorealistic setting. Note, though, that this is not necessarily linked to technology prowess but it is more about the artistic use of colors to make graphics attractive regardless of the actual number of pixels (see Figure 2.20).

FIGURE 2.18 In *Captain Blood* players have to figure out how to communicate with different alien species and express themselves via an articulated icon-driven system to get the information they need to progress in the game. (© 1988 Infogrames.)

The AGE Framework may be seen then as a canvas where we can use any of these elements to explain how games successfully manage to engage players emotionally and how emotions and instincts are ultimately the driving forces that make the players act in the game.

For example, as summarized in Figure 2.21, we can imagine a horror game that manages to scare the player with a sudden encounter with a zombie in a dark room. Scaring the player will trigger his survival instinct, and this will instantaneously push him to find a way to answer the threat, for example by escaping and avoiding the danger, which will be made

FIGURE 2.19 Uncovering the secrets of a mysterious world is a very effective way to engage players in narrative-based games and adventures: here, *Myst*. (© 1995 Broderbund.)

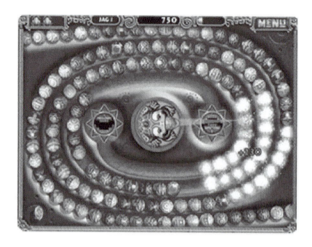

FIGURE 2.20 *Zuma Deluxe* wouldn't be that attractive if all the marbles were just different shades of gray.... (© 2004 PopCap.)

possible by the actions provided by the game, such as the ability to run or to hide somewhere.

To better understand how this theoretical framework can help us to figure out how a game can successfully build an engaging and enjoyable experience in practice, let's take a look at the classic arcade game *Frogger* (Konami, 1981).

In *Frogger*, players control a small frog that, starting from the bottom of the screen, they have to bring to safety by crossing a trafficked highway and a river.

Our analysis can proceed either in a top-down approach, from the experience to the actions, or the other way around, in a bottom-up style. Let's start with the latter, by identifying the actions first and then go up to toward the experience (see Figure 2.22).

So, what are the actions in *Frogger*? Let's start playing the game and ask ourselves "What can I do in the game?" An easy answer is simply to check out the actions mapped on the game controls.

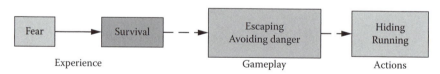

FIGURE 2.21 Experience, gameplay, and actions for a generic horror game: the survival instinct is what motivates the player to escape (gameplay) by using the available abilities at his disposal (actions).

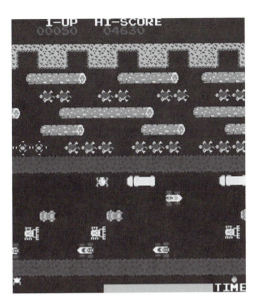

FIGURE 2.22   *Frogger*: Was it an engaging and fun game? Why? (© 1981 Konami.)

In *Frogger*, this analysis is extremely simple becasuse we only have a joystick that allows us to move left, right, forward, and backward. If, on the other hand, we were analyzing a more modern and far more complex game, the study of the actions might have required a little bit more time and attention, as shown in Figure 2.23.

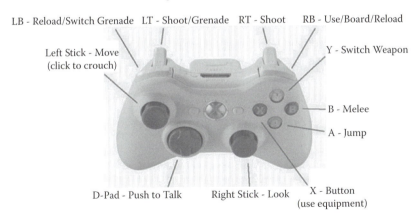

FIGURE 2.23   If we have problems identifying the available actions in a given game, we can start by checking the control scheme and see what the different joysticks and buttons are used for. Here we see the control layout and consequent actions for the multiplayer version of *Halo 3*. (© 2007 Microsoft.)

Going back to *Frogger,* we can now proceed to the next stage and analyze the gameplay. To do so, we should ask ourselves something like "What are the game rules allowing us to do?" Or, more simply, "What are we actually doing in the game? What are we using the actions for?" These are the questions we need to answer here.

In the case of *Frogger,* we are trying to avoid the speeding cars and then jumping on the floating logs to reach a safe haven at the top of the screen. In game design terms, we can say the gameplay is about "avoidance" of different hazards together with a "race to an end" component. By describing the gameplay in these terms we have also explicated the goal of the game, and we are then ready to analyze the emotional experience. We now have to ask ourselves "How do I feel while playing the game?"

This is the most subjective part of the analysis and can obviously be quite tricky, but we can rely on the 6-11 Framework to guide us in the process.

Most likely, we would point out that, while playing the game, we were excited by the fast action of moving across the highway and river and then happy for successfully reaching the end. Notice that we have already identified the two main emotions that make *Frogger* fun and enjoyable, but why were we happy? Because we felt proud for our achievement.

Right! Pride plays an important role here and, in fact, it usually resolves into joy and happiness. We have another emotion to describe our experience. Now, what is the achievement we are proud of? Surviving the perils we had to face while crossing the road and river! So, survival is the main instinct at play here, and it actually drives us toward the goal of the game. We may also realize that, by looking at the cars approaching us from all directions, we might have felt a bit scared, and we may have unconsciously taken the role of the frog, i.e., we identified with it.

The whole analysis can then be summarized into a simple diagram like the one shown in Figure 2.24.

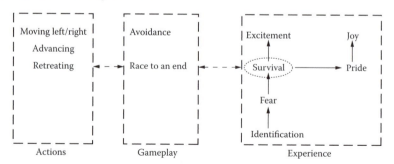

FIGURE 2.24   AGE analysis for *Frogger.*

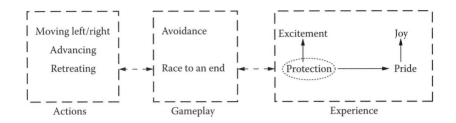

FIGURE 2.25 Alternative AGE analysis for *Frogger:* we are not the frog, we are just there to help it.

As stated earlier, analyzing the experience can be quite subjective, so some players may see things a bit differently.

For example, they may not have thought they were taking the role of the frog in the first place, but, on the other hand, they simply thought their role was to "help" the unlucky frog to safely reach the pond. In this case, identification, fear, and survival wouldn't play any role in their emotional experience, and they would feel protective instead. Here the frog is not an avatar, but it simply acts as a character the player has to rescue.

Under this assumption, the resulting AGE analysis would be like that shown in Figure 2.25.

What if instead we decide to analyze the game following a top-down approach?

Again, we start our analysis by playing the game, but this time we try to figure out the experience first by asking ourselves "How is the game trying to motivate me? How do I feel while playing?" This should lead us to question our relationship with the playable character: Is it an avatar ("I'm playing as this little frog who has to cross the street"), which will lead us to the identification-fear-survival route? Or is it just a character we have to protect ("I have to help this poor little thing!"), leading us to the model motivated by protective feelings? Once the emotional analysis is in place, we can proceed downward with the questions we saw earlier for identifying the gameplay and the actions.

Regardless of our starting point, either the actions or the experience, we should arrive at the same result at the end of our analysis.

TAKE AWAY

In this chapter we discussed a methodology for analyzing and understanding how games work at different levels, namely, *actions, gameplay,* and emotional *experience*. We will use this approach to get insights on different game concepts and to design our own prototypes in the forth-coming chapters.

EXERCISE

Select a mobile or web-based game of your choice and try to analyze it by playing it critically, breaking it down into actions, gameplay, and experience as seen in this chapter for *Frogger*.

CHAPTER 3

About Games and Ideas: Dream vs. Reality

EVERY ASPIRING GAME DEVELOPER has plenty of very ambitious ideas for the next blockbuster. On the other hand, any professional developer will tell you that, in the game industry, grand ideas are worth nothing. All that matters is execution. And this is where things get difficult: unfortunately, time and resources are very limited, so, while I hate to wake you from your daydreaming, a reality check is needed.

Fantasizing about the next *Halo* or *Uncharted* will bring you nowhere: unless you have someone backing you up with $100 million, a large team of experienced professionals, and enough patience to allow for a development cycle spanning several years, your efforts and big dreams are destined to be crushed by the harsh reality we live in.

This doesn't mean we have to stop dreaming! Successes as diverse as *Brain Age* (Nintendo, 2006), *FarmVille* (Zynga, 2009), and *Angry Birds* (Rovio, 2009) were developed by small teams with small budgets within realistic timeframes. What really matters is knowing ourselves, our strengths, and our limitations and then setting our goals accordingly.

Today we are very lucky to have modern and powerful tools, like Construct 2, that have lowered the barrier of entry into web-based, mobile, and even social games to a level such that anybody can make and distribute games to an almost unlimited audience.

These types of games, though, are much different in concept and appeal than the AAA titles you may be playing on your home console systems and that likely made you interested in game development in the first place, so we may have to revise game ideas and concepts accordingly.

Individual developers or members of small independent teams made up of friends or schoolmates should focus on games that implement straightforward concepts with clear and easily understandable goals.

Levels should also be structured for playing sessions lasting only a few minutes at a time so that, when played on mobile devices on the go, they can be picked up quickly and stopped any time (see an example in Figure 3.1).

Interestingly, games with these characteristics are not a new concept that emerged recently due to our modern and busy lifestyle or due to the popularity of new mobile devices. These were actually common traits of most games during the 1980s and early 1990s. At that time, in fact, technology couldn't really support extensive and complex games, like those we have today, on the hardware that was available at that time, so developers had to make that kind of design approach a necessity.

Indeed, it may be surprising for the younger generation to realize that old games still have a lot to teach us about game design, about what works and what doesn't. Playing the classics can actually be a neverending source of inspiration and ideas for new game concepts!

FIGURE 3.1 *Angry Birds*: an easily understandable but addictive concept where playing each level takes no more than a couple of minutes. This makes it perfectly suitable for a mobile experience on the go while commuting, for example. (© 2009 Rovio.)

While 30-year-old games do look extremely primitive and lack all the bells and whistles we are used to today, this lack of detail and technological prowess is actually helpful for exposing all the gameplay elements that made such games popular back in the day and, thus, are very useful learning tools.

This is also the reason why more and more university degrees on game development are incorporating classes on game history. If you follow industry events like the Independent Game Festival (IGF),* you will soon notice that many of the winning games often showcase gameplay and aesthetics clearly inspired by games of the past.

The influence and inspiring force of these old "relics" shouldn't be underestimated, and I truly encourage you to spend some time rediscovering old classics or little-known games for systems like the Atari 2600, Intellivision, Commodore 64, Nintendo Entertainment System (NES), PC-Engine, Sega Genesis, and the like. Look beyond the blocky and low-resolution graphics and see if you can relate their core concepts to newer games or, maybe, even get new ideas on how to reinterpret them in a modern way for a new audience.

To exemplify how an old game can still be relevant in a modern setting, let's see some actual examples where we can find specific gameplay ideas reinterpreted and adapted into something original across a multitude of genres, from casual games to high-budget AAA productions (see Figures 3.2–3.8 for some examples).

In the end, while game development is still a very young field, it is important to be aware that it has an exciting and fascinating history, with many interesting concepts that can be explored in novel ways. Knowing more about it can only help the new generations of developers to build further on that solid foundation, exactly as writers and artists learn from the works of the people who preceded them in their respective fields.

To stress the relevance of research to inspire new game ideas, the prototypes we are going to develop in the next chapters will be first introduced by an analysis of the early classics they are referencing.

---

* The Independent Game Festival is held annually in conjunction with the Game Developers Conference (http://www.igf.com).

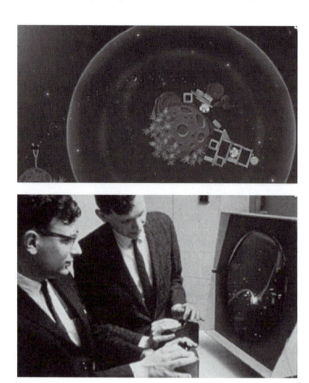

FIGURE 3.2   In *Angry Birds Space* (top, © 2012 Rovio), the player bends his shots using the gravity field of the nearby planets. We can find the same idea in one of the first computer games ever created, *SpaceWar!* (bottom, developed by Steve Russell et al. at MIT in 1962), where players had to shoot at each other while taking into consideration the gravity field of the star at the center of the screen.

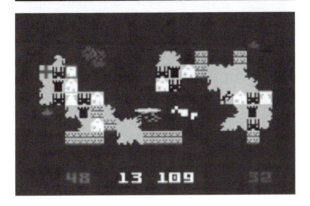

FIGURE 3.3 The *Civilization* franchise, started by Sid Meier in 1991 with the original game published by MicroProse (top, © 1991 MicroProse), keeps pushing the strategy genre to new heights with each new release, innovating from a core set of ideas that can be traced back to 1981, when a truly groundbreaking game, *Utopia* (bottom, © 1981 Mattel, developed by Don Daglow), was released for the Intellivision console.

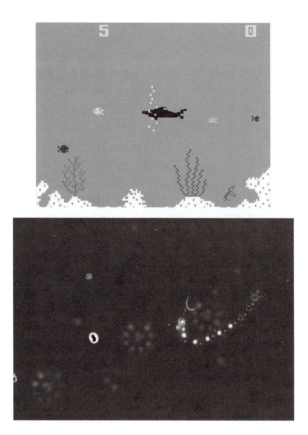

FIGURE 3.4   Still on the Intellivision console, Mattel released *Shark!Shark!* in 1982 (top, © 1982 Mattel). It was a very addictive arcade-style game where the player started as a little fish who had to eat smaller ones to grow while avoiding being eaten by bigger creatures. We can find the same basic concept, this time with plankton-like microorganisms, in the acclaimed experimental title *flOw* by Jenova Chen (bottom, © 2006 thatgamecompany). In *flOw*, though, gameplay is made much more interesting by enabling players to freely experiment with difficulty levels. This allows them to find the right match for their skills, making it possible to enter into a so-called state of flow, where the player's ability and game's challenges are in equilibrium.

FIGURE 3.5 Managing and caring for the life of a virtual character (and his dog) was the main idea behind *Little Computer People* (top, © 1985 Activision); here, we made our little friend do some aerobic exercises to keep fit. The concept was then upgraded and expanded into a whole community with *The Sims* (bottom, © 2000 Electronic Arts).

FIGURE 3.6 Quick Time Events (QTEs) are an integral part of many modern games, like *Asura's Wrath* (top, © 2012 Capcom) and have evolved into a very effective tool for building a stronger connection with in-game characters and delivering an engaging story, as in *Heavy Rain* (middle, © 2010 Sony Computer Entertainment America). They are nothing new, though; QTEs got started with the adventures of Dirk the Daring in *Dragon's Lair* many years ago (bottom, © 1983 Cinematronics).

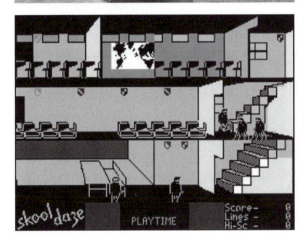

FIGURE 3.7   Before getting a modern treatment with *Bully* (top, © 2006 Rockstar Games), managing a busy class schedule while fighting classmates and avoiding teachers was already the setting for a very original game on the ZX Spectrum and Commodore 64: *Skool Daze* (bottom, © 1983 Microsphere).

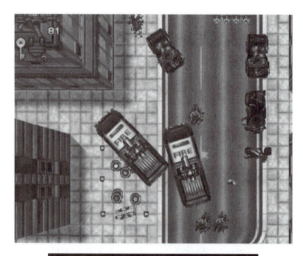

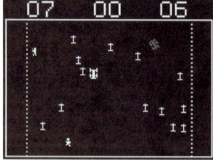

FIGURE 3.8 The *Grand Theft Auto* (*GTA*) franchise has always drawn much controversy, starting from its first installment (top, © 1997 BMG Interactive Entertainment) in which the player could steal a car and run over pedestrians, leaving a trail of blood behind him. Surprisingly, though, there was an arcade game with gameplay based on chasing and running over people more than twenty years earlier: *Death Race* (bottom, © 1976 Exidy). That game, loosely based on the movie *Death Race 2000* featuring Sylvester Stallone and David Carradine, put the player at the wheel of a car with the task of running over as many zombies as possible; zombies that are run over leave a cross behind them. Most people saw no difference between zombies and pedestrians and, indeed, like *GTA* in modern times, the game stirred a huge antigaming debate back in the day.

TAKE AWAY

- Don't stop dreaming, but dream about something you can actually achieve!

- Playing old games critically is an invaluable learning experience that can inspire new ideas and game concepts.

CHAPTER 4

Game Design Documentation for Indies

" To document or not to document? That is the question: whether 'tis nobler in the mind to suffer the slings and arrows of outrageous and sudden ideas, or to take arms against a sea of troubles and begin by writing everything down?"

If Hamlet were an indie game designer, he might have thought something like that. Indeed, most indie developers ask themselves something similar when beginning a new project: why make the effort of documenting our ideas and trying to crystallize them before the actual work starts? Is it really useful? Or should we just go along day after day, iteration after iteration, and see where our inspiration leads us? And, if we decide to document, which format is most suitable for a given project? Will anyone really read it?

In this short chapter we'll try to answer these questions and see how to approach design documentation effectively from an indie perspective.

In professional settings, game design documents still take the shape of the infamous "Game Design Bibles," tomes often spanning 100+ pages outlining every possible detail in the game. Every studio has its own specific formats, but in general, most tend to include sections covering the following topics:

1. **Introduction/general information:** A high-level description of the game, just one paragraph to capture the attention of the reader.

2. **Detailed game description:** The nuts and bolts of the game, in as much detail as possible, usually including several subsections:

   (a) Core gameplay and its elements (e.g., race to an end, territorial acquisition, etc., and how they are implemented)

   (b) Game flow (e.g., whether the game is structured in chapters, levels, etc.)

   (c) Characters/units (including detailed descriptions in terms of classes, abilities, and eventual statistics)

   (d) Game physics

   (e) Artificial intelligence (purposes and approaches used)

   (f) Multiplayer (how it works and which specific game modes it is used for)

   (g) Walkthrough (a step-by-step guide for the whole game or at least for the first few levels)

3. **Level requirements and progression:** How the game progress is structured, including the following:

   (a) Level diagrams and maps

   (b) Flow diagrams (usually accompanying the maps, describing what is going to happen in each area of the levels)

   (c) Description of puzzles (if any)

   (d) Assets (which are used in each level and how/when they are presented to players)

4. **Story:** If story plays an important role in the game, it should have its own dedicated section.

   (a) Backstory and world description (for example, describe the lore of the fantasy world the game takes place in)

(b) Character descriptions (go more in depth on histories and backgrounds of both playing characters and nonplaying characters)

(c) Game text, dialog requirements (how we are going to tell the story to players)

    i. Sample scripts

5. **Graphical user interface (GUI):** All the information and options that are displayed to the player across the game, from the first menu screen onward.

(a) Flowchart (how the different screens are linked, e.g., menus, options, etc.)

(b) Functional requirements (what kind of information do we need to display?)

(c) Buttons, icons, pointers, bars, text (e.g., how and where score, health/mana bars, dialog windows, etc. are displayed)

(d) Mock-up (an overall view of how the GUI will look)

6. **Art:** The general graphic style used and eventual references: in particular,

(a) Goals, style, mood, references

(b) Two-dimensional art and animation

(c) Special effects

(d) Three-dimensional art and animation

(e) Cut scenes

7. **Sound and music:** Special effects, voice-overs, and music

(a) Goals, style, and formats used

(b) Sound effects

    i. GUI (e.g., mouse clicks)

    ii. In game

(c) Music

    i. System screens (opening music in the splash screen, options menu, credits, etc.)

    ii. Level themes (background music across the different levels and areas of the game)

    iii. Events (jingles and themes triggered by specific events, e.g., finding a clue, advancing to the next level, etc. Also more elaborate and dynamic music systems that can change according to different gameplay situations)

    iv. Cut scenes (what kind of music is featured in each cut scene?)

This extremely detailed approach has some good points: by creating it, we do actually have to think of the whole game in detail. In addition, everything is in one single place for easy reference, at least in theory. But these also bring some undesired side effects: game development is an iterative process. Ideas change throughout the early (and sometimes not-so-early) stages of development, and such a document is difficult to update, track changes, and manage. Also, its length makes it difficult to search it in practice and makes people less inclined to sit down and read it.

This is actually an interesting point that is worth discussing a little more in detail. Many game designers soon realize that no one in the team actually reads their design documents! While this may seem a bit hard to believe at first, I found this to be true both in my personal experience and also confirmed by many other people. One of the funniest anecdotes I heard was from Chris Natsuume, cofounder of the casual game developer Boomzap.* Before founding his own studio, he was a producer for the AAA title Far Cry (developed by Crytek and published by Ubisoft in 2004) and, to check whether their comprehensive documentation was actually read by his colleagues, he started adding notes to some random pages like "if you read this line, come over to me and I'll give you $10." Guess what? No one ever went over to ask for the $10!

If no one reads it, can we just skip the documentation entirely then and just start working on actual development? No, I highly discourage this, even if you are working solo, since writing down your ideas is the best

---

* www.boomzap.com

way to think things over and analyze problems before they even happen. Anyway, we definitely need to find a much more agile way of doing things.

At Boomzap, for example, they try to concentrate all the most relevant information we saw in the canonical bible approach by using a very visual style, mostly via mock-ups of different screenshots to discuss how the gameplay would develop. The whole documentation usually takes less than 20 pages.

An even more drastic approach, to outline a design in the most focused way possible, has also been proposed by Electronic Arts/Maxis Creative Director Stone Librande in his highly popular Game Developer's Conference talks[*] discussing a "One-Page Designs" format.

The idea is to identify and discuss only the main elements of the game and their relationships. Note that this doesn't necessarily mean the whole game documentation is going to fit onto one page. Different features or sections, such as concept art to discuss the theme and mood of the game, GUI, storyboards, relationships between units and their stats, and different maps/levels, may require their own pages, but the important point is that each sheet we draft should stand alone and should discuss in enough detail one or more related aspects in a visual and easily understandable way.

A possible format for approaching design documentation in this way is showcased in Figure 4.1.

In general, good guidelines to design such one-page documents are to start with a title and version (don't forget to date the document!), write a synthetic description of the topic under discussion, and then draw a main central picture or diagram to illustrate the topic. This can have a more detailed description to clarify important concepts, including sub-pictures showing further details, callouts to identify items and functionalities, and more.

The remaining part of the page can be used to illustrate other related diagrams, flowcharts, bullet points/checklists, high-level goals, or other meaningful information.

It is also important to leave some white space around diagrams to facilitate reading and comprehension of the material presented. Although you may want to squeeze as much information as possible on the page, an overly cluttered layout won't incentivize people to go through it, undermining the very reason of this approach: we want our documents to be actually read and not silently ignored!

---

[*] Stone's original slides can be retrieved from his website: www.stonetronix.com/gdc-2010/

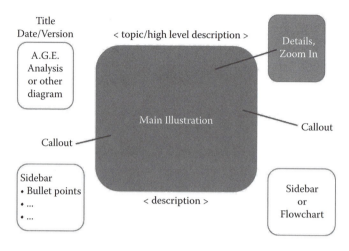

FIGURE 4.1   A possible template for one-page design documentation.

In the next chapter we will start using this approach in practice to document our ideas.

TAKE AWAY

In this chapter we discussed the importance of documenting our ideas, an often overlooked area in indie game development. We discussed different approaches, from documents potentially spanning hundreds of pages to much more synthetic design documents. One-page designs, in particular, are a very useful tool to think and formalize our ideas while also providing an easily readable format for anyone involved in the project.

EXERCISE

Write a one-page design document for the game *Frogger*, which we analyzed in Chapter 2.

CHAPTER 5

Moon Wolf, a Space Arcade Game

A RCADE GAMES AND space shooters were all the rage in the early days: from *Space Invaders* to *Asteroids*, from *Tempest* to *Defender*, many classics were made around this theme.

The genre is still a very good playground to hone our skills as game designers because it is usually built around a simple yet engrossing gameplay demanding good hand-eye coordination and fast reflexes, which are still relevant in many mobile games. Here, gameplay has to be carefully fine-tuned as the player progresses across waves of enemies, making also for a good playtesting and balancing exercise.

Our first prototype will fall into this category of arcade-like space games. We will model the core actions and gameplay after an old but engaging arcade game of the early 1980s: *Solar Fox*. As an homage to our source of inspiration, our game will be named *Moon Wolf*.

5.1 *SOLAR FOX*: ANALYSIS

Solar Fox is an arcade game released by Bally Midway in 1981. In it, the player has to drive a starship across a series of grids to retrieve solar cells while avoiding different types of enemies and hazards. To defend himself, the player has a limited range fire, which can momentarily halt the sentinels patrolling the grid perimeter, can destroy incoming shots, and can speed up/slow down his ship to predefined cruise speeds.

With taglines like "Bally-Midway's *Solar Fox* speeds through a video universe of challenges" and "Speed and Strategy are all you have and they

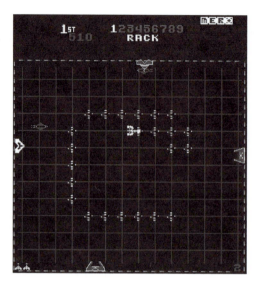

FIGURE 5.1   A screenshot of the original *Solar Fox*. Players had to move around the two-dimensional grid at different speeds to gather all cells while avoiding enemy fire. (© 1981 Bally Midway.)

just might be enough!" *Solar Fox* was relatively popular, so much so that it was even featured in the 1983 movie *Joysticks** (see Figure 5.1).

To gain a better insight on the game, let's analyze it with the AGE framework, starting with the actions.

What actions can we do in the game? Let's check the controls: the joystick allows us to move around the two-dimensional grid, while two buttons allow us to change speed, from low to high or vice versa (according to the game difficulty we select when starting the game) and shoot a short-range missile.

What are we using the actions for? By shooting and moving around we can avoid enemies and grab the available cells. In game design terms, we can then say we have a gameplay centered around themes like avoidance (avoid being hit by the enemies), race to an end (we have to find a path to reach the next cell we are targeting), and taking/hoarding all cells in the level.

Finally, regarding the experience, the goals here are simply to reach and grab all cells while avoiding incoming fire. Our collecting instinct will push us to clear the level, which, in turn, should make us happy and proud of our success. Our survival instinct would also play an important role,

---

* Despite featuring *Solar Fox* and some other great games, *Joysticks* isn't really a movie worth remembering: it's an example of the low-quality, rowdy teen sexy comedies that were common in the 1980s, and it's no surprise it is currently scoring an abysmal 3.3 out of 10 rating on the Internet Movie Database! http://www.imdb.com/title/tt0085764/

FIGURE 5.2 The control panel for *Solar Fox*: note the attractive joystick to add realism to the space flying experience. (Image taken from the International Arcade Museum, www.arcade-museum.com).

making us react as fast as possible to enemy shots. Both collecting and survival would be stronger if the game manages to make us feel like we are actually in command of the spaceship (identification), something that the original arcade game tried to achieve subconsciously by providing a joystick shaped like a futuristic airplane control, in addition to the attractive and aggressive artwork on the cabinet (Figure 5.2).

Our analysis is summarized in the AGE diagram in Figure 5.3.

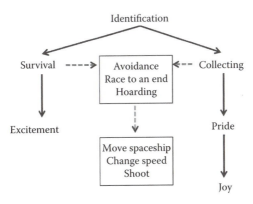

FIGURE 5.3 AGE analysis for *Solar Fox*.

Inspired by this classic, we can now start designing our own take on the genre.

5.2 *MOON WOLF*: DESIGN

Our space arcade game will retain the main elements of *Solar Fox* but will simplify a few things while adding something new as well.

First of all, we won't have the fancy flying joystick at our disposal, but we can still try to engage the player by providing a simple background story to make the setting a little more exciting. For example:

> A mysterious alien force is amassing deadly weapons behind our moon. As the famed Commander Wolf, you are Earth's only hope: infiltrate enemy lines and steal all their energy reserves while avoiding their sentinels!

Our gameplay would essentially remain the same as the original, but we can change a few aspects to make it our own: for example, shooting is not really the main part of the action, so, for simplicity's sake, we can just focus on the avoiding and collecting aspects instead.* On the other hand, we may want to add a resource-handling element, making the change speed feature limited and, thus, more meaningful: the player can only accelerate as long as he has enough fuel for boosting its speed. This means we should also give opportunities for refilling our fuel tank, though, and we can do so by deciding that every time we collect a cell, there is a 10% probability to spawn a recharge battery. The battery should recharge 20 units of fuel when picked, for example. Instead of four sentinels like in the original arcade game, we can also limit our design to just one main antagonist that would roam the full screen perimeter and shoot straight missiles. To make the action more varied and challenging, we can add different types of hazards, like asteroids that can randomly travel across the screen. In addition, the player would start with only one life: getting hit means game over. When all cells have been collected, the game restarts with a new wave, replacing all the cells and making the sentinel, as well as the asteroids, move faster and shoot at a higher fire rate.

All these ideas are summarized in our one-page design document shown in Figure 5.4, which will serve as a reference throughout the development process that we will start in the next chapter.

---

* Indeed, this is what the home conversion for the Atari 2600 console did back in the day.

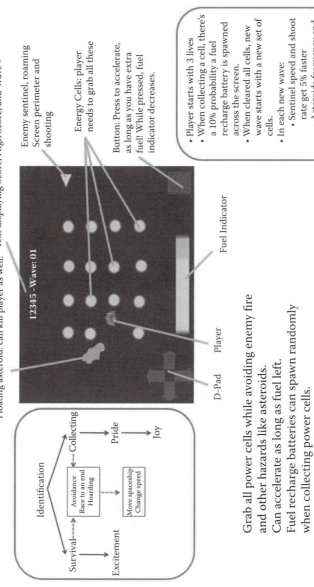

Moon Wolf
26-04-13/V.1.0

"A mysterious alien force is amassing deadly weapons behind our moon. As the famed Commander Wolf, you are Earth's only hope: infiltrate enemy lines and steal all their energy reserves while avoiding their sentinels!"

Floating asteroid: can kill player as well! Text displaying Score, High Score, and Wave #

Enemy sentinel, roaming
Screen perimeter and
shooting

Energy Cells: player
needs to grab all these

Button: Press to accelerate,
as long as you have extra
fuel! While pressed, fuel
indicator decreases.

- Player starts with 3 lives
- When collecting a cell, there's a 10% probability a fuel recharge battery is spawned across the screen.
- When cleared all cells, new wave starts with a new set of cells.
- In each new wave:
  - Sentinel speed and shoot rate get 5% faster
  - Asteroids frequency and speed increase as well

12345 - Wave: 01

Fuel Indicator

D-Pad   Player

Identification

Collecting

Pride → Joy

Avoidance
Race to an end
Hoarding

Move spaceship
Change speed

Survival

Excitement

Grab all power cells while avoiding enemy fire
and other hazards like asteroids.
Can accelerate as long as fuel left.
Fuel recharge batteries can spawn randomly
when collecting power cells.

FIGURE 5.4   One-page design document for our first game: *Moon Wolf.*

Finally, note also that all these rules and corresponding values are just a starting point. Most likely we will have to change them and fine-tune everything once we start playtesting our first prototype. Remember: nothing in a game design document, no matter how verbose or concise it is, is ever set in stone.

TAKE AWAY

In this chapter we discussed our first game concept: a simple arcade space game inspired by *Solar Fox*, a classic arcade game released in 1981 by Bally Midway. We analyzed the game using the AGE framework and then summarized our ideas in a one-page design document that will serve as a reference during our development work.

CHAPTER 6

Moon Wolf Development

It's time to start developing our first game with Construct 2! First, we will define the layout and touch controls. We will also add some background music and preview our work locally on a browser. Adding cells and a scoring system will come next, followed by the implementation of the speed change, fuel bonuses, and simple animations. Last but not least, we will add the sentinel and asteroids to create challenges and complete the game plus a basic game loop to keep playing at a higher difficulty level once all cells have been collected or to restart after the game is over.

Before we begin, a general reminder: don't forget to save your ongoing project often! Note also that Construct 2 automatically keeps one or more previous saves as backup copies. (You can specify how many from the **File** menu, look for the **Preferences** icon and then pick the **Backup** tab. The default is one.)

6.1 GETTING STARTED

If you have a demo project still open, close it and start by creating a new empty one either from the **File** menu or the **Start** page. Once you are more experienced, it is recommended you use the provided templates to speed up the early development stages, but for now, it's a good idea to go through every step to get a better understanding of what we are actually doing and why.

The first thing we should take care of is to define the screen size for our game and define how it is going to scale when it's played on devices having different screen resolutions.

Luckily for us, Construct 2 handles scaling very well, so let's change the **Full screen in browser** property in the **Configuration settings** for the project to **Letterbox scale** (to access these, click on an empty area in the layout to display the **Layout properties** in the right panel, then click on the **Project properties view** link). But what resolution will we develop in? Considering we want our game to work on many devices, from Windows 8 based PCs to tablets and smart phones across different models and generations, it's a good idea to start with something average that can be scaled accordingly, up or down, by the game engine itself.

For our game, I decided to target a resolution of 800 × 480 pixels, which can be a good starting point for many wide-screen devices and is adopted by several 7 inch Android-based tablets as well as smart phones. Feel free, however, to change the resolution to fit any specific device you have in mind.

Our project settings should then look like those shown in Figure 6.1.

Now let's start by setting up our first layout, by default named "Layout 1," as the game layout, where we will prototype our gameplay. Rename "Layout 1" as "Game" (you can do this from either the **Project** or the

Project settings	
Name	**Moon Wolf**
Author	Roberto Dillon
Description	**Our first C2 game!**
Version	1.0
First layout	Game
Use loader layout	No
Pixel rounding	Off
Window Size	800, 480
Configuration Settings	
Preview browser	Chrome
Fullscreen in browser	Letterbox scale
Use iOS retina display	**Never**
Hide address bar	No
Enable WebGL	On
Sampling	Linear
Loader style	Progress bar & logo
Pause on unfocus	No
Clear background	Yes
More information	Help

FIGURE 6.1 The **Project settings** for our first game. Here we define the window size and how it should scale on devices with different resolutions. Note that the exact field names, values, and order may be slightly different across different versions of Construct.

Properties windows by clicking on the layout name) and its "Event Sheet 1" as "Game Sheet." In case the **Layout properties** are not displayed, click anywhere on the layout to see them, and be sure our event sheet is correctly associated with it (check in the **Layout properties**).

We can now add a background and a spaceship.

Note that, in this game, I will be using the free space assets that come with Construct 2 (we saw them already in the *Space Blaster* Construct 2 demo: they can be downloaded from http://www.scirra.com/freebundle.zip). This book is not about art assets: you may also check Appendix A for a list of alternative resources available online, or simply use boxes and triangles of different colors to prototype your ideas, as we did in the mock-up image used in the one-page design document to explain the game concept. Don't forget that great graphics don't make great games, great game design does!

Our background image will be background1.png, by default located in the **Sprites/space/backgrounds** folder where we unzipped the assets. However, feel free to use any background image you like.

To add any other object to the game, double click or right click anywhere on your empty layout and select **Insert new object**. Since now we want to add an image, choose **Sprite**. Change the default name to **Background** and click **Insert**.

Note that now the cursor changed into a crosshair. Click anywhere inside the layout to open the **Sprite editor** window. Once there, open the folder icon and select your background image.

Once the image has been imported, you may also want to change the picture origin and bring it to (0,0) so that it will be easier to move it later by using coordinates. To do this, click on the origin icon (shown in Figure 6.2) and then select the origin point, by default placed in the middle of the image. Move it to (0,0) by clicking close to the upper left corner of the image and then moving it by using the arrow keys as needed.

Close the editor window and you will be back to the layout. Now we can either resize the whole image to fit the 800 × 480 pixels view of our layout or we can simply position the big image in a way you like and display only a portion of it.

Once this is in place, repeat the previous process to add a new sprite to the game, but this time let's choose an image suitable for the player's ship. I used the Crescent008.png file, but if you don't have a nice sprite at hand don't worry: you can just draw a triangle like the one in *Asteroids* (have it point toward the right) and your game will still work pretty well!

FIGURE 6.2   Moving the origin of an image to a more convenient position.

Click on the crop icon and your sprite should look like the one in Figure 6.3.

Close the **Edit image** window and place your spaceship anywhere you like. If, for any reason, it is not automatically displayed in the layout, we can drag and drop it from the **Project** panel on the right (look into the **Object types** folder). Resize it so that our game view will allow for enough room for proper maneuvering. For example, I rescaled the ship to (33,42). Then click on **Behaviors**, as shown in Figure 6.4. Add one by clicking on the plus (+) sign and select **8 Direction** under the **Movements** section.

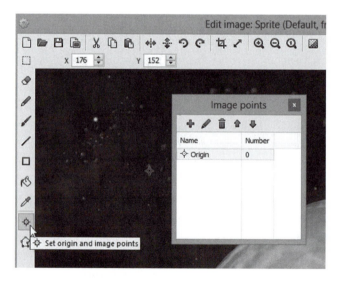

FIGURE 6.3   Our player sprite, cropped, in the image editor.

⊟ Object type properties		
	Name	Player
	Plugin	Sprite
	Global	No
⊟ Common		
	Layer	Layer 0
	Angle	0
	Opacity	100
⊞	Position	51, 73
⊞	Size	33, 42
⊟ Instance variables		
	Add / edit	Instance variables
⊟ Behaviors		
	Add / edit	Behaviors
⊟ Effects		

FIGURE 6.4   We can easily add predefined and very useful behaviors to selected objects.

This behavior allows us to control our spaceship right away by using the arrow keys. Before we try it, we should be sure to add touch controls as well so that our game can be played on mobile devices and tablets via a touch screen.

This is not as difficult as it sounds. First, we should keep things neat. It is a good practice to keep the graphical user interface (GUI) on a separate layer, so add a new layer that we are going to call "UI." To do so, in the panel on the right, click on the **Layers** tab next to the **Projects** tab, click on the plus sign and rename the new layer as shown in the Figure 6.5. We can also rename the original layer, "Layer 0," something a bit more meaningful, for example "Action," if we like. From now on we can simply select, show, or lock a layer by clicking on the corresponding icons, and we can

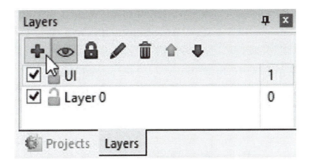

FIGURE 6.5   Adding a layer. Layers are a huge help in keeping our game structure neat by separating different groups of elements, for example, the GUI. Note that in the free edition we can add up to four layers only.

FIGURE 6.6 Our control GUI: a directional pad (D-Pad) made by four big arrows that, when touched or clicked, will be highlighted and move our ship in the corresponding direction.

also change their order by dragging a layer up or down the hierarchy in the panel.

Now it's time to start defining the control GUI: we are going to have four big arrows placed in the lower left corner of the screen that will highlight when touched and move our ship at a default speed. Each arrow has to be defined as a new sprite, which we can call "Control_Up," "Control_Down," and so on. After we add each sprite to the project and draw the arrows in the image editor, we should have something like what is shown in Figure 6.6.

Note that I scaled each arrow to be 50 × 50 pixels with an Opacity of 30 (a value of 0 means invisible). We will be using this property to simulate the touching highlight effect.

Next, we need to add the "Touch" control object to the game. Double click on an empty area of the layout and select what we need (Figure 6.7).

FIGURE 6.7   Select the **Touch** object to insert it in our game.

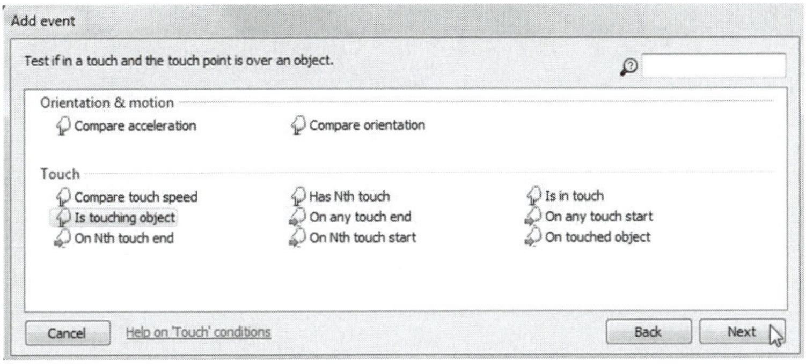

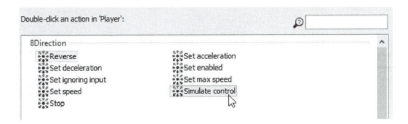

FIGURE 6.8   Adding a new event via the **Touch** object. In this case, we want the event to be triggered when a specific object is being touched.

Once added, it is time to start coding the events to make our spaceship move. Select the **Game Sheet** tab (or **Event Sheet 1** if you haven't renamed it yet), and add the first event by clicking on **Add event**.

Double click the **Touch** object, choose **Is touching object** (Figure 6.8), and click on the **Next** button.

In the **Parameters for touch** dialog, select the **Control_Up** arrow sprite as the **Object to be touched** and press **OK**. Now click on the **Add action** text next to the event we just created, select the **Player** sprite, and choose **Simulate control** (Figure 6.9).

Finally, in the **Parameters** dialog, pick the **Up** key from the list. From now on, whenever we run the project, touching or clicking the arrow sprite will have the same effect as pressing the up cursor key on the keyboard and will move the related sprite (the player ship in this case) up according to the speed defined in the **8 Direction** behavior (which is shown in the **Properties** panel whenever we select the player sprite in the game layout,

FIGURE 6.9   The event will trigger an action on a related object. In this case, we are going to simulate a specific control key. As you see, we can also add actions to control many other movement-related features, including acceleration and speed.

Behaviors	
8Direction	
Max speed	200
Acceleration	600
Deceleration	500
Directions	8 directions
Set angle	360 degree (smooth)
Default controls	Yes
Initial state	Enabled
Add / edit	Behaviors

FIGURE 6.10 A detail of the **Properties Panel** showing the current properties of the **8 Direction** behavior, defining the ship speed, among other things.

see Figure 6.10) or by setting up a new action via the **Set speed** and **Set max speed** parameters shown in Figure 6.9.

We also want to simulate the press button highlight effect, so add another action, this time choosing any of the control sprites and then selecting the **Set opacity** command and specifying a value of 100 (Figure 6.11).

Since we also want the arrow to go back to its original opacity value when not touched, we have to add another event right after the touching one and, specifically, an **Else** event where we set the value back to 30 (to do this, we can simply select the event, then right click on it, move on the **Add** submenu and choose **Add "Else"**).

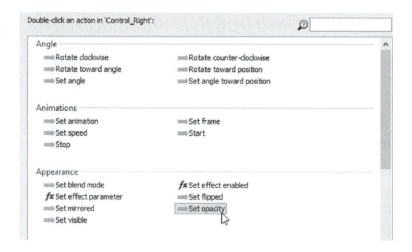

FIGURE 6.11 After selecting one of our control GUI sprites, we can choose different actions for it, including changing its opacity via the **Set opacity** action.

Allow for touch besides keyboard controls				
🔲 Touch	Is touching ➡ Control_Right	🚀 Player	Simulate ⊞ 8Direction pressing Right	
		➡ Control_Right	Set opacity to *100*	
		Add action		
⚙ System	Else	➡ Control_Right	Set opacity to *30*	
		Add action		
🔲 Touch	Is touching ⬅ Control_Left	🚀 Player	Simulate ⊞ 8Direction pressing Left	
		⬅ Control_Left	Set opacity to *100*	
		Add action		
⚙ System	Else	⬅ Control_Left	Set opacity to *30*	
		Add action		
🔲 Touch	Is touching ⬆ Control_Up	🚀 Player	Simulate ⊞ 8Direction pressing Up	
		⬆ Control_Up	Set opacity to *100*	
		🚀 Player	Reverse ⊞ 8Direction	
		Add action		
⚙ System	Else	⬆ Control_Up	Set opacity to *30*	
		Add action		
🔲 Touch	Is touching ⬇ Control_Down	🚀 Player	Simulate ⊞ 8Direction pressing Down	
		⬇ Control_Down	Set opacity to *100*	
		Add action		
⚙ System	Else	⬇ Control_Down	Set opacity to *30*	
		Add action		

FIGURE 6.12 The overall events we need to define for controlling our spaceship and for changing the opacity of the control GUI sprites accordingly. Note also that we can add comments (the top line in the figure) by right clicking on the event sheet and selecting the **Add comment** option. We can also move comments and events around simply by dragging them.

After repeating this for all four directions, we should have a set of events like those in Figure 6.12.

Now we have to be sure our spaceship remains in the visible area, so we need to set up a series of events that check the ship position and block it if necessary.

Let's add a new event having the **Player** as object and **Compare X** as condition (Figure 6.13). We can then add an action to this event with **Player** as object where we set its coordinate (via **Set X**) accordingly.

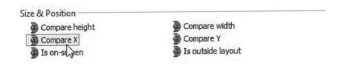

Size & Position
- 🎮 Compare height
- 🎮 Compare X
- 🎮 Is on-screen
- 🎮 Compare width
- 🎮 Compare Y
- 🎮 Is outside layout

FIGURE 6.13 Choosing the **Compare X** condition for a newly defined player event.

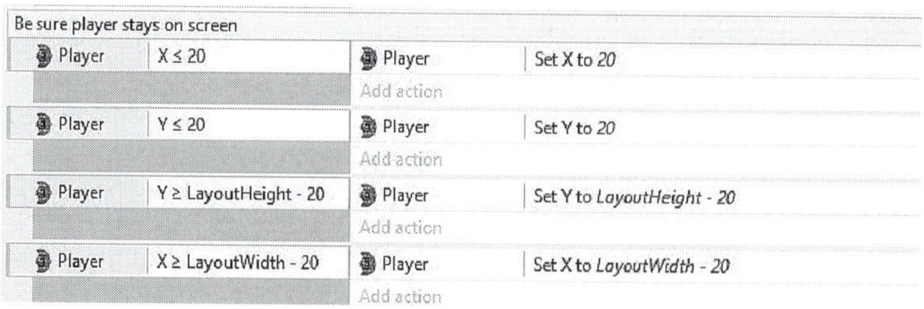

Be sure player stays on screen

Player	X ≤ 20	Player	Set X to *20*
		Add action	
Player	Y ≤ 20	Player	Set Y to *20*
		Add action	
Player	Y ≥ LayoutHeight - 20	Player	Set Y to *LayoutHeight - 20*
		Add action	
Player	X ≥ LayoutWidth - 20	Player	Set X to *LayoutWidth - 20*
		Add action	

FIGURE 6.14 The set of events we need to keep the player within the screen boundaries.

So, if our X coordinate is less than or equal to 20, we automatically replace it with a value of 20 pixels so that we stop just before reaching the left border of the screen (remember the upper left corner of the screen has 0,0 coordinates). For the rightmost value we can reference the **LayoutWidth** variable and subtract 20 and then proceed in the same way for the up and down boundaries. Once done, our section of the event sheet will look like Figure 6.14.

The last thing we should do before trying our game for the first time is adding some background music to make our space cruising a little more engaging! Go back to the **Game** tab and add the **Audio** object to the project (see Figure 6.15).

For this example I'll be using the WeirdSynth.ogg and -.m4a files included in the **asset-bundle/Ambient FX** folder that comes with the personal license, but, as usual, you can use any file you have around in formats like mp3, ogg, or wav.

Import the files by right clicking on the **Music** folder in the **Projects** tab (see Figure 6.16).

Note that importing audio wave files in Construct is recommended, since Construct will automatically convert them to ogg and m4a. Ogg

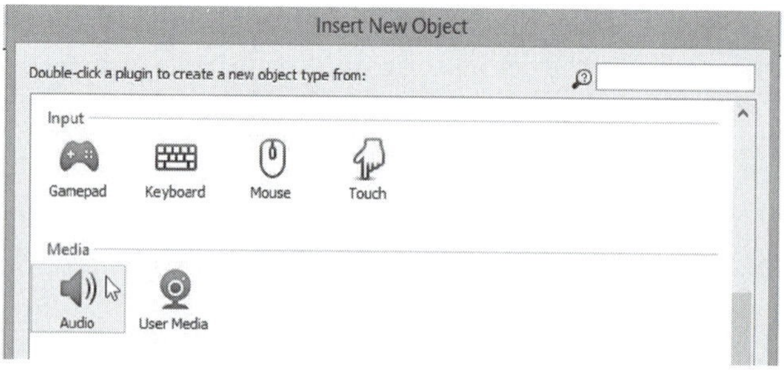

FIGURE 6.15 Adding the **Audio** object to our game.

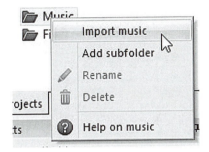

FIGURE 6.16   Importing music directly from the **Projects** tab.

files are the standard for browsers like Chrome, Firefox, and Opera, while Internet Explorer 9 and Safari need files in m4a. Be sure to have both if you want your audio to be playable on as many devices as possible!

Also, be aware of a subtle difference between the **Sounds** and **Music** project folders: files in the **Sounds** folder have to be downloaded completely before we can play them in the game, while files in the **Music** folder are streamed, hence we can start playing them almost immediately.

Once the files have been imported, we can call them from the event sheet to start playing them as the game starts.

We want the music to start as the game begins, so we add a new event directly from the **System** object, **On start of layout,** which is called as soon as the layout starts running. The event will use the **Audio** object and, specifically, the **Play** function, where we specify the filename we want to play, whether it loops or not, and its starting volume (0 means maximum volume, i.e., no attenuation) as seen in Figure 6.17.

Parameters for Audio: Play

Choose the audio file to play.

Audio file	WeirdSynth
Loop	looping
Volume	0
Tag (optional)	""

Cancel   Help on expressions   Back   Done

FIGURE 6.17   Setting up the audio file to play.

FIGURE 6.18 **On start of layout** we want to start playing our background music, looping with no attenuation.

In the end, we will have a new event like the one shown in Figure 6.18.

Now save your project, if you didn't do so already, and get ready to play what we have done so far in the browser of your choice. To do so, be sure you are displaying the game layout and click on the **Run Layout** button: you can then control the spaceship by using either the arrow keys, clicking the arrow controls with your mouse, or just touching the controls if you have a touch enabled screen! (See Figure 6.19.)

While not available in the free version, once you register for the Personal or Business Edition license, Construct 2 will actually offer another very useful way of previewing a game on different computers and tablets directly via local area network or wifi. This would allow for an easy way to test a project across different setups and hardware, without the need to export and download the project on each different machine.

This type of testing may require a relatively complex setup, though, spanning some network and firewall settings. You can check the "How to preview on a local network" tutorial online at Scirra's own website under "Tutorials/Beginner/Workflow/" or by going directly to this address: https://www.scirra.com/tutorials/247/how-to-preview-on-a-local-network.

FIGURE 6.19 Testing our work in progress in a browser: we can freely move the ship around by using the keyboard or by clicking/touching the on-screen controls!

Since all this has already been covered very well online by Construct's own developers, I won't cover it here again, and we will move on with *Moon Wolf* development instead.

6.2 ADDING CELLS AND A SCORING SYSTEM

Let's add a new **Sprite** object anywhere in our game layout as usual. Once in the **Image Editor,** make your own cell design or import a suitable graphic file. In this case, I'll be using the "saucer_blades000" sprite located in the **asset-bundle/Sprites/Space/Enemies** folder. Crop the image and then go back to the layout. Click on the new sprite to show its properties (on the left) and rename it "Cell." Also, resize it to make it proportioned to our ship and screen; here, 30 × 30 pixels should work well (Figure 6.20).

Now duplicate the sprite several times and spread the copies around the layout in any way you feel appropriate. We can do this by standard copy and paste keyboard shortcuts or by pressing Ctrl while clicking on the sprite of choice and then dragging it on a different area of the layout (be sure the layers you copy from and to are the same! In our case, we want all our in-game objects to be on the **Action** layer).

At the end of this process we should have something like Figure 6.21. Note that each new sprite added to the layout will, by default, be at the top of the layer it belongs to. This means our spaceship is now at the bottom and, most likely, we want it to fly on top of the other objects instead. To do so, right click on the **Player** sprite, select **Z Order** and bring it to the top of the layer once again (Figure 6.22).

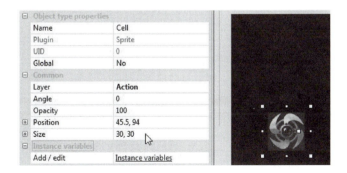

FIGURE 6.20 Adding a sprite to act as the energy cells we have to collect in the game. Rename the object properly, "Cell" in this case, and resize it to match the screen size and other objects.

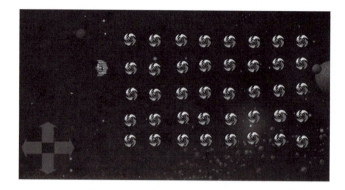

FIGURE 6.21 A possible layout for our game, showing all the cells ready to be collected.

Before coding what happens when the player collides with a cell, let's plan ahead a little bit and start defining another important element of our GUI: a text line that should display the current score, the high score, and the current level/wave number.

Add a new object and choose **Text** under the **General** category and rename it "Score_txt." After you put it in the layout, check in its properties window to select a font you like together with a suitable size and a bright color. Be sure the text window is big enough for your font size (resize it if necessary) and that our object is on the UI layer. I suggest we resize the

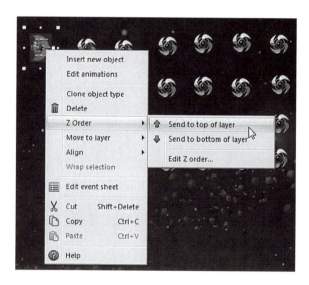

FIGURE 6.22 Bringing the player's ship on top of the layer.

Object type properties	
Name	Score_txt
Plugin	Text
UID	50
Global	No
Common	
Layer	UI
Angle	0
Opacity	100
⊞ Position	2, 11
⊞ Size	800, 46
Instance variables	
Add / edit	Instance variables
Behaviors	
Add / edit	Behaviors
Effects	
Blend mode	Normal
Add / edit	Effects
Container	
No container	Create
Properties	
Text	Text
Initial visibility	Visible
Font	Lucida Console(14)
Color	☐ 255, 255, 204
Horizontal alignment	Center
Vertical alignment	Top
Hotspot	Top-left
Wrapping	Word
Line height	0
More information	Help

FIGURE 6.23   Setting up the text for displaying player's scores.

text window to cover the whole width of our layout and then change the **Horizontal alignment** property to **Center** to have the text automatically centered across our window. In the end we should have a set of properties like those in Figure 6.23.

Now we need to define some variables to keep track of the score. Move to our event sheet and right click on an empty area. Select **Add global variable** from the menu (Figure 6.24), and then fill it with the relevant data (Figure 6.25).

Do the same for two more variables, named **Highscore** and **Level**, setting them to 0 and 1, respectively. Global variables will be displayed on top of the event sheet. We want to display these variables as soon as the game starts, so we will add a corresponding action in the **On start of layout** event. Click **Add action** and select the **score_txt** object. Click **Next** and

FIGURE 6.24 Right click in an event sheet for creating a global variable, i.e., a variable visible and accessible from anywhere in the game.

then scroll down until you see the **Set text** option. Alternatively, when looking for a specific action across a long list of options, use the **Search** field in the top right corner of the window to type what you are looking for. Click **next** and we can define the text we want to display. Here we can mix characters and variables and append each to the other by using the ampersand (&).

Note also that another window on top of your text line will pop up (with transparency, you may have to roll over with the mouse pointer to make it fully visible) displaying all **Objects with expressions** available.

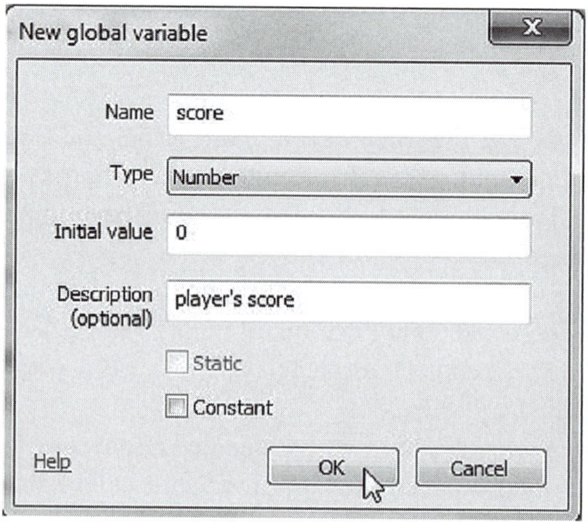

FIGURE 6.25 We name our variable score and set its type to number with a starting value of 0.

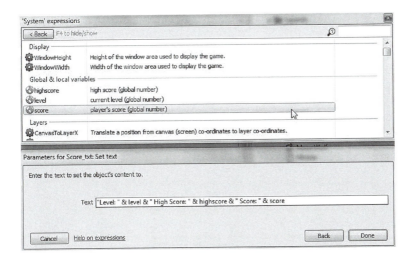

FIGURE 6.26 Setting up the string for the **Score_txt** object. The window on top allows us to easily include different objects and variables in the expression we are building. In this case we selected the **System** object, since we are interested in the game global variables we defined earlier.

This is quite handy for retrieving variables or other objects we want to interact with. In this case we can select the **System object** and insert all the variables we need in our string simply by clicking on each of them.

The result should be something similar to Figure 6.26.

And the **On start of layout** event will then look like Figure 6.27.

The next step is to check for the collision between the ship and any of the cells. When this happens, we want the cell to disappear and award 10 points to the player. To do so, we define a new event for the player object.

Click on **Add event,** and select the **Player** sprite. Look for the **Collision** section of possible events and click on **On collision with another object**. After this, we have to select the cell object in the new popup window (Figures 6.28 and 6.29).

FIGURE 6.27 The **On start of layout** event updated to display the score text line when the game begins.

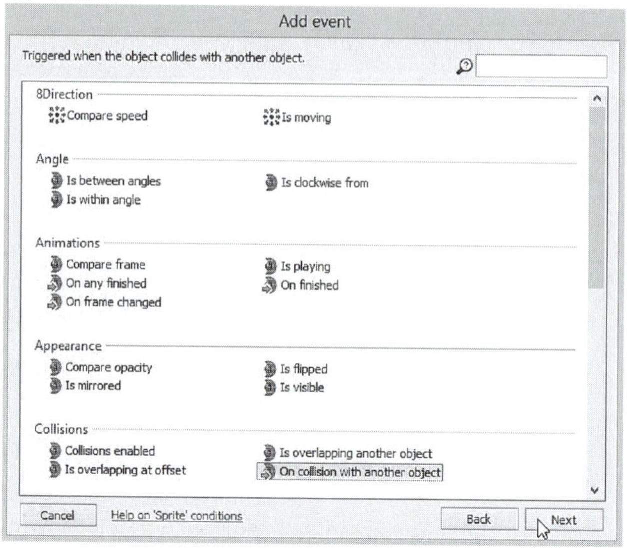

FIGURE 6.28 Setting up collision detection between two sprites is a very straightforward process in Construct 2: we simply need to select the collision event and then the object we will be colliding with.

Now that the collision event is defined, we need to add the corresponding actions we want to perform when the event is triggered (i.e., a collision is detected).

First, we need to remove the cell, since we just picked it up. Click on **Add action**, select the cell object, and select the **Destroy** action in the **Misc** section.

For updating the score, add another action, select the **System** object and then choose the **Add to** in the **Global & local variables** section. In the new window, select the score variable and write "10" in the **Value** field. At

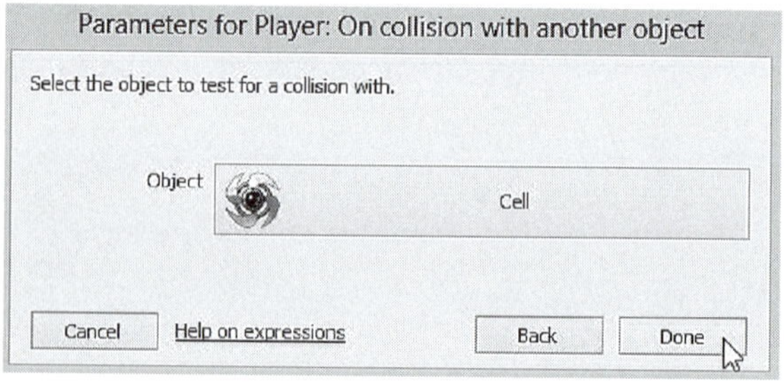

FIGURE 6.29 Selecting the cell object for our collision event.

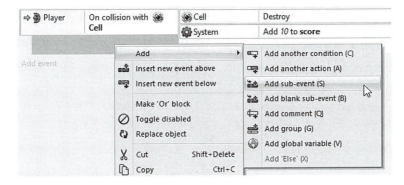

FIGURE 6.30 Defining a subevent for checking if we need to update the high score as well.

this point we may also want to check whether we have beaten the current high score and update it as well.

To do so, we need to introduce a subevent that compares two values and, eventually, triggers the desired action.

Right click on the empty area of the collision event and select the **Add subevent** in the **Add** menu (Figure 6.30). Click on the **System** object and then **Compare variable** in the **Global & local variables** section. Here choose score > **Greater than highscore** as shown in Figure 6.31.

Then, we add an action to the subevent to update the high score value as well (select the **System** object and then the **Set value** command where the value is set to our **score** variable).

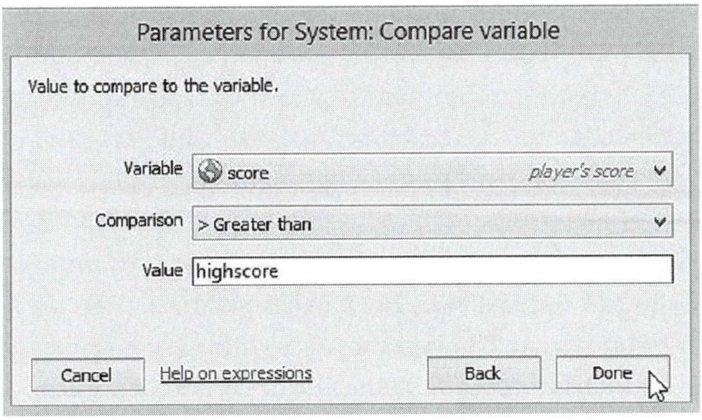

FIGURE 6.31 Comparing **score** and **highscore** variables.

Checking for collision between Player and Cells				
⇒ 🐦 Player	On collision with 🐦 Cell	🐦 Cell	Destroy	
		⚙ System	Add 10 to score	
		T Score_txt	Set text to "Level: " & level & " High Score: " & highscore & " Score: " & score	
		◀)) Audio	Play OK - 1 not looping at volume 0 dB (tag "")	
		Add action		
⚙ System	score > highscore	⚙ System	Set highscore to score	
		T Score_txt	Set text to "Level: " & level & " High Score: " & highscore & " Score: " & score	
		Add action		

FIGURE 6.32 The collision event. It takes care of updating the score and, eventually, the high score, and it also destroys the specific cell.

The last step is to update the display. To do so, we can simply copy and paste the **score_txt** action as defined in the **On start of layout** event in both the main collision event and its subevent.

If we also want to add some polish, we can add a sound to be played when the collision happens. Right click on the **Sounds** folder in the **Projects** tab and select a sound you think is suitable. I chose the **OK-1. wav** sound in the **Asset-bundle/SoundFX** folder, but you can also design a new one with a tool like SFXR, as described in Appendix A. Add another action to the main body of the collision event and select the **Audio** object. Select the **Play** action under the **General** group and then select the file you just imported, not looping and with a volume of 0 dB (i.e., no attenuation).

The Player/Cell collision event in its entirety is shown in Figure 6.32. Save the project and test the game!

6.3 SPEEDING UP

In this section we are going to add the speeding up functionality, triggered when moving in any direction while pressing a specific button. We will need to design new GUI elements and objects and, in doing so, we will also introduce new concepts like Instance Variables and Particles.

As we see in our one-page design document, we need to add the fuel bar and a button. Start by creating these elements: each is a new **Sprite** object.

The fuel bar is made by two sprites: a background and a foreground image. We can call the first **fuel_bg**, and simply fill the 256 × 256 pixel (we can stretch it out later in the game layout) with a bright blue tone of your choice in the sprite editor. Close the editor to go back to the layout and change the y dimension of the sprite to 30 pixels. Also change the opacity to 50, and place the sprite at the bottom of the screen.

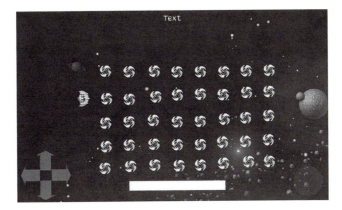

FIGURE 6.33 The game layout after adding the GUI elements for the speeding up effect: a fuel bar and a button.

Now repeat the process for a new sprite called **fuel_fg**, but this time we fill it with a bright yellow color. Once back to the game layout, let's resize it to something like 245 × 24 pixel and an opacity level of 70. Then place this on top of the blue background bar.

Add one more GUI sprite and name it **speedup_btn**. In the editor either draw a rectangle filled with a bright red color, or select a big sized brush (e.g., 256 to cover the entire sprite image) and a high hardness value (e.g., 90 or more), since we don't need a halo effect around it. Go back to the layout, resize the button to 80 × 80 pixel, for example, and change its opacity level to 30, like we did previously for the virtual D-pad.

We should then have a GUI like in Figure 6.33. Be sure that all its elements are placed in the UI layer!

We need now to implement the events we want to trigger when pressing the button, i.e., lighting it up, progressively reduce the fuel_fg image, and change the speed of our ship (as long as we have fuel left). All these will be handled in a way similar to what we just did for the D-pad.

Switch to the event sheet and add a new event, choose the **Touch** object, then select **Is touching object**, and finally choose the **speedup_btn** as the object being touched.

After this, we add the actions for changing the button opacity to 100. Changing the fuel bar X size is a little trickier and requires us to introduce something new: **instance variables**.

To keep track of its width, in fact, we should define first an instance variable, i.e., a variable tied to a specific object in the game. We can do so through the property window once we select the object on the **Game**

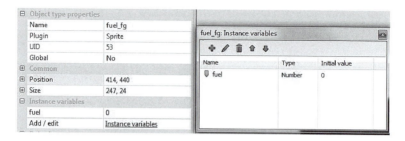

FIGURE 6.34   Adding an instance variable named fuel of type number to the fuel bar foreground to keep track of its level.

layout and we click on the **Add/edit Instance variables** line in the object properties (Figure 6.34).

We should initialize this variable at the beginning of the game with the original bar width. The **On start of layout** event is a suitable place for doing it: add an action, pick the **fuel_fg** object, choose **Set value** in the **Instance variable** section and then pick the **Width** property from the **fuel_fg** object (Size & Position group) as shown in Figure 6.35, or simply write **fuel_fg.Width** directly in the value field.

The **On start of layout** event will then be updated as in Figure 6.36.

We are now ready to change the bar width in real time as we press the button.

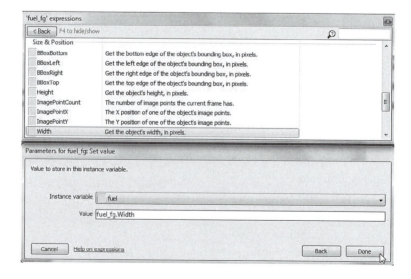

FIGURE 6.35   Initializing the fuel variable with the object's own width.

FIGURE 6.36   Updating **On start of layout** event to reflect the initialization of **fuel_fg** instance variable.

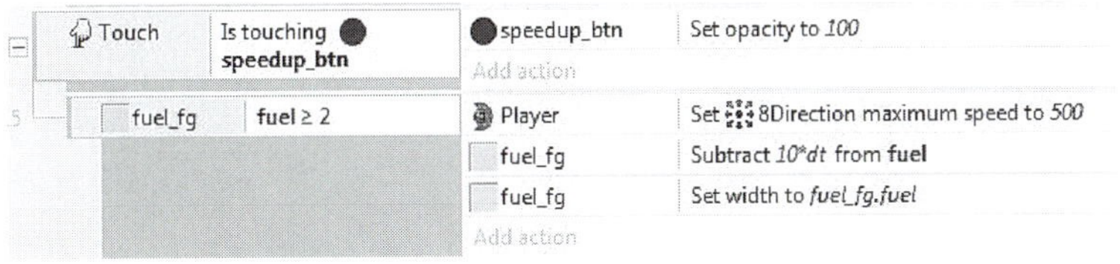

🖐 Touch	Is touching ⬤ **speedup_btn**	⬤ speedup_btn	Set opacity to *100*		
	fuel_fg	fuel ≥ 2	🎮 Player	Set ⠿ 8Direction maximum speed to *500*	
			fuel_fg	Subtract *10*dt* from fuel	
			fuel_fg	Set width to *fuel_fg.fuel*	

FIGURE 6.37   The event and subevent needed for giving a boost to the player's ship and update the GUI, as long as we still have enough fuel!

Note also that we want this to happen only when we have enough fuel left. The first thing we should do is **Add a subevent** where we check whether the fuel variable of the **fuel_fg** object is still greater than a minimum value, let's say 2. If this condition is satisfied, we can proceed to update the player's speed to, let's say, 500: select the **Player** object and add an action to the subevent we just created, then pick **Set max speed** in the **8 Direction** group. Finally, we have to decrease the variable and resize the bar.

For the former, we want the decreasing rate to be constant, like 10 pixels per second, and not dependent on the specific frame rate of the machine the game is running on. Construct achieves frame independence by using the system expression **dt**, which returns the time elapsed in seconds between two frames,* so let's add a new **Subtract from** action for the **fuel_fg** object where we subtract **10 * dt** from its instance variable **fuel**. After that, we add another **Set width** action where we update the width of **fuel_fg** width to the new vale of **fuel** as shown in Figure 6.37.

If we playtest the game now (by the way, remember to save often!) and press the button, most likely we will see something unexpected: the **fuel_fg** yellow bar will remain centered where it is, giving the impression it is shrinking from both sides! This happens simply because we didn't change its origin point yet and, by default, this is located in the center of the image.

---

* Note that predefined behaviors like **8 Direction** have dt already built in, so we don't need to add it when working with them.

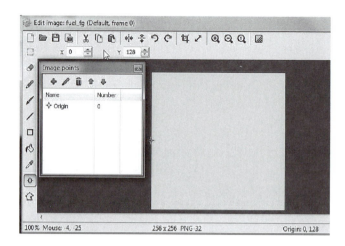

FIGURE 6.38   Image coordinates in the layout refer to its origin point. If we want the left side of our bar to remain next to the left side of **fuel_fg**, we need to move the origin point from the center to the edge of the image.

To fix this, open the sprite in the image editor and move the origin point to 0,128 like in Figure 6.38.

Now that this is fixed, we need to restore the player's speed, as well the button's opacity when we stop pressing the button. We can do so by adding an **else** condition to the **Touch** event where we reset the opacity and maximum speed variables. **Else** is part of the **System** object and has to be added as an event right after the condition we want to check, as shown in Figure 6.39.

Unfortunately, for the button press, we don't have a simple way to simulate the event as we did with the **8 Direction** for movement, so we need to handle this case specifically if we want to also enable keyboard input, for example by pressing the space bar.

Touch	Is touching speedup_btn	speedup_btn	Set opacity to *100*
		Add action	
fuel_fg	fuel ≥ 2	Player	Set 8Direction maximum speed to *500*
		fuel_fg	Subtract *10°dt* from **fuel**
		fuel_fg	Set width to *fuel_fg.fuel*
		Add action	
System	Else	speedup_btn	Set opacity to *30*
		Player	Set 8Direction maximum speed to *200*
		Add action	

FIGURE 6.39   Restoring the variables when we stop touching the button.

▦ Keyboard	**Space** is down	🚀 Player	Set ⋮⋮ 8Direction maximum speed to *500*
fuel_fg	**fuel** ≥ 2	fuel_fg	Subtract *10°dt* from **fuel**
		fuel_fg	Set width to *fuel_fg.fuel*
		Add action	
⚙ System	Else	🚀 Player	Set ⋮⋮ 8Direction maximum speed to *200*
		Add action	

FIGURE 6.40 Handling keyboard input in addition to the touch controls for speeding up the spaceship.

To do so, add the **Keyboard** object to the project first, then add a new event, choose the newly added **Keyboard**, and then choose the **Key is down** condition. Then click on <**click to choose**> and press the space bar to associate it with the key down event. We also need to check that we have enough fuel by adding an additional condition in the same event (or as a subevent, as we did in Figure 6.39 when touching the **speedup_btn**). In the end, our keyboard event will be defined as in Figure 6.40.

But there is an instructive problem here. Assuming the keyboard event is placed after the one for the touch button, if we play the game we will soon realize that, while the space bar works as planned, clicking on the red button has no effect on the speed! Why? Because the **else** condition after the keyboard event is going to be checked *after* the touch control changed the speed value, and it will be executed since the space bar is not pressed, setting the speed back to 200 regardless of what the touch button event did previously!

This means we need to reorganize our code in a more efficient way. We can actually delete the action resetting the player speed in the **else** part of the touching button event, as well as the whole **else** part of the keyboard event.* What we should do instead is a common event that gets triggered when neither the button nor the space bar are pressed and only then resets the speed to the original value of 200.

Add a new event and start by copying and pasting our two conditions, **Touch/Is touching speedup_btn** and **Keyboard/Space is down**. Now click on each to select them individually, right click, and choose **Invert** from the menu. This will add a red cross next to each condition and make the event run only when both are false, i.e., space bar *is not* pressed and button *is not* touched.

---

* Note that we can temporarily disable an action or event, instead of deleting it, by right clicking on it and then selecting **toggle disabled** in the menu. This is very handy when testing and looking for different ways of doing things.

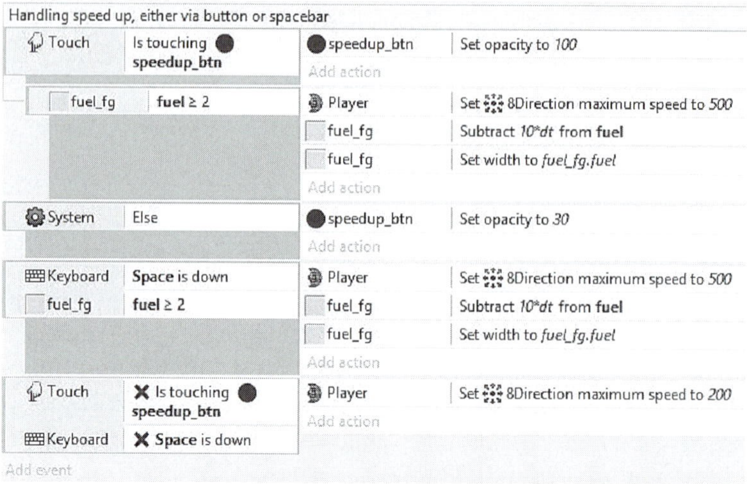

Handling speed up, either via button or spacebar

🖐 Touch	Is touching ● speedup_btn	● speedup_btn	Set opacity to *100*	
		Add action		
fuel_fg	fuel ≥ 2	🅐 Player	Set 8Direction maximum speed to *500*	
		fuel_fg	Subtract *10*dt* from fuel	
		fuel_fg	Set width to *fuel_fg.fuel*	
		Add action		
⚙ System	Else	● speedup_btn	Set opacity to *30*	
		Add action		
⌨ Keyboard	Space is down	🅐 Player	Set 8Direction maximum speed to *500*	
fuel_fg	fuel ≥ 2	fuel_fg	Subtract *10*dt* from fuel	
		fuel_fg	Set width to *fuel_fg.fuel*	
		Add action		
🖐 Touch	✗ Is touching ● speedup_btn	🅐 Player	Set 8Direction maximum speed to *200*	
⌨ Keyboard	✗ Space is down	Add action		
Add event				

FIGURE 6.41 All the events for handling the speed boost via either on-screen button or space bar and then properly resetting the value.

The final set of events is shown in Figure 6.41.

When we boost the player speed, it would be nice to show some visual feedback, so this is a good time to introduce **particle effects**.

Particles are just another predefined object we can easily add into our project and layout (we find it under the general section next to the **Sprite** object), so let's add one and name it "boost." As soon as we place it in the layout or double click on it, the image editor opens up: we can now draw our own particles. For this example, we can first reduce the size of the image from the default 256 × 256 to 32 × 32 via the resize icon (it is next to the crop icon) and then draw a small bright colored circle with the brush tool (I used a size 32 with a hardness value of 25).

Back in the layout we can see our **Particle** object: select it and do some experiments to understand how to manipulate and fine-tune the various effects. Note that by clicking on **help** at the bottom of **Properties** tab we are taken to the online manual page with a detailed description of all the different parameters. For this simple example, most default values are fine: we may just change the **Spray cone** property to 30 or 45 degrees and a **Timeout** property to 0.2 seconds to have a more focused jet. We may also want to fine-tune the individual particle size to match the current screen resolution and player sprite more precisely, for example, by reducing the **Size** to 16 (in the **Initial particle properties** section).

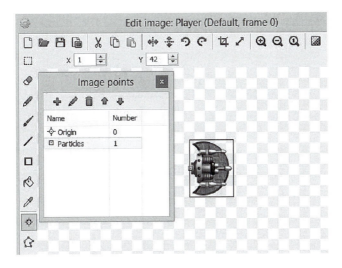

FIGURE 6.42 Adding an image point to the player: that is where the particle effect will be attached.

What we really need to do now is to attach the particle to the player and switch the effect on and off together with the speed boost.

To do so, we should first add a specific **Image point** to the player sprite that we will use as an anchor for the particles. Open the **Player** sprite in the Image editor, select the **origin** icon and add a new one-image point. Call it "Particles" and place it on the ship exhaust system as in Figure 6.42. Note that the new point has an index number of 1.

The particles should be off when the game starts, so we should add an Action to the **On start of layout** event to do so: select the **boost** particle object and then pick the **Set visible** option in the **Appearance** section. In the following menu, select **Invisible**.

We then need to turn the particles on whenever we speed up the player, i.e., when we either press the button or the space bar and we have fuel left. Add a **Set Visible** action for the particles in both those events and then add another event to make the particle invisible again if neither is pressed. The updated events should be like those in Figure 6.43.

We are now ready to use the player image point we defined earlier to display the particles properly. This should be done every frame so we can add a new **System** event, **Every tick**, and then add a new action for the **boost** object, specifically the **Set position to another object** (in the **Size & Position** group), which we tie to the **Player** sprite and its image point 1. We should also add a **Set Angle** action to the particles for adjusting their

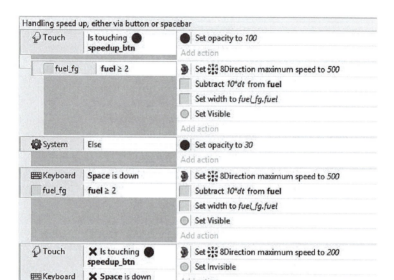

Handling speed up, either via button or spacebar		
🐾 Touch	Is touching ● speedup_btn	● Set opacity to *100*
		Add action
☐ fuel_fg	fuel ≥ 2	🖉 Set ⁝⁝⁝ 8Direction maximum speed to *500*
		☐ Subtract *10*dt* from **fuel**
		☐ Set width to *fuel_fg.fuel*
		◎ Set Visible
		Add action
⚙ System	Else	● Set opacity to *30*
		Add action
⌨ Keyboard	Space is down	🖉 Set ⁝⁝⁝ 8Direction maximum speed to *500*
☐ fuel_fg	fuel ≥ 2	☐ Subtract *10*dt* from **fuel**
		☐ Set width to *fuel_fg.fuel*
		◎ Set Visible
		Add action
🐾 Touch	✖ Is touching ● speedup_btn	🖉 Set ⁝⁝⁝ 8Direction maximum speed to *200*
		◎ Set Invisible
⌨ Keyboard	✖ Space is down	Add action

FIGURE 6.43 Updating different events to switch on and off the boosting particle system (here identified by the filled yellow circle).

Every frame we update the position and alignment of the particles		
⚙ System	Every tick	◎ Set position to 🖉 **Player** *(image point 1)*
		◎ Set angle to *Player.Angle-180* degrees
		Add action
Add event		

FIGURE 6.44 Every tick, i.e., every frame, we need to adjust the particles' position and angle.

angle, which should be set to **Player.Angle-180 degrees**, so that the particles are emitted backward (Figure 6.44).

In the game design document we also discussed a rule about fuel refills: "every time we collect a cell, there is a 10% probability to spawn a recharge battery. The battery should recharge 20 units of fuel when picked," so we should work on this feature now.

This will allow us to explore how to instantiate objects dynamically, but, first, we need to draw or import a suitable image for our batteries. I decided to go with the image Spikey0000.png[*] in the usual **asset-bundle** folder, but this shouldn't necessarily affect your choice.

---

[*] Asset-bundle/Sprites/Space/Enemies/Spikey0000.png.

Name your object something meaningful, like **FuelBattery**, crop the image, and resize it as necessary (I resized it to 34 × 30 pixel). Now don't bring it into the visible layout, but leave it off the screen: this instance is going to work as a template that we are going to reference for the new ones we will be creating and destroying.

What we are going to do is this: we define an instance variable in a suitable game object, the player for example, and every time we trigger the collision event between the player and a cell, we randomly generate a new value for this variable within a specific range. If the value is in the top 10% of the range, we spawn a new battery fuel in a random location of the screen. Finally, when the player picks the battery, we refill the fuel reserve as long as it doesn't reach its maximum level.

Defining instance variables should be easy by now: in the game layout, select the **Player** sprite and then add the variable through the **Properties** panel. Set it to the type "number," and give it a name related to its purpose, like "spawnb." Now we need to extend the actions in the **Player On collision with Cell** event: first, let's add the action to update the spawnb variable and see if we are lucky enough to get a fuel recharge. Select the player, choose set value and, in the value field, write "random(1,100)." The random instruction is also accessible through the **System** object, in the **Values** group and, as we can imagine, it will generate a random number between 1 and 100 excluded. Now we can add a subevent to check for the random value outcome: if spawnb is greater than or equal to 90, we trigger an action where, from the **System** object, we choose **create object** (in the **General** section), select the **FuelBattery**, and then we write the specific coordinates where we want the new object to be created. We want these values to be random within the screen so we can write something like

round(random(20, LayoutWidth-20))

for the *x* axis and

round(random(20, LayoutHeight-20))

for the *y* axis (Figure 6.45).

Once the battery is spawned, we need to program for picking it up, destroying the battery, and updating the fuel bar accordingly, i.e., adding 20 fuel units and filling it up only to its maximum level, for example 245,

FIGURE 6.45   The player/cell collision event updated to include the possibility of spawning a fuel recharging battery.

which is the original full length of the bar after we resized it according to our screen dimensions.

While we could easily hard code the required values of 20 (for the refill) and 245 (for the maximum level of fuel) directly in our event, this is never considered to be a good programming practice: having values stored in variables makes the resulting code much easier to manage and update when the logic behind our programs starts getting more complex. For this reason, before proceeding with the event, let's add an instance variable named **refill** to the **FuelBattery** and another one named **maximum** to **fuel_fg**. Both should be of type number and be initialized with a value of 20 and 245, respectively.[*]

I'll let you write down this new event as a little exercise without further instructions. The result is shown in Figure 6.46, where I also added a new sound clip to be played when the fuel battery is picked up.

6.4 ADDING ENEMIES AND A BASIC GAME LOOP

Our game is now starting to take shape: we can roam around, speed up, pick up the cells, and increase our score. We are still missing one of the main components, though: enemies to make the action challenging and exciting!

As defined in the game design, the main opponent here is an alien spaceship, roaming the screen perimeter and shooting around. So let's add two more sprites: one for the enemy, which we call **sentinel**, and one for its missiles, which we simply name **rocket**. For these, I'll be using the sprites

---

[*] These could also be declared as global constants by selecting the checkbox while declaring a new global variable, but here I preferred to keep them within the objects they relate to.

Picking up a battery partially refills the fuel, unless the fuel reserve is full already

⇨ 🎲 Player	On collision with ✻ **FuelBattery**	✻	Destroy
		🔊	Play **OK - 4** not looping at volume 0 dB (tag "")
		⬜	Add *FuelBattery.refill* to **fuel**
		⬜	Set width to *fuel_fg.fuel*
			Add action
fuel_fg	**fuel ≥ fuel_fg. maximum**	⬜	Set **fuel** to *fuel_fg.maximum*
		⬜	Set width to *fuel_fg.fuel*
			Add action

FIGURE 6.46   The event handling player/fuel battery collision, with a subevent checking we don't add anything beyond the maximum level. Instance variables have been used for defining how much fuel each battery provides (FuelBattery. refill) and how much we can store (fuel_fg.maximum).

in asset-bundle/Sprites/Space/Enemies/bug_eye0000.png for the alien and asset-bundle/Sprites/Space/Rockets/rocket_type_C0004.png for the rocket (note that the image is oriented toward the right: if you draw your own sprite, use the same convention). While cropping the image in the editor, we should also be sure to set up image points properly so that, when the sentinel shoots a rocket, this gets spawned from the right position, i.e., in front of the spaceship. As shown in Figures 6.47 and 6.48, a new point

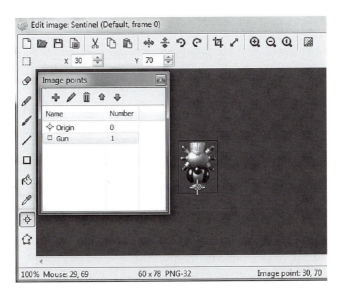

FIGURE 6.47   Adding an image point named **Gun** to the **Sentinel** sprite. This is the point where we will spawn enemy rockets.

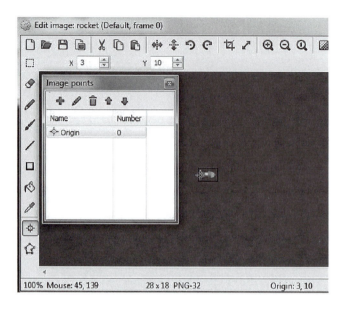

FIGURE 6.48   Moving the origin point of the rocket to its tail.

called **Gun,** having index number 1, is added to the sentinel's gun, while the origin point of the rocket is moved to its tail.

We will get back to the rocket in a moment when we implement the shooting action (for now, place it outside of the playing area), but we should take care of the sentinel movement first.

We want the sentinel to roam the perimeter of the screen. To do so, let's start by placing it in the upper right corner. We have to make it move straight to the opposite corner on the left, rotate clockwise 90 degrees, and go down to the bottom left corner, rotate 90 degrees again, and so on. There is a predefined behavior called **bullet** that would help us a little bit here. The bullet behavior simply makes an object move forward at a specified angle. In our case, we are going to let the sentinel move straight and simply turn when it reaches the edges of the screen. The exact boundaries should be selected according to the actual size of our sprite and to the location where we want the sprite to start. In the **Sentinel** object, we also need to define an instance variable called, for example, **side** (of type number) to keep track of the side along the perimeter the sentinel is moving on. This is needed to avoid the sentinel getting stuck in a corner and keep turning around forever. The resulting events and actions are shown in Figure 6.49.

Sentinel Movement			
🦊 Sentinel	X ≥ LayoutWidth-25	🦊	Rotate *90* degrees clockwise
🦊 Sentinel	Y ≤ 40	🦊	Set **side** to *1*
🦊 Sentinel	**side** = 0		Add action
🦊 Sentinel	X ≥ LayoutWidth-25	🦊	Rotate *90* degrees clockwise
🦊 Sentinel	Y ≥ LayoutHeight-40	🦊	Set **side** to *2*
🦊 Sentinel	**side** = 1		Add action
🦊 Sentinel	X ≤ 25	🦊	Rotate *90* degrees clockwise
🦊 Sentinel	Y ≥ LayoutHeight-40	🦊	Set **side** to *3*
🦊 Sentinel	**side** = 2		Add action
🦊 Sentinel	X ≤ 25	🦊	Rotate *90* degrees clockwise
🦊 Sentinel	Y ≤ 40	🦊	Set **side** to *0*
🦊 Sentinel	**side** = 3		Add action

FIGURE 6.49 Planning for the **Sentinel** movement. We compare its x and y coordinates, and every time we get close enough to a corner, we turn 90 degrees clockwise to move along the other side of the playing field. Note how the different checks can be grouped together as additional conditions within the same event (right click on the event and select **Add condition** to do so).

For the shooting, let's define two more instance variables for the sentinel: **shoot**, a random number between 0 and 100, and **trigger**, a threshold value we will compare **shoot** with: if **shoot** is higher than or equal to that, the sentinel will actually shoot a missile. The updated properties for the sentinel are shown in Figure 6.50, where we also see the rocket placed outside of the visible playing area.

To complete the shooting process, we now have to work on the rocket. First, we need to add, via the **Properties** panel, the **Bullet** behavior to it, and then set its speed to 400. We should also add another behavior, **DestroyOutsideLayout**: since we don't want the rockets to travel forever, we should destroy the object as soon as it walks out of the screen. This behavior takes care of this for us automatically.

After this, we can define the needed events and actions: specifically, in the **Every tick** (i.e., every frame) event, we need to add an action to pick a number for the **shoot** variable (**sentinel** object, **Set value**, select **shoot** variable, and specify **random(0,100)**). **Shoot** will then be compared in a subevent, to be triggered if its value is higher than the **trigger** variable (choose the **sentinel** object, **Compare instance variable,** and pick the two

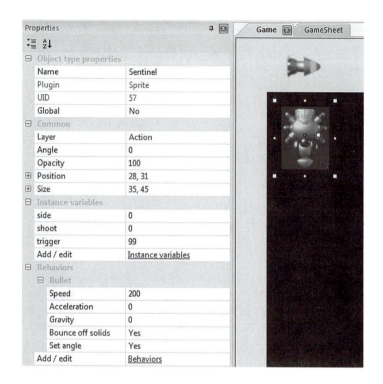

FIGURE 6.50 Updated properties for the **Sentinel** object. We added three instance variables to keep track of the movement (**side**) and define the shooting rate (**shoot** and **trigger**). The behavior **Bullet** was also added, with a starting speed set at 200 pixels per second. Finally, note the rocket sprite placed outside of the screen: it will be used as a template for spawning all the rockets the sentinel will shoot at the player during the game!

variables). If so, we select the **sentinel** object again and its **Spawn another object** action (which is in the **Misc** section), where we choose the rocket as well as the layer and the image point the object should spawn from (pick image point 1, i.e., the **gun** point we defined earlier in Figure 6.47). Last, we add another action to rotate the rocket 90 degrees clockwise and align it with the sentinel sprite. The new events are shown in Figure 6.51.

We can follow the same procedure for adding other enemy types, for example, asteroids, as discussed in the game design document.

After having added a new **Sprite** object, drawn or imported an asteroid image (I'll be using asset-bundle/Sprites/Space/Rocks/rock-type-A0000. png), and done any eventual resizing and cropping, we can now think of the game logic we want for it. For example, we can decide that, at the

Every frame we update the position and alignment of the particles. Sentinel may be shooting!			
⚙ System	Every tick	◯ Set position to 🔹 **Player** *(image point 1)*	
		◯ Set angle to *Player.Angle-180* degrees	
		🔸 Set **shoot** to *random(0,100)*	
		Add action	
🔸 Sentinel	**shoot ≥ Sentinel. trigger**	🔸 Spawn 🚀 **rocket** on layer **0** *(image point 1)*	
		🚀 Rotate *90* degrees clockwise	
		Add action	

FIGURE 6.51   Updated **Every tick** event to include the sentinel shooting action.

beginning of the game, there is 0.25% probability that an asteroid starts moving across the screen, entering at a random position and angle.

As for the rocket, we should start by placing the asteroid sprite out of the visible playing area (it will act as a template for the instances we will spawn dynamically) and add two behaviors to it: **bullet** for its movement (with a starting speed of 100, for example) and **Destroy outside of layout** to get rid of the instances once they are no longer needed. To handle the asteroid's appearances, we need to add two more instance variables of type number to the sentinel. Call them **spawn_ast** and **trigger_ast**: these will work like those we declared previously to handle the shooting of rockets. Set **trigger_ast** at 399.

In the **Every tick** event we should now add another action to set the value of **spawn_ast** randomly between 0 and 400 and then check this against **trigger_ast** in another subevent. Implementing this section will follow the same steps we did for the rockets. The only difference is that here we want to give the impression the asteroids are floating into the playing field so they should spawn up randomly at the top of the screen (for example with Y set to 1: remember that the asteroid objects will be destroyed automatically once they are off screen, so if we spawn them outside the layout they also will be destroyed right away!) and then moving downward by setting an angle between 0 and 180 degrees.

The revised **Every tick** event is shown in Figure 6.52.

Now that we have all the objects in place, we should worry about the collision detection between the player and all the hazards: sentinel, rockets, and asteroids!

Basically, they will all work the same way: if we hit any of them, we should have some explosion effect and display a button with "game over" text to restart the game.

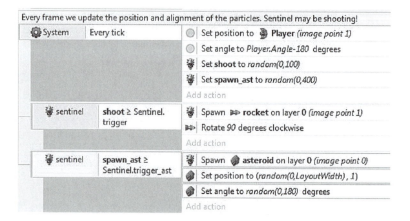

Every frame we update the position and alignment of the particles. Sentinel may be shooting!		
⚙ System	Every tick	◯ Set position to 🎮 **Player** *(image point 1)*
		◯ Set angle to *Player.Angle-180* degrees
		🐝 Set **shoot** to *random(0,100)*
		🐝 Set **spawn_ast** to *random(0,400)*
		Add action
🐝 sentinel	**shoot** ≥ Sentinel. trigger	🐝 Spawn 🚀 **rocket** on layer 0 *(image point 1)*
		🚀 Rotate *90* degrees clockwise
		Add action
🐝 sentinel	**spawn_ast** ≥ Sentinel.trigger_ast	🐝 Spawn 🪨 **asteroid** on layer 0 *(image point 0)*
		🪨 Set position to *(random(0,LayoutWidth)* , *1)*
		🪨 Set angle to *random(0,180)* degrees
		Add action

FIGURE 6.52 Updated **Every tick** event to include the spawning of asteroids, handled in the background by the sentinel object.

For the explosion effect, let's try to make some cool particles. Add a new particle object, name it **Explosion,** and draw some fancy, multicolored dots with the brush tool, for example, like those shown in Figure 6.53, but you can also import an image if you have something suitable, of course (in this case, in the Explosion properties, change blend mode to **Additive** so that each particle blends properly with the background and with the

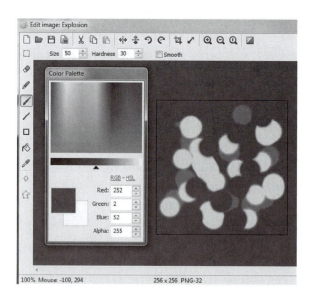

FIGURE 6.53 Possible particles for our explosion effect. Parameters will be set so that particles are emitted in all directions in a single burst.

other particles as well). Experiment with different settings until you find a combination you like. For example, we may select **Spray cone** to 360 (we want the explosion to be all over the place), set it to **One shot** type and have a **Rate** of 100 (for a one shot type of particle, this is the total number of particles we are creating), a **Speed** of 200, and a **Size** of 50. Check the effect by previewing the game in your browser and then move it outside the layout.

Now let's add the collision related events: we pick up the player object and we put together three **Is overlapping** conditions, one for each of the possible hazards: the sentinel, the rocket, and the asteroids. Then select the event, right click on it, and choose **Make 'OR' block** like in Figure 6.54. This will make the actions fire whenever any of those collisions happen.

In the actions we take the **Player** object to spawn a new **Explosion** particle in its default image point, and then we simply destroy the player as well as the object that hit us.

We are still missing something important: a "Game Over" message and Restart button! For simplicity, in this example we are going to merge the two, so add a **Button** object in the game (you will find it in the **Form controls** group in the **Insert new object** window), change the name to game over, the text to "Game Over," add a tooltip saying something like "Click

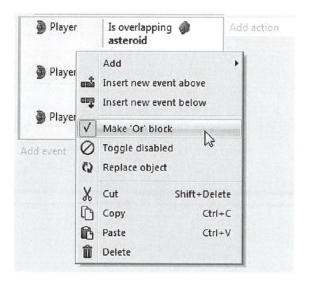

FIGURE 6.54 Turn an event with multiple conditions into an 'Or' block: any of the defined conditions will fire the related actions.

FIGURE 6.55 The collision events and related actions.

to Restart!" and resize it so that it is big enough to be noticed. Place it in the middle of the screen but be sure its **Initial visibility** is set to **Invisible**.

We will turn it to **visible** in the collision event like in Figure 6.55.

When clicked, the button should restart the layout by also resetting the relevant variables. The event is shown in Figures 6.56 and 6.57.

Don't forget to add a suitable explosion sound to make things nicer!

To properly complete the game loop, we still need to allow the player to start playing again at an increased challenge level when all cells have been picked up. To do so, we need, first of all, to keep track of how many cells we have gotten so far.

Add an instance variable to the Player object and call it **cells**. Be sure it is set to 0 when the game starts. Now, every time we pick up a cell we need to increase the value of this variable by one, so add a corresponding action to the Player/Cell collision event. Since we know we placed 40 cells in our layout, we could simply check to see whether our counter cell is equal to that number and proceed, but we are smarter than that! As said earlier in this chapter, hard coding values is never a good idea: what if we want to expand the game to have different cell layouts and different numbers? Every time we would need to remember to update the values, otherwise

FIGURE 6.56 The different actions we have to do to restart the game once we click on the button.

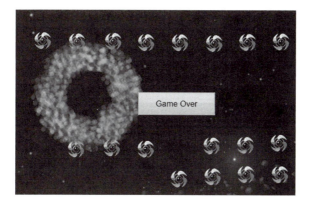

FIGURE 6.57 The player was hit by a rocket, triggering the "ring of fire" explosion effect we created together with the **Game Over** button.

we would get very unexpected results. Flexibility should be planned in advance, so it is a much better idea to add one more instance variable of type number to the **Player**. Let's name it **total**. Then, in the **On start of layout** event, we add a subevent where we use the **System** object and its **For each** action, which we can use to cycle through all cell instances we placed in the level and count them by adding 1 to the total variable (Figure 6.58).

Only then we can proceed in defining the event that will compare the player cells variable against the total: if the two match, we destroy all objects and display a new button that allows for replaying the level with faster and more deadly hazards (Figure 6.59).

When a new level starts, we should also update the shooting rate and speed of the different hazards, as suggested in the game design document. We can define simple formulas for these changes that we should implement in the start of layout, making sure that everything works consistently for the very first level (Figure 6.60).

⇨ 🔧 System	On start of layout	🔊 Play **WeirdSynth** looping at volume 0 dB (tag "")
		[T] Set text to *'Level: ' & level & ' High Score: ' & highscore & ' Score: ' & score*
		▢ Set **fuel** to *fuel_fg.Width*
		◯ Set Invisible
		Add action
⤷ 🔧 System	For each 🔩 **Cell**	🎲 Add *1* to **total**
		Add action

FIGURE 6.58 The updated **On start of layou**t event, now including a counter to keep track of how many cells we have in the level.

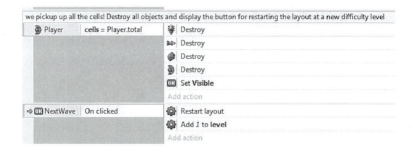

FIGURE 6.59 The event to be triggered once all cells have been cleared, followed by the click event for the new button we have to add to restart the level.

As a final note to this chapter, I want to briefly discuss debugging. If you didn't already, you will soon realize that, when testing your work in progress, most of the time things don't run as expected, and we have to find out why. To do so, developers look at all the relevant variables in the program and track them down to see where things go wrong. Starting from the beta release n.140, Construct 2 added a built-in tool for displaying all relevant information about the game, from frames per second and CPU usage to specific objects and variables. Debugging a layout can be started by using the keyboard shortcut Ctrl+F5 or any of the corresponding shortcuts in the ribbon and quick-launch bar. Alternatively, to simply track a few relevant data, we could also add a specific **debug** layer for showing a couple

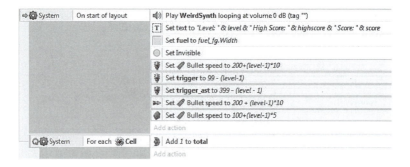

FIGURE 6.60 The final **On start of layout** event, including also actions for updating different variables according to the current level: the sentinel, rockets, and asteroids will get gradually faster, and the shooting rate will also increase. Remember we should playtest the game throughout to fine-tune these values properly and find a sweet spot with a difficulty curve that doesn't frustrate or bore players.

of text fields displaying only the information we are interested in, such as variables and flags being triggered when important events, like collisions between two sprites, for example, get registered. Needless to say, the debug layer has to be removed (or at least turned invisible) when we build the final version to be released to the public.

Last, another option to track down variables would be to use the **Browser** object and write to the browser's own console window via the **Log to console** action.

TAKE AWAY

This chapter was packed with useful information and many different concepts. We introduced GUI and touch controls, variables, particles effects, collision events, and even programmed a basic movement pattern for the sentinel spaceship built around the bullet behavior. Most importantly, though, we developed our first game, complete with a simple game loop to restart after a game over or to continue with a more challenging level if the player manages to survive.

EXERCISE

Try adding a shooting functionality to the player's ship, for example, for destroying asteroids.

CHAPTER 7

Kitty & Katty, a Platformer

F ROM *SPACE PANIC* (A 1980 arcade game developed by Universal) to *Super Meat Boy* (developed by Team Meat in 2010), platform games have always been a fundamental genre that every aspiring game designer needs to master, especially if interested in developing two-dimensional games.

To start defining our own, we will look at the first platform game that incorporated a swift jumping action: *Donkey Kong*. This was the game that, thanks to its innovative qualities and groundbreaking success, made platformers a staple in gaming literature ever since, and is still played competitively to this very day.

7.1 *DONKEY KONG:* ANALYSIS

Donkey Kong was the first game designed by Shigeru Miyamoto at Nintendo in 1981. It was a truly original concept: not only did it add jumping to the platforming model pioneered by Space Panic one year earlier, defining a fundamental game action common to most platform games ever since, but it also introduced brief cut scenes to describe a simple story. To support these, it also featured easily recognizable characters that were destined to become game icons, starting from Jumpman the carpenter, soon to be renamed Mario the plumber.

The simple cut scenes are actually extremely important to set the tone of the game and to involve the player emotionally in the action. Watching Pauline, originally named Lady, being abducted by Donkey Kong and then desperately crying for help throughout the game (Figure 7.1) was sure to push the player into Jumpman's shoes and raise our protection instinct: who can resist such a charming and defenseless damsel in

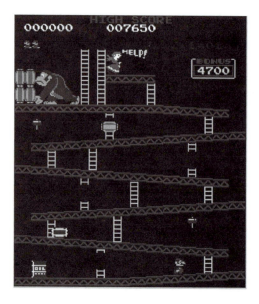

FIGURE 7.1 Lady Pauline screaming for help in *Donkey Kong* first stage: how can we resist such a desperate cry? Off we go, no matter if we will get run over by rolling barrels! (© 1981 Nintendo.)

distress? The protection instinct is indeed the main driver behind the gameplay, which is a simple race to an end (we need to reach Pauline) while avoiding different hazards (barrels, flames, etc.). The game also gives Jumpman a chance to defend himself for a short while by giving him a hammer to smash the incoming barrels, though doing so prevents him from climbing ladders and advancing toward Pauline. Later stages also add a few of Pauline's belongings, like an umbrella or a bag, adding a **collecting** component to add some variety and reinforce the experience. The AGE framework analysis for *Donkey Kong* is summarized in Figure 7.2.

7.2 *KITTY & KATTY:* DESIGN

Our platform game will take *Donkey Kong* as a model, maintaining a gameplay built around avoidance and race to an end and relying on our protection instinct to save... a damsel in distress? No, we saved too many already. Let's try to be a little more original this time!

Our player is going to play the role of a guy having a relaxing holiday in a chalet on the Alps with his two beloved cats, named Kitty and Katty.

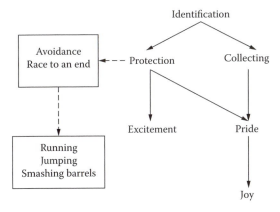

FIGURE 7.2   AGE analysis for *Donkey Kong*. Protection clearly drives the game-play motivating the player. Collecting is also present in some stages, where we can pick up different bonus objects.

One morning he wakes up and realizes his cats are missing: they must have adventured off the beaten path on the nearby mountain peak, and now they are lost somewhere, unable to get back home. We need to rescue them!

The game will include moving platforms in the shape of clouds, vertical paths working as ladders we can climb on, and, to make things challenging, two different types of boulders falling off from the top of the mountain. Note that we will not script the path for the boulders: we will use the underlying physics engine instead, with gravity being responsible for moving the boulders down toward the valley.

The player will start with three lives and will be able to run, jump, and climb in his quest for rescuing Kitty and Katty.

This time we should also take more care in programming a proper game structure: we will design a splash screen and a high score table, and we will also plan for different levels that get unlocked as we proceed in the game.*

All these ideas, including the AGE analysis, are summarized in the one-page game design document shown in Figure 7.3.

---

* We will design only the first stage though, leaving the others as practical exercises to the attentive reader. If different stages are planned, an additional game design documentation page should also be added to describe the various layouts and sequences.

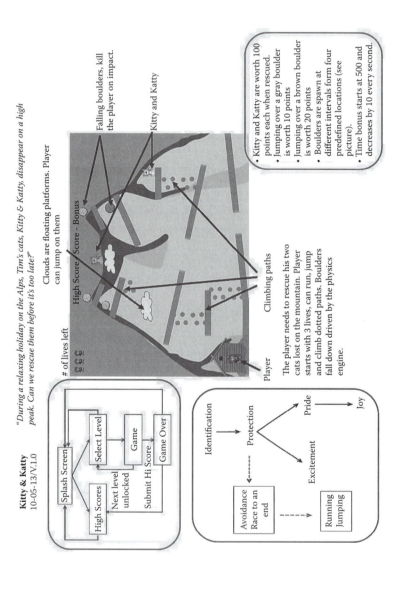

FIGURE 7.3   One-page design document for our platform game: *Kitty & Katty*. Note that the AGE analysis doesn't explicitly include the collection instinct, which was present in *Donkey Kong*, because we didn't plan for extra bonus objects to be spread around the level.

TAKE AWAY

For our second game, we decided to reference an evergreen classic: *Donkey Kong*, taking it as a model for a platform game with simple physics-driven features. Like in *Donkey Kong,* we are going to rely on players' protection instinct to motivate them to climb the mountain and rescue two little cats who couldn't go back home otherwise. This game will also feature a proper game structure and framework, including a splash screen, a high score table, and a stage selection screen.

CHAPTER 8

Kitty & Katty Development

*K*ITTY & *KATTY* IS going to be developed as a PC/browser game, so our starting resolution should be on the low end of the spectrum to allow people with old computers and monitors to enjoy it without big issues: limiting our window size to 800 × 600 pixels would be fine in this case.

Start a new project and define the layout and screen dimensions accordingly, together with a "letterbox scale" option to easily accommodate larger (or smaller) resolutions. The first thing we should take care of now is setting up the game structure as described in Figure 8.1.

8.1 GAME STRUCTURE

To implement the game structure we just defined, we need to add different layouts to the project, one for each part: splash screen, high score table, level selection, and then the actual levels. We can add them one by one by right clicking on the **Projects** tab, **Layouts** folder, and select **Add layout** as shown in Figure 8.2.

When adding a new layout, Construct will also ask us if we'd like to add a new event sheet to be associated with it. Let's do so as well (event sheets can be added any time by right clicking on the event sheet folder and selecting the appropriate command, so don't worry if you forget about this while adding a layout).

In the end, after we rename and resize all layouts accordingly, we should have something like Figure 8.3, and then we should update our project properties so that the application knows which layout needs to be loaded first. In our case it will be the splash screen, as shown in Figure 8.4.

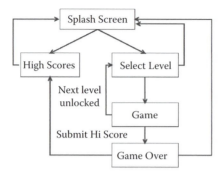

FIGURE 8.1   The game structure we want to implement for *Kitty & Katty*.

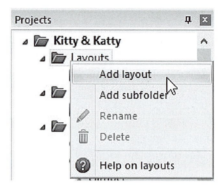

FIGURE 8.2   Adding a new layout.

FIGURE 8.3   Layouts and event sheets for our game.

Properties		⊠
About		
Name	Kitty & Katty	
Version	1.0.0.0	
Description	Rescue Kitty & Katty in this high altitude a...	
ID		
Author	Roberto Dillon	
Email	roberto@programandplay.com	
Website	adsumsoft.programandplay.com	
Project settings		
First layout	splashscreen	⌄
Use loader layout	No	
Pixel rounding	Off	
Window Size	800, 600	

FIGURE 8.4   Deciding the first layout to load in the project properties.

Let's start by implementing the splash screen then. We are going to keep things extremely simple here (but you can of course let your imagination and artistic creativity run wild), so all we will have is a big text with the game title and, possibly Kitty and Katty sprites.* Once we set this up, we need to implement the most crucial component of the framework: its navigation system.

We already used buttons in *Moon Wolf*, and, indeed, using buttons to navigate from layout to layout is clearly the easiest route. However, we won't do that here. The reason is that the **Button** object is specific to the Web and might not work on other platforms if later we decide to port and wrap our HTML5 game by using other tools. Even if we are planning this game to be a PC/web title only, it is always a good practice to keep as many opportunities open as possible.

For this reason, we are going to make our own buttons by using sprites, but there is also another aspect we should consider before choosing our approach: web games can also be played in countless different resolutions, and sprites may not always scale that well. To work around this problem, Construct 2 offers the **9-patch** object. A 9-patch image is subdivided in nine different areas, eight small ones encompassing the edges and one big central one (Figure 8.5), so when we need to stretch the image to fit a different resolution, we can have much finer control on each area and decide whether to "stretch" or "tile" them ("tile" means repeating the same section over and over)

---

* I'll be using free PD art from www.clker.com.

FIGURE 8.5   A sprite button subdivided in nine different areas covering its edges and center. Each margin can be set through the object properties.

Properties		
Image	Edit	
Left margin	16	
Right margin	16	
Top margin	16	
Bottom margin	16	
Edges	Tile	⌄
Fill	Stretch	
Initial visibility	Visible	
Hotspot	Top-left	
Seams	Overlap	

FIGURE 8.6   A section of the 9-patch object properties where we can set up the width of each area by changing the margin positions and whether we want edges and center (here named Fill) to be stretched or tiled when the object gets resized.

to improve the final result. The different parameters for the 9-patch object are shown in Figure 8.6.

Before proceeding further, we should first have at least a couple of images ready, including a default and a highlighted/pressed state. For simplicity, we will be using the same graphics for all buttons. We could make a simple round or square looking button in the image editor or use free tools like GIMP.* Once we have the images, go back to Construct. To simulate

---

* GIMP is a great free image editing program which you should definitely check out if you don't know it already: www.gimp.org.

the button effect, we are going to have three different elements per button: two 9-patch objects, one each for the **off** and **on** button state (with the latter starting as invisible and placed to exactly superimpose on the former) plus a text object to be placed on top of the graphics to identify the different functions.

Overall, we are going to need buttons for accessing the level selection screen (we will call the two 9-patch objects for this button **btn_play_off** and **btn_play_on**), displaying the high score table (**btn_hi_off, btn_hi_on**), and for going back to the main menu (**btn_menu_off, btn_menu_on**).

In the splash screen layout only the first two will be needed, so let's start by adding the corresponding 9-patch objects, importing the images in the editor, and then resizing/positioning as appropriate (take some time to experiment with the 9-patch parameters so you understand how they work). When you are happy with the result (be sure the **on** image starts as **invisible** and is above the **off** one: this can be done by changing the z-order by right clicking on the object and selecting the z-order option), add the corresponding text object on top of the images.

In the end, our splash screen should look something like Figure 8.7.

Now we have to program the highlight button effect and the action that should be triggered when each button is clicked. To do so, we need to add the **Mouse** object to the game first. As usual, double click any empty area across the layout and then select the mouse from the different options available (it's in the input section). Now go to the splash screen event sheet.

Double click on the empty sheet to add the first event: choose the mouse object and select **On object clicked** as shown in Figure 8.8.

FIGURE 8.7 Our simple splash screen featuring buttons for navigating to different parts of the game. Each button is made by three components: a first underlying 9-patch image for the off state, visible by default, a highlighted image right on top of it, invisible by default (but still displayed in the editor), which is going to be switched to visible once clicked, and finally a text object identifying the specific button function.

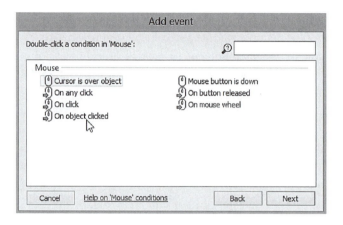

FIGURE 8.8 Our buttons will respond to mouse clicks thanks to the **On object clicked** mouse event.

To complete the event, select the object we want to interact with (in this case, one of the **on** state buttons, let's start with **btn_hi_on** for example), choose the type of click and specific mouse button we want (we can leave the default values here, i.e., single click on the left button). For the action, let's pick the **btn_hi_on** object and change its **visibility property** to **visible**.

We now need to take care of two things: first, if we move the cursor away, without releasing the click first, we should restore the **on** button image to invisible and nothing else should happen. On the other hand, if we release the mouse left button while on the image, hence completing the clicking process and requesting a new layout (the high score table in the case of the **btn_hi** object), we need to load and display it.

The first event implies checking that the mouse cursor is not overlapping the image any more. In the event sheet we can do this by selecting the **cursor is over object** event and then **inverting** it by right clicking on the event and then selecting the **Invert** option.

For the second condition, instead, we need to check for two mouse events: **On left button released** and, again, **Cursor is over object**. If these conditions are met, we reset the button **on** state to **invisible** once again (otherwise it will still be on once we come back to this screen after a game) and load the desired layout (accessible through the **system** object, **Go to layout (by name)** action).

The events are displayed in Figure 8.9.

1	⇒ (ᵇ) Mouse	On **Left** button **Clicked** on ⟺ **btn_hi_on**	⟺ btn_hi_on	Set Visible
			Add action	
2	(ᵇ) Mouse	✖ Cursor is over ⟺ **btn_hi_on**	⟺ btn_hi_on	Set Invisible
			Add action	
3	⇒ (ᵇ) Mouse	On **Left** button released	⟺ btn_hi_on	Set Invisible
			⚙ System	Go to layout "**highscores**"
	(ᵇ) Mouse	Cursor is over ⟺ **btn_hi_on**	*Add action*	

FIGURE 8.9 All the events needed for having a working button made by two overlapped images.

Repeat the same procedure for the other button, this time directing the player to the **levelselect** layout.

Let's now move on to the **highscores** layout and add a button to go back to the splash screen in the same way we just did for the splash screen and its own buttons (use **btn_menu_off, btn_menu_on**). We won't do anything else on this layout for now: we will come back to it later to implement the actual high score table once the game is done. Let's now focus on the **levelselect** layout for selecting a specific level instead and add a button to go back to the main menu here as well. To do so, we can simply copy and paste both objects and related code across layouts from **highscores** to **levelselect** and the corresponding event sheets.

Once done, we should add a sprite image for each level we will be having in the game. I'll be adding three now as an example: for simplicity's sake, just three big squares with the level number displayed on them. After this we need to define how to show a specific level is locked. For example, we can manipulate the image transparency level to show they are not available yet or superimpose another image, like a lock or a cross, which we then remove once the level is accessible. In our case, the layout would then look something like Figure 8.10.

But how should we handle the lock/unlock of a level?

The idea here is to have a Boolean variable (i.e., true/false) associated with each image telling us whether the specific level is accessible or not. If not, we show a cross/lock sprite and we don't process any mouse click on it. Moreover, if we want the player to be able to start at different levels across different playing sessions to save her progress, we also need to store this piece of information locally on the computer.

Let's start by adding three sprites, one for each possible level, together with an **instance variable** of type **Boolean** and another one of type

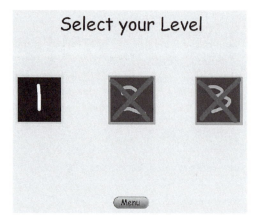

FIGURE 8.10 A level selection screen. At the beginning, only the first level should be accessible, while the others are locked.

number to each of them. We can call the first **unlocked** and we can have it instantiated to **false** by default. The second one can be called **lvl** (short for level) and have it set to 1, 2, or 3 according to the specific level image. We should also define a **global variable** at the beginning of the event sheet of type **number** (remember that this, like any other global variables, will be accessible from any layout). Let's name it **player_level** and instantiate it with a starting value of 1.

Now, the comparison between this and each level icon's specific **lvl** variable should be performed when the layout starts. To do so, add a **System/On start of layout** event followed by a **System/compare two values** subevent. If **player_level** is greater than or equal to the specific **lvl** variable, we set **unlocked** to true. If not, we need to add an **else** condition and act accordingly: right click on the subevent we just defined and select **Insert new event below,** then choose the **System** object and, among the **Special conditions** group, select **Else.** In the action part of the sheet, we pick the **System** object again and use it to create a new instance of the cross/lock sprite we prepared earlier, placing it exactly on top of the still locked level image. The event sheet should then look like that in Figure 8.11.

Note that, in the **On start of layout** event, we should have a subevent like the one just described for each level icon displayed on the screen.*

---

* We actually don't need to check for the first level, since it will be unlocked by default. Anyway, we are including it here as well to verify the code is actually working properly when the game starts.

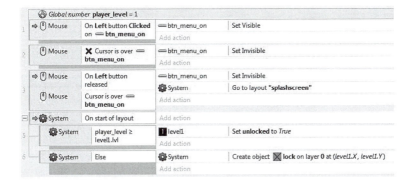

FIGURE 8.11 Event sheet for the level selection screen, showing the back to splash screen button and, most importantly, the events for updating a level's unlocked variable and superimposing a predefined lock object (the red cross in this case) if necessary. Note that an instance of the lock object must be placed somewhere outside the visible part of layout if we want to create more during runtime.

Now we need to process the mouse click on any unlocked image. This should be very straightforward by now, and all we need to do is create an event with two conditions: a mouse event checking for the left click on the level object and a check that the unlocked variable for the specific image is true (the condition to choose is **Is Boolean instance variable set**, in the **Instance variable** section). If so, we go to the specific level layout. The resulting events for all three levels are shown in Figure 8.12.

At this point it is good to introduce the **WebStorage** object: double click anywhere on a layout to add a new object to our project and look for it in the **Data & Storage** section. This object can store data locally on the

⇒ Mouse	On Left button Clicked on ▮ level1	System	Go to **level1**
▮ level1	Is **unlocked**	Add action	
⇒ Mouse	On Left button Clicked on ▮ level2	System	Go to **level1**
▮ level2	Is **unlocked**	Add action	
⇒ Mouse	On Left button Clicked on ▮ level3	System	Go to **level1**
▮ level3	Is **unlocked**	Add action	

FIGURE 8.12 Checking mouse clicks and status of unlocked variable to start different levels. In our prototype, though, we will have only one playable level, so clicking on any image will always start the same level. It will be up to you to make levels 2 and 3 as an exercise at the end of this chapter!

WebStorage	Local key "LevelReached" exists	System	Set player_level to *WebStorage.LocalValue("LevelReached")*
		Add action	
System	Else	WebStorage	Set local key "LevelReached" to 1
		Add action	

FIGURE 8.13   Checking for the existence of a **LevelReached** key to initialize the **player_level** variable when the game starts. If it doesn't, we define it once and for all.

player's device, which we can then retrieve later when needed, allowing us a simple way to store player's progress and other data.* In our game, we need to store the level reached by the player and the different high scores for the leaderboard. We will discuss the high scores later, but we can take care of saving the player's level already. In fact, instead of simply setting up the global variable **player_level** to 1 like we did earlier, at the beginning of the game we could check whether a specific value has been previously saved. If so, we instantiate our global variable to that number. If not, meaning that is the first time we ever run the game, we create such value and instantiate it to 1.

All this can be done simply via the **WebStorage** object: let's move to the event sheet associated with the first layout our game loads, i.e., **splashscreen_ sheet**, and add a new event. Select **WebStorage** and its **Local key exist** option, naming the key, for example, **"LevelReached"** (between quotes). If the key exists already, we define an action assigning its value to our global variable **player_level** (via the **System** object). If not, we create an **Else** event via the **System** object where we take **WebStorage** and define **LevelReached**, initializing it to the value of 1. These events will look like Figure 8.13.

The last thing we should do before we start programming the actual gameplay is to design a simple game over screen. We already defined the specific layout, so go on and add a fancy "Game Over" sign together with a button to go back to the splash screen. Leave some space though: we will revise this later in case of a high score to allow players to input their names!

8.2 BACKGROUND AND PLATFORMS

Off to the actual game now! Open the game layout (in Figure 8.3 we called it **level1**) and start drawing a sprite or importing an image for the background mountain (for this, like for most other assets in this game, I took

---

* For a full state save, suitable for complex action or role-playing games where we want to take a "snapshot" of the whole game to continue it later, Construct 2 provides a proper save and load feature through the **System** object.

an image from the public domain clipart collection website Clker.com). You may also want to change the layout background color to a nice light blue to simulate a bright summer sky day. This is actually done via the layer, so select the main layer where the action takes place and, in its properties tab, change the background color. For example, I picked one with RGB values of 0, 204, 255.

Once the mountain background is in place, we should add a series of platforms to help our hero climb around and reach the mountain peak. Add a new sprite, naming it, for example, **path**. This can be a simple brown filled rectangle that we are then going to stretch and modify to make platforms of different sizes across the mountain.

Place the path sprite in the layout and click on **Add/Edit Behaviors** in its **Properties Tab**. To define the typical behavior we would expect from a platform, Construct gives us two options: a **solid** behavior and a **jump through** one. The difference being that the latter allows for characters to jump on them from underneath while, on the former, we would just bump our head on a solid wall and fall back. Here, we are going to use **jump through**. Once this is done, add also the **Physics behavior** and set the values as in Figure 8.14. This is not necessary for having a proper platforming action, but it will be needed for interacting with the boulders, whose movements will be controlled by the physics engine.

Behaviors	
Physics	
Immovable	Yes
Collision mask	**Bounding box**
Prevent rotation	No
Density	1
Friction	0.3
Elasticity	0.2
Linear damping	0
Angular damping	0.01
Bullet	No
Jumpthru	(no properties)
Add / edit	Behaviors

FIGURE 8.14 The physics properties for the path sprites, needed later when we will also add the falling boulders. Be sure **Immovable** is set to **Yes** and that we are using **Bounding box** as collision mask.

There are two more important elements we should add to make our platformer more interesting: moving platforms and stairs.

For the first, let's add a new sprite in the shape of a fluffy cloud. We will place this in the upper part of the mountain, and we will let the player jump and ride it to provide an original way to the mountain top. This means we should add the **jump through** behavior to the sprite as well.

The "stairs" here can take the shape of a vertical, rocky path for the player to climb. For this, let's add a **tiled background** object instead of a simple sprite. This will allow us to define just a small part of the image, which will be repeated over and over as we stretch it: we can make stairs as long as we like without actually deforming the sprite image! It is the same idea we used earlier with the 9-patch images when designing buttons, and it works really well. I designed the vertical path to be just a few dark gray circles (Figure 8.15), which will be repeated as needed while drawing the vertical paths in the layout.

Now we have all the elements for designing our levels, i.e., platforms and paths we can use to make them challenging yet possible, so it's high time to start making your own actual level! Mine is shown in Figure 8.16, where you will see I also added a small hut at the lower left corner: this is where the player will start his adventure.

One more thing before moving on to the next section and adding the main characters to our game. We talked about the clouds being

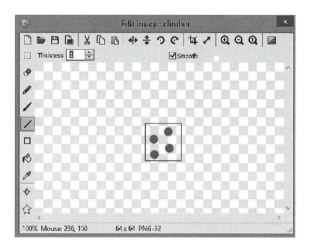

FIGURE 8.15 A simple image we can use for identifying vertical paths across the mountain. Just a few dots to be repeated over and over as needed by the **tiled background** object.

FIGURE 8.16 The layout for the first level of the game, featuring different platforms (which we can also rotate slightly) and vertical paths to climb. Note that the image for the vertical path is repeated automatically and not stretched, since it is defined as a tiled background object and not as a simple sprite. We will make the player spawn at the hut in the lower left corner of the screen (think of the big blue barrel in *Donkey Kong*!).

moving platforms, and this is something we can do now already without adding any additional event: we simply need to add another behavior to them, specifically the **Sine** to make them move back and forth. Once added, we can specify the actual movement through its properties (Figure 8.17).

Behaviors	
Jumpthru	(no properties)
Sine	
Active on start	Yes
Movement	Horizontal
Wave	Sine
Period	8
Period random	0
Period offset	0
Period offset random	0
Magnitude	200
Magnitude random	0
Add / edit	Behaviors

FIGURE 8.17 The sine behavior properties for the clouds. Here we can define how fast and how far the clouds can go and if the movements should also have random components or not. Experiment till you find the values that suit your level most!

FIGURE 8.18 A detail of the level layout, showing Kitty and Katty ready to be rescued.

8.3 KITTY, KATTY, AND THE PLAYER

Now that we have the first level designed, we need to populate it. Let's start by importing a suitable image for Kitty and Katty, if we haven't done so already, and then place them in some not so easy places to reach. For example, we can place one at the very top of the mountain, accessible only by jumping on a cloud, while the other could be on the midlevel platform on the right, as shown in Figure 8.18. There's no need to add any behavior to them.

We can now start thinking about our main character.

For designing our hero, I decided to use the Tim character sprites from the famous award-winning game *Braid* by Jonathan Blow, since David Hellman, the artist responsible for *Braid*'s gorgeous graphics, has generously made these assets freely available to the indie community.[*]

To start, insert a new sprite object in the layout and call it **Tim**, in honor of *Braid*'s protagonist.

Once in the image editor, we can start adding the graphics. I divided all Tim images into individual frames but, naturally, Construct 2 also allows you to import sprite sheets (all frames included in one single, big image) so you can choose the approach you prefer for this.

Let's start with the Default animation, which is not really an animation, since we are going to use only one frame. Let's rename it **Idle** and import the still Tim sprite. To add another animation, right click on the **Animation** window of the image editor and select the proper command (Figure 8.19).

We have to do this a few times: starting with a **Running** animation that will look like in Figure 8.20.

---

[*] http://www.davidhellman.net/braidbrief.htm

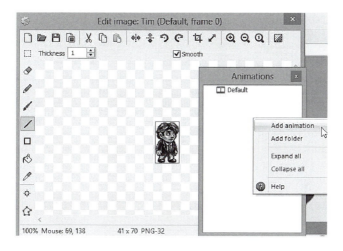

FIGURE 8.19   Adding a new animation in the image editor.

Note that, as we said, each frame can be added individually or by importing a sprite sheet where all frames, each having exactly the same dimensions, are spread regularly across the image. This can be done from a specific menu, as shown in Figure 8.21.

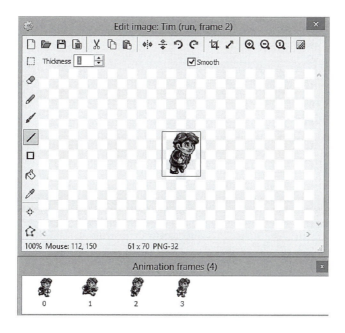

FIGURE 8.20   The running animation, made by four frames.

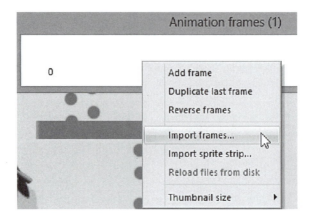

FIGURE 8.21   Right click on the **Animation frames** window to import frames from individual images or a sprite sheet (here called **sprite strip**).

The running animation also should have a left counterpart. We will do this at runtime, but it's useful to know we can easily reverse an entire animation if needed in the editor itself by shift clicking on the reverse icon as shown in Figure 8.22.

Once the running animation is done, we also have to add a jumping animation (one single frame that we will use also for falling) and a simple two-frame animation for climbing. In the end we will have all the animations as shown in Figure 8.23.

Let's not forget running and climbing animations need to loop: we can set this, and other parameters like animation speed, via the **Animation properties** tab displayed when we select a specific animation in the Image Editor (Figure 8.24).

We need now to set up our character and play the different animations as appropriate. Construct provides us with a very helpful **Platform**

FIGURE 8.22   Mirroring an animation is a very simple process that can be done in two different ways: we can specify a running left animation on its own in the image editor by copying and mirroring an existing one frame by frame (like in this figure) or mirroring the whole animation later at runtime via events (this is actually what we will be doing in our game).

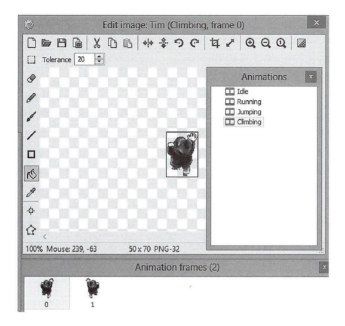

FIGURE 8.23   We will need all these different animations in our game. Here a frame from the **Climbing** animation.

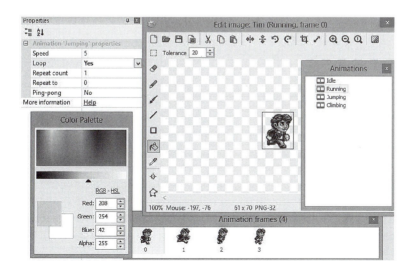

FIGURE 8.24   Setting the **running animation loop** property to **yes.**

behavior that takes care of all the low-level work for us, but there is a small caveat. Adding the **Platform** behavior to the animated sprite itself can give us collision problems due to the changing nature of animated sprites, with weird results like our character getting stuck on a platform or ledge if a collision is registered during any animation frame, for example. It is then recommended to have a very simple sprite, like a rectangle, of the same size of the character (possibly a few pixels smaller, depending on the shape of your sprite and how you want to trigger the contact with the platforms) and add the **Platform** behavior to this instead. The animated sprite will then be attached to this sort of invisible **mask** and follow it accordingly.

Add a new sprite, name it **Player**, and resize it to be like our idle Tim character. Then add the **Platform** behavior to it while also adding the **Pin** behavior to Tim. Figure 8.25 shows both Tim and its Player mask in the layout editor.

To stick the **Player** sprite to the animated **Tim** sprite by using the **Pin** behavior, we need to move to the event sheet. Once there, add a new event for Tim, selecting the **Pin/Is pinned** event. Invert it (by right clicking on the event and selecting the **invert** command) so that the event is triggered only if Tim has not been pinned yet, and then define an action for Tim by

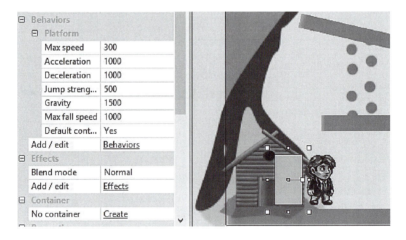

FIGURE 8.25   Tim with its mask in the layout, also showing the mask's **Platform** properties. I filled the latter with a bright yellow color so I could easily see it against the background when testing. You can start with these values for speed, jump strength, etc. and then tweak them while playtesting to make the overall movement feel more natural in your specific level. Don't forget to add the **Pin** behavior to make it stick to Tim and change the mask's **Initial visibility** property to **Invisible** to make it disappear during an actual game!

FIGURE 8.26   The event sheet for our **level1** layout, here superimposing and pinning the animated Tim sprite to the invisible Player object.

using the **Pin** object and pinning it to the **Player** as shown in Figure 8.26. If we play the layout now, we will be able to move Tim around (with no animations yet) by using the cursor keys, but, in reality, we are actually controlling the underlying Player sprite, and Tim is simply being dragged around thanks to the Pin behavior!

To finally play the animations, we need first to check the status of the **Player** sprite (whether it is on the floor or jumping, for example), then check which key is actually being pressed (are we going left or right?) and finally trigger the right animation sequence.

Let's go in order and let's begin with the running action. We need to start with the **Player** sprite and select its **is on floor** event from the **Platform** behavior. This is to be followed by two subevents, one for each running direction, i.e., a **keyboard** event for the right cursor key, **key is down**, and one for the left cursor key. For the corresponding actions we need to choose our animated sprite, **Tim**, and pick the **select animation** action, writing the name of the animation we want to play (**running**, in this case) while leaving the **from Beginning** parameter set so that the animation will always start from its first frame.

Now, if you followed these steps so far, we should not forget we have Tim running only toward the right, and we still have to mirror the whole animation when running left! To do so we need to add another action: select **Tim** and, in the **Appearance** group, pick the **Set mirrored** action. Set the flag to **mirrored** when running left and **not mirrored** when running right.

We also want the animation not only to stop immediately when we release the cursor key, but to go back to its idle state right away. For this we need to add another subevent for the **Player** object. Among its events, select **On stopped** among its **Platform: Animation triggers** group, and then add an action for **Tim** setting the animation to **idle**. The sequence of events is shown in Figure 8.27.

Now we need to do something similar when we are jumping or falling.

3 ⊟	▯ Player	🐾 Platform is on floor	Add action	
4	⌨ Keyboard	Left arrow is down	🏃 Tim	Set animation to "**Running**" (play from beginning)
			🏃 Tim	Set **Mirrored**
			Add action	
5	⌨ Keyboard	**Right arrow is down**	🏃 Tim	Set animation to "**Running**" (play from beginning)
			🏃 Tim	Set **Not mirrored**
			Add action	
6	⇒ ▯ Player	🐾 Platform On stopped	🏃 Tim	Set animation to "**Idle**" (play from beginning)
			Add action	

FIGURE 8.27 The events for animating the sprite while running left and right and resetting the animation to idle as soon as we stop moving.

Make a new event with two conditions: **Player/Platform On fall** and **Player/Platform On jump**. Then select both, right click on the event, and choose **Make 'Or' block** so that the following action will be triggered when either of the two events happen (obviously, they can't happen together!). The action will simply take Tim and set the animation to **Jumping**, since both are sharing the same animation frame.

Last, we need to take care of resetting things once Tim touches the ground, so we need a new event **Player/Platform On landed** bringing back the **Idle** frame. But what if we touch the ground and keep running right away without stopping first? We need to take care of this case as well, so let's add a subevent to the event we just defined to be triggered if the sprite is moving, i.e., **Player/Platform is moving** where we restart the **Running** animation. All this sequence is exemplified in Figure 8.28.

Now that we can run and jump, as well as fall from a platform, we need to take care of climbing.

The first thing we need to do is check whether we are overlapping with one of the possible vertical paths, named **climber** in my case, we placed in the level earlier. Pick the **Player** object and select the **Is overlapping**

7	⇒ ▯ Player	🐾 Platform On fall	🏃 Tim	Set animation to "**Jumping**" (play from beginning)
		- or -	Add action	
	⇒ ▯ Player	🐾 Platform On jump		
8 ⊟	⇒ ▯ Player	🐾 Platform On landed	🏃 Tim	Set animation to "**Idle**" (play from beginning)
			Add action	
9	▯ Player	🐾 Platform is moving	🏃 Tim	Set animation to "**Running**" (play from beginning)
			Add action	

FIGURE 8.28 The events for having Tim behave properly when jumping, falling, and also hitting the ground running!

another object event in the **Collisions** group, then we need to define two subevents to check whether we have an up or down key press and move accordingly, while also setting the proper climbing animation.

There is something tricky here that requires our attention though: the **Platform** behavior won't allow us to move properly! So we need to define an action first that disables the Platform behavior through the **Set enabled** action. Only then we can proceed in moving our player up or down a specific amount, which we can define as an instance variable for the **Player** object (named, for example, **ClimbingSpeed**). Once we are back on the ground (i.e., overlapping with a **path** object again or not overlapping anymore with the **climber** path), we need to remember to restore the **Platform** behavior once again or the game won't be playable any more! All these events and actions are exemplified in Figure 8.29.

Now that we can move around properly, we need to be sure we stay within the layout boundaries. Left and right edges are easy to control: we can either check for player's coordinates through events or add a new sprite, naming it "**wall**," add a solid behavior to it, and then use two instances of it to frame the layout, placing them just outside the viewable game field to stop the player from running away. To minimize the number of events in the game (don't forget the free version of Construct 2 allows only for 100 events in a game), I'd suggest we take the latter approach.

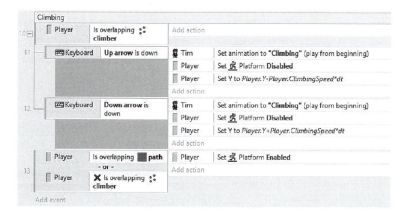

FIGURE 8.29 The events related to climbing: we need to disable the Platform behavior when climbing and reenable it as soon as we get back on the platforms. The climbing speed is defined by an instance variable set, for example, to 20 pixels per second (note the **dt** in the formula when updating the *y* coordinate since now we are not using a predefined behavior for handling movement).

Once this is done, we still need to take care of the hole in the middle of the lower path in Figure 8.16. If we fall in there we also want the player to lose a life and then respawn at the hut.

Let's proceed in order. First, we add an instance variable to the Player, name it **Lives,** and initialize it to 3. We should also display the lives indicator in the top right corner of the screen. The simplest way to do this is to add a new sprite for each life. We can call these **life1**, **life2**, and **life3** and add them to the GUI layer. Import the Tim idle sprite for each of them, and place them on the top right corner of the screen, in order from life1 to life3, as in Figure 8.30.

When Tim dies, we want the game to remove these accordingly. We can achieve this effect in several ways, and I will use this opportunity for introducing the concept of functions. As in any programming language, functions are used here to define snippets of code that can be called any time it is needed from another part of the program. To enable the use of functions in Construct 2, we need first to add the **Function** object to the game. Do so now. Then let's define a new event for the **Player** sprite and select **Is outside of layout** (within the **Size & Position** group). The corresponding actions would be to change the Player position in front of the hut, subtract 1 to its instance variable **Lives,** and then call the proper function to take care of removing one life indicator, eventually going to the **game over** layout if there are no lives left.

When using the **Function** object, we can call a specific one by name and also add eventual parameters to be passed for further comparisons and processing. In our case, let's call the function **LifeLost,** and we also add the player lives as parameters, as shown in Figure 8.31.

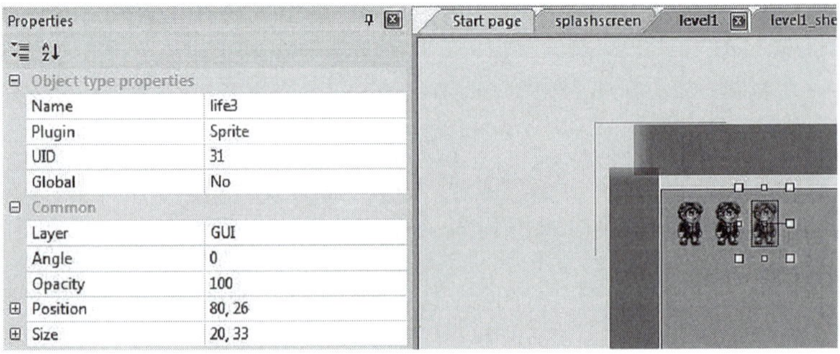

FIGURE 8.30 The three life indicators in place.

Parameters for Function: Call function

The name of the function to call.

Name | "LifeLost"
Parameter 0 | Player.Lives

Add parameter - Remove parameter

Cancel | Help on expressions | Back | Done

FIGURE 8.31   Calling a function named **"LifeLost"** and passing it one parameter, namely, the **Player.Lives** instance variable.

We have to declare the function now. Add a new event and select the **function** object. Select **On function** and then specify its name (**LifeLost**). The next step is to add three different subevents where, in each, we check the value of the parameter and destroy one life indicator accordingly. When lives get to 0, we also go to the Game Over layout. The function is shown in Figure 8.32.

Try to play the game, and have fun falling in the crevasse to check the function is actually working!

8.4 RESCUING OUR PETS AMIDST FALLING BOULDERS

After testing that everything done so far works as expected, it is time to add a score system, save Kitty and Katty, and add falling boulders to build excitement and keep players on their toes.

15⊟	⇒🗘 Function	On "LifeLost"		Add action	
16	🗘 Function	Parameter 0 = 2	🐾 life3	Destroy
				Add action
17	🗘 Function	Parameter 0 = 1	🐾 life2	Destroy
				Add action
18	🗘 Function	Parameter 0 = 0	🐾 life1	Destroy
			⚙ System	Go to **gameover**
				Add action
	Add event			

FIGURE 8.32   The function handling player's deaths: removing indicators one by one and, eventually, loading the game over screen.

2	⇒ System	On start of layout	Tim	Set animation to **"Idle"** (play from beginning)
			System	Set **Score** to 0
			System	Set **Bonus** to 500
			txt_Score	Set text to *"Score: "* & *Score*
			txt_HiScore	Set text to *"Hi Score: "* & *HighScore*
			txt_Bonus	Set text to *"Bonus: "* & *bonus*

FIGURE 8.33 Taking care of initializing and displaying score and bonus information when the game starts.

Let's start with the score. We decided in our game design document to display the current score, the high score, and also a time bonus, starting at 500 and decreasing by 10 every second. To make things look a little better compared to *Moon Wolf*, this time we should have each number in its own **Text** object. Add one text object for each element and call them something like **txt_Score**, **txt_HiScore**, and **txt_Bonus**. Place them appropriately in the top part of the screen.

We also need to add related global variables, i.e., **Bonus**, **Score**, **HighScore**, which we can initialize to 500, 0, and 0, respectively (we will take care of the **HighScore** later). Finally, in the **On start of layout** event, we need to add instructions for displaying these values when the game begins, like in Figure 8.33.

The bonus works like a timer, and we can implement it simply by decreasing the **Bonus** variable through an event including two conditions: **Every X seconds**, which we find in the **Time** section of the possible events for the **System** object, and also a check on the current bonus value, i.e., we want to stop decreasing Bonus once it reaches 0. The event for doing this is shown in Figure 8.34.

For saving Kitty and Katty, all we have to do is to check for a collision between their sprites and the player. When this happens, we increase the player's score by 100 as defined in the game design document.

To make sure things are working properly, though, we also need to define two more instance variables in the **Player** object to keep track of

Time Bonus				
3	System	Every **1.0** seconds	System	Subtract *10* from **Bonus**
	System	**Bonus** ≥ 10	txt_Bonus	Set text to *"Bonus: "* & *bonus*
			Add action	

FIGURE 8.34 Setting up the bonus: we subtract 10 every second as long as it is greater than or equal to 10 so that it never goes below 0.

Instance variables	
ClimbingSpeed	20
Lives	3
Kitty	false
Katty	false
Add / edit	Instance variables

FIGURE 8.35 The instance variables for the Player object, now including also two Boolean flags, set to false, for keeping track of our progress in saving Kitty and Katty.

the pets we saved. These should be Boolean variables, initially set to false[*] (Figure 8.35). When both are toggled to true, we know we have accomplished our mission, and we can proceed to the next stage by updating the player's level.

The actions we need to take when we register a collision between the player and a cat are the following:

1. Toggle the related instance variable in the **Player** object, setting it to true.

2. Add 100 to the global variable **Score**.

3. Update **txt_Score** accordingly.

4. Remove the cat from the layout (somewhat ironically, this actually means "destroying" her, even if we just saved her!).

The corresponding events, together with the event for ending the level and going back to the selection screen with the next challenge unlocked, are shown in Figure 8.36.

Once all these have been implemented, we can take care of making the game challenging and exciting by adding the falling boulders from the top of the mountain.

Back in our game design, we decided to have two different types of physics driven boulders, but we didn't really specify other details like the spawn rate, and so on, so now we have to fill in all the details, starting from the exact location where they should spawn. By referencing the mock-up screenshot in the game design document, we have four possible

---

[*] While not strictly needed since the **Player** object is created every time we load the level, it is definitely good practice to initialize these in the **On start of layout** event as well.

Checking if we rescued Kitty and Katty				
⇨ Player	On collision with 🐾 Katty		Player	Toggle **Katty**
		⚙ System	Add *100* to **Score**
		T txt_Score	Set text to *"Score: " & Score*
		🐾 Katty	Destroy
		Add action	
⇨ Player	On collision with 🐾 Kitty		Player	Toggle **Kitty**
		⚙ System	Add *100* to **Score**
		T txt_Score	Set text to *"Score: " & Score*
		🐾 Kitty	Destroy
		Add action	
Both rescued! Unlock next level!				
	Player	Is **Kitty**	⚙ System	Add *Bonus* to **Score**
	Player	Is **Katty**	⚙ System	Set **player_level** to 2
			📇 WebStorage	Set local key "LevelReached" to player_level
			⚙ System	Go to **levelselect**
			Add action	

FIGURE 8.36 All the different steps we need to take to update the score when reaching one of our cats and also for moving to the next stage. For the latter, note how we check if both the Kitty and Katty instance variables are true (**Is Kitty** means the Kitty variable is set to true). If so, we update the score by adding any bonus left and also update the local key in the WebStorage object to save the player's progress before moving back to the level selection screen. Once there, we will see the second stage now unlocked.

spots at the top of the mountain that we should now store into a suitable data structure.

In my layout these four points are identified by the following coordinates: (230,155), (570,115), (260,50), and (525,50). A good way to save them is to use a two-dimensional array: add the **Array** object to the project and then, in the **On start of layout** event, add an action to define a new array object via the **Set size** option. Construct's array object is made to handle up to three-dimensional arrays, where each dimension is labeled as width, height, and depth (i.e., *x*, *y*, *z*) so, for a 2D array having four elements on the *x* axis (indexed from 0 to 3) and two on *y* axis, we need to specify the values (4,2,1).

After this, we can proceed in adding each point one by one as shown in Figure 8.37.

We are now ready to finally add the boulders. Find or draw a suitable image and import it in a newly created sprite object named "boulder." In my case I picked a simple public domain clipart[*] that was actually depicting the moon, but I thought it could make for a nice falling and rolling

---

[*] Once again, found on www.clker.com.

⇒ 🔧 System	On start of layout	🏃 Tim	Set animation to "**Idle**" (play from beginning)
		🔧 System	Set **Score** to *0*
		🔧 System	Set **Bonus** to *500*
		T txt_Score	Set text to "*Score:* " *& Score*
		T txt_HiScore	Set text to "*Hi Score:* " *& HighScore*
		T txt_Bonus	Set text to "*Bonus:* " *& bonus*
		Player	Set **Kitty** to *False*
		Player	Set **Katty** to *False*
		⊞ Array	Set size to *(4, 2, 1)*
		⊞ Array	Set value at *(0, 0)* to *230*
		⊞ Array	Set value at *(0, 1)* to *115*
		⊞ Array	Set value at *(1, 0)* to *570*
		⊞ Array	Set value at *(1, 1)* to *115*
		⊞ Array	Set value at *(2, 0)* to *260*
		⊞ Array	Set value at *(2, 1)* to *50*
		⊞ Array	Set value at *(3, 0)* to *525*
		⊞ Array	Set value at *(3, 1)* to *50*
		Add action	

FIGURE 8.37   The **On start of layout** event now updated to include the 2D array structure for storing all the points where we will spawn the boulders.

boulder anyway. Then, to make the second boulder type, to be named "boulder2," I simply changed its colors from gray to brown and resized it to be slightly bigger than the original one. Once the images are ready, we can proceed in adding the physics behavior to them.

The first boulder and its properties are shown in Figure 8.38.

Once you determined a set of values that feel appropriate for the different physics parameters, place the boulders off screen and let's see how we can spawn them once the game starts. We also want the player to score points when he successfully jumps above them, and we want him to lose a life if he is hit by the boulders. Let's start from the latter problem.

Losing a life is very straightforward: we can simply check for the collision between the player and the specific boulder, decrease the Player's **Lives** instance variable, respawn the Player at the hut, and finally call the **LifeLost** function where we remove one life indicator and, eventually, move to the Game Over screen. The event is depicted in Figure 8.39.

But how can we determine if we jump above them? We need a small trick here: like for the **Player** sprite being actually an invisible mask under Tim's animation, we should use an invisible mask approach here as well, place it above or below the boulder, and award points when we register a collision between **Player** and this instead.

Start by adding two new sprites, call them **boulder_mask** and **boulder2_mask**. Fill them with any color you like: I used red for the first and

⊟ Object type properties	
Name	boulder
Plugin	Sprite
UID	25
Global	No
⊟ Common	
Layer	action
Angle	0
Opacity	100
⊞ Position	-145, 142
⊞ Size	30, 30
⊟ Instance variables	
Add / edit	Instance variables
⊟ Behaviors	
⊟ Physics	
Immovable	No
Collision mask	Circle
Prevent rotation	No
Density	1
Friction	0.1
Elasticity	0.2
Linear damping	0
Angular damping	0.01
Bullet	No

FIGURE 8.38 The first boulder and its properties after having added the **Physics** behavior. Be sure to set collision mask to **Circle** and experiment with the different parameters like density, friction, and elasticity to find the settings that feel more natural within your level. Note that the object's mass is calculated as its density multiplied by the area of its collision mask.

green for the second so that they could stand out easily during testing (needless to say, these should be turned to invisible when we release the game). Resize them according to the size of the boulders and the height of player jumps. They should be thin but long, like 15 × 70 pixels for example. We should also move their origin point to the bottom of the image. This will allow for an easier placement when we attach the mask to the boulder,

Being hit by a boulder: Player loses a life. We call the same function we defined when falling into the pit.				
⇨ Player	On collision with 🔘 boulder		Player	Set position to (hut.X, hut.Y - 5)
	- or -		Player	Subtract 1 from **Lives**
⇨ Player	On collision with 🔘 boulder2		⇄ Function	Call "**LifeLost**" (Player.Lives)
			Add action	

FIGURE 8.39 Handling the collision with both types of boulders by combining the two events in an **or** block.

whose origin we left in the center. Once back in the layout, add the **Pin** behavior to the masks.

We are now ready to handle the spawning. For example, we can set these at regular intervals, like every 2 or 3 seconds (to make the game a little easier) for the smaller gray boulder and 3 (or 4) seconds for the bigger brown one. We can also randomize the exact location by choosing one of the points we stored earlier in the 2D array.

Let's do all this step by step as usual: first of all, add a new **System** event, **Every X seconds**, from the **Time** group. Let's set the interval X to 2 seconds, meaning we are going to work on the smaller boulder. Now we have to choose a specific spawn point. To do so, add a new global variable, call it **SpawnPoint**, and then add a **System** object action, **Set value**. Here we set the value by using the instruction "**choose(0,1,2,3).**" As its name implies, this command chooses one number at random among those listed. We will use this to pick the coordinates of a specific element in our 2D array. This can be done while creating the boulder through the **System/Create Object** action, where we specify the array element we want to pick, in its *x* and *y* coordinates as shown in Figure 8.40.

After this, we need to create the **boulder_mask** object. We can proceed in the same way, but its *x* and *y* coordinates have to be set to the boulder's own *x* and *y*. The last step is to use the **Pin** action of the Pin behavior to

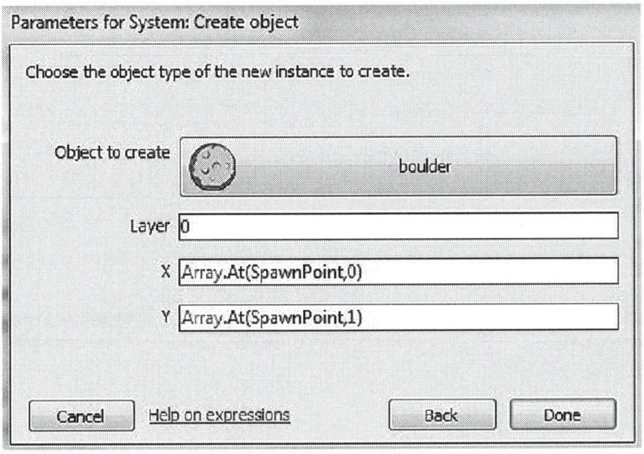

FIGURE 8.40 Specifying *x* and *y* spawning coordinates for the boulder by referencing the array created previously. **SpawnPoint** is a variable having a random value among 0, 1, 2, and 3.

stick it to the boulder we just created. Be sure to select **Position only** or the mask will rotate with the boulder!

We should also be sure to destroy the boulder and the mask once they roll out of the layout. To do so, define a new event having an **Is outside of layout** condition for both objects, and then simply destroy them.

Finally, the scoring: if we register a collision between the player and a mask, we update the score variable as well as the text displaying it.

The same steps have to be performed for the other boulder as well. In the end, we will have the events listed in Figure 8.41.

The game in action will now look like Figure 8.42.

8.5 THE HIGH SCORE TABLE

Once Tim has no more lives left, we automatically move to the **gameover** layout. Here we have to check whether the player did well enough for her score to be recorded and displayed in the high score table. Right, the table! We didn't define it yet. Let's go back to the splash screen. Add a global variable named **FirstPlay** and initialize it to 0. We will use this as a flag to identify whether the game has just been launched. We also need to initialize the high score table. Add another **array** object to the layout and call it

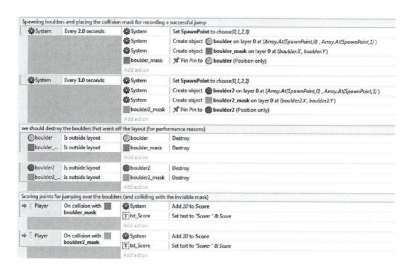

FIGURE 8.41 All the events and actions needed for spawning boulders in a random location, pinning another object to act as an additional collision mask, destroying them once they are outside the playing layout, and, finally, updating the score if a successful jump is registered (i.e., a collision between the player and the pinned mask, which has been placed above the boulder).

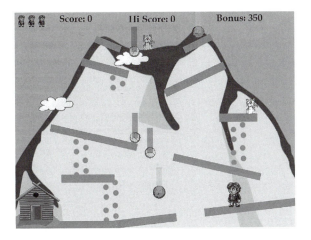

FIGURE 8.42 Rolling boulders in action! Don't forget to set the mask object property **Initial visibility** to **Invisible** once you are done testing!

something meaningful, e.g., **HighScoreTable** (you don't have to be creative when assigning names: just be straightforward and pick self-explanatory terms!). What we need now is a **System/On start of layout** event with a **System** subevent to check for the **FirstPlay** variable (i.e., **System/Compare variable**). In the corresponding Actions, we will then define the array size (we will limit this leaderboard to five scores only so the size will be **(5,2,1)**) and then populate the data one by one with dummy values (i.e., Players' names and scores) like the old arcade games used to do (Figure 8.43).

Once this is done, we can go back to the **Game Over** layout and start implementing the high score feature. Let's add some new elements in the layout first: we need a new text object to congratulate the player when achieving a high score, a **Textbox** object to let players input their name (add also a Boolean instance variable to this and name it **update**—we are going to use this as a flag to signal the need to update the table when leaving the layout), and a button to load the high score layout if the player wishes to do so (Figure 8.44). All these new elements should start as invisible: we don't want to display them if the player didn't get a top score! This can be done by setting the corresponding value in the **Properties** tab for each element or by coding it in the **On start of layout** event as shown in Figure 8.45. We also need to add a global variable of type **Text** to store the player's name. We can simply call it **name** and give it a default value of "Player."

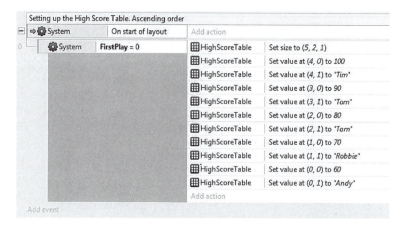

Setting up the High Score Table. Ascending order			
⊟ ⇨ 🔧 System	On start of layout	Add action	
0 🔧 System	FirstPlay = 0	⊞ HighScoreTable	Set size to (5, 2, 1)
		⊞ HighScoreTable	Set value at (4, 0) to 100
		⊞ HighScoreTable	Set value at (4, 1) to "Tim"
		⊞ HighScoreTable	Set value at (3, 0) to 90
		⊞ HighScoreTable	Set value at (3, 1) to "Tom"
		⊞ HighScoreTable	Set value at (2, 0) to 80
		⊞ HighScoreTable	Set value at (2, 1) to "Tam"
		⊞ HighScoreTable	Set value at (1, 0) to 70
		⊞ HighScoreTable	Set value at (1, 1) to "Robbie"
		⊞ HighScoreTable	Set value at (0, 0) to 60
		⊞ HighScoreTable	Set value at (0, 1) to "Andy"
		Add action	
Add event			

FIGURE 8.43 Setting up the **HighScoreTable** array. Note that the array is popu-
lated in ascending order (i.e., element (0,0) is the lowest score while (4,0) is the
highest). This will make things easier for us later on, since the **Sort** method implemented in Construct's **Array** object sorts elements in ascending order as well.

Note that in Figure 8.45 we are also setting the **FirstPlay** global variable
to 1 so that, when we are back to the splash screen, we don't reinitialize the
whole table once again, aside from setting the previously defined **update**
variable of the **AskName Textbox** object to **false**.

The next event we have to define is the one checking for a high score.
All we have to do is check the player score against the lowest score in the

FIGURE 8.44 The game over layout in the editor after adding different objects to
congratulate players for achieving a high score, letting them input their names.

⇒ System	On start of layout	a̱ AskName	Set **update** to *False*
		System	Set **FirstPlay** to *1*
		btn_hi_off	Set Invisible
		btn_hi_on	Set Invisible
		T txt_hi	Set Invisible
		a̱ AskName	Set **Invisible**
		Add action	

FIGURE 8.45   Making the high score related elements invisible when the layout starts.

table. If it is equal or higher, we have a high score, which will turn all those objects visible (Figure 8.46)!

By checking Figure 8.46 you should also notice that, when clicking on the **btn_hi_on** object, we are calling a new function named **UpdateTable** before moving to the **highscores** layout. This function, which we should call also when clicking on the **btn_menu_on** button before going back to our splash screen, is where we actually update the high score table (Figure 8.47).

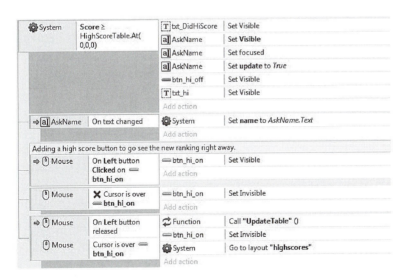

System	Score ≥ HighScoreTable.At(0,0,0)	T txt_DidHiScore	Set Visible
		a̱ AskName	Set **Visible**
		a̱ AskName	Set focused
		a̱ AskName	Set **update** to *True*
		btn_hi_off	Set Visible
		T txt_hi	Set Visible
		Add action	
⇒ a̱ AskName	On text changed	System	Set **name** to *AskName.Text*
		Add action	
Adding a high score button to go see the new ranking right away.			
⇒ Mouse	On **Left** button **Clicked on** btn_hi_on	btn_hi_on	Set Visible
		Add action	
Mouse	✗ Cursor is over btn_hi_on	btn_hi_on	Set Invisible
		Add action	
⇒ Mouse	On **Left** button released	Function	Call "UpdateTable" ()
		btn_hi_on	Set Invisible
Mouse	Cursor is over btn_hi_on	System	Go to layout "highscores"
		Add action	

FIGURE 8.46   If the player's **Score** is higher than the lowest score in the high score table (whose values are stored in ascending order), we turn all new objects visible. We also give focus to the textbox (via **Set focused**), set its **update** instance variable to true, and also update the global variable **name** as the player writes his or her name (via the **On text changed** event for the **textbox** object). The last subevents are for handling the navigation button to the high score layout while also calling a function for actually updating the high score table with the specified name and score.

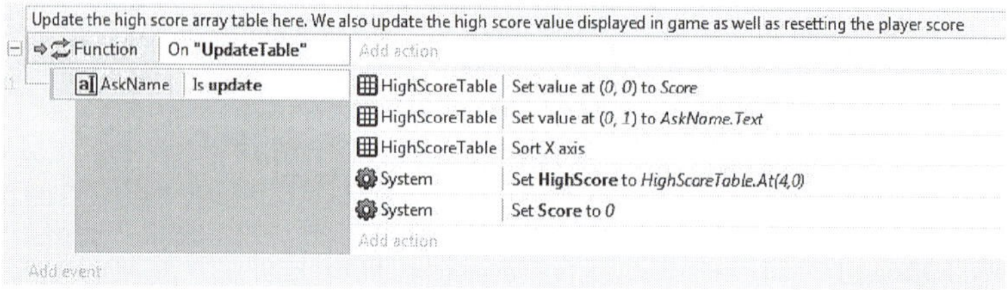

FIGURE 8.47 The function handling the table update and related global variables. Note that all the updating code is actually in a subevent triggered by the **update** instance variable in the textbox object. If we were not adding this check, and still call the function from the **btn_menu_on** object for going back to the splash screen, we would always overwrite the lowest score in the table, even if the player scored less than that.

We do so by overwriting the lowest score in the table with the new one together with the player's name, and then we sort the 2D array based on the *x* axis values (i.e., the scores) so that our new value gets inserted in the right place. We also refresh the **HighScore** global variable (we display it during the game) and reset the player's score to 0 for the next game.

With these latest addition, a basic version of *Kitty & Katty* featuring all the aspects we talked about in the game design document is finally complete.

Congratulations in delivering your second prototype!

TAKE AWAY

In this chapter we expanded our knowledge of Construct 2 quite significantly: we saw how to use the WebStorage component to save values locally and retrieve them later in another game session, we learned how to use arrays, add functions, use physics in our games, and, last but not least, make customized buttons via the 9-patch object, helping us to deliver a more flexible GUI that can self-adapt to many different devices and screen resolutions.

EXERCISES

Kitty & Katty is a fully working prototype now, but there are still lots of things we can do to improve it and make it a much more interesting and fun game. Here are some suggestions:

- Make the hut a "safe house" so that the player can't be killed when there (hint: we could do this in many different ways, either checking the player's position before proceeding in removing a life or by destroying the boulders when they hit the hut, for example, or even by changing the level design so that they can't even reach there!).

- Add music and special effects.

- Design a second and third level layout.

- Add a death sequence for Tim after he is hit by a boulder (hint: no need to draw new frames for a new animation from scratch. Be resourceful with what you have already: you can take the idle sprite, rotate it 90 degrees, and then have it fade away by changing the opacity value).

- Save the high score table (hint: value by value via WebStorage or, much better, exploring the other possibilities Construct 2 offers for saving and loading data files).

CHAPTER 9

Turky on the Run, a Puzzle Game

PUZZLE GAMES have always been a staple of gaming, and masterpieces like *Tetris* are there to remind us of how popular and long lasting a simple yet perfectly designed puzzle can be.

A centuries old puzzle concept we are all familiar with is the so-called "game of 15," where a 5 × 5 grid is filled with 14 tiles leaving only one space empty, thus allowing the player to maneuver the existing tiles around and ultimately reach a specific configuration. This could be, for example, an orderly sequence of numbers or a picture. Perhaps surprisingly, not many video games used this concept despite a pioneering attempt by Konami with *Loco-Motion,* a 1982 arcade game that also served as an inspiration for *Turky on the Run,* a small game recently released on iOS and BB10 devices. This is the game we are going to discuss here and then proceed in developing it step-by-step throughout the next chapter.

9.1 *LOCO-MOTION:* ANALYSIS

In *Loco-Motion* the player is presented with a grid and a set of railroad tiles that have to be moved to form a proper railway system, thus allowing a small locomotive to pick up all passengers waiting at the stations just outside the map (Figure 9.1).

The locomotive can't be stopped and can't be controlled directly: it will simply follow the trail it is on, so we have to herd it around by shifting tiles accordingly. If it gets in a dead end, falls into the empty square, or gets

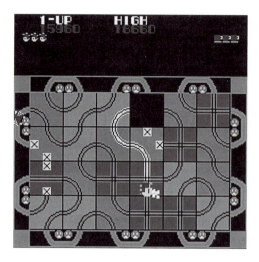

FIGURE 9.1   Can we manage to drive the locomotive toward the waiting passengers on the edges of the map and pick them up without crashing somewhere?

caught by any crazy trains or loop sweepers that pop up if the player takes too long in reaching the commuters, it will crash, and the player loses one of the three available lives.

The railroads could also be manipulated to make the crazy trains and sweepers crash into each other, scoring bonus points. This feature is actually very important to enhance the playing experience further by engaging players' revenge instinct against the bad trains that keep chasing after the small locomotive, henceforth complementing the collecting instinct (i.e., picking up all the waiting passengers), which is at the core of the game appeal as exemplified by the AGE framework analysis in Figure 9.2.

9.2 *TURKY ON THE RUN:* DESIGN

Like any other sliding tile puzzle, our game will rely on players' spatial reasoning skills, but its theme and settings are going to be much different from *Loco-Motion*. Instead of a locomotive going to pick up passengers, here we are going to have a little turkey, aptly named Turky, who needs to reach his peacock sweetheart for a date across the tile-based maze. Lady's patience is limited though, so our game will be time based and not lives based like most other games: if Turky is unable to reach his girlfriend in time, the game will be over. Also, Turky, while by no means a very smart guy, won't be moving around crashing in dead ends if no paths are available: if the path ends abruptly, he will try to go back looking for an

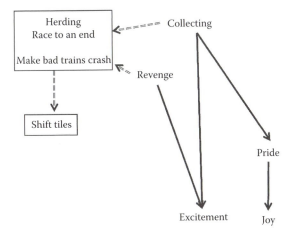

FIGURE 9.2 AGE analysis for *Loco-Motion*. Collecting is the main instinct driving the gameplay, while revenge plays a complementary role by offering the secondary objective of destroying the locomotive chasers.

alternative route, or, if there is no way back, he will stay still waiting for us to help him out.

Making the character stare helplessly at the player, waiting for him to act, is also likely to enhance our protection instinct: hopefully, most players will feel the impulse to see a happy ending and bring Turky safe and sound to the end of the maze to hug Picky the Peacock!

Setting up the path won't be the only challenge, though: like the crazy trains in *Loco-Motion*, here we have three different bad guys chasing after Turky: two cats, who roam the maze like Turky, and an owl, who appears only in later levels and flies randomly around. If they catch Turky, our Romeo will have to restart from a random spot on the left side of the maze with a time penalty.

While the tile that Turky is on or the tile he is moving to can't be shifted, players can help Turky by moving the tiles the cats are on to avoid a clash. This is also an effective way to take revenge against the two annoying chasers: bonus points will be awarded, but the cats will then respawn randomly, possibly right on top of Turky!

Turky also has another option to defend himself: pick up a SuperPower power-up that will make him invincible for the current level. This is only one of several power-ups granting points, speed, or extra time that we can use to add variety to the gameplay, while also adding a collecting element. All these ideas, including the AGE analysis, are outlined in the one-page game design document shown in Figure 9.3.

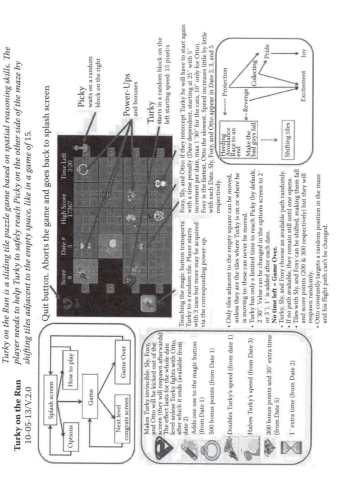

FIGURE 9.3   One-page design document for *Turky on the Run.*

TAKE AWAY

Puzzle games are an important genre in the gaming landscape, offering game designers opportunities to craft apparently simple systems that can nonetheless deliver a very engaging and addictive gameplay.

In our specific case, it is instructive to realize how, despite the fact that *Loco-Motion*, the game we drew inspiration from, and *Turky on the Run* are essentially sharing the same basic actions and gameplay, the use of a different theme and settings can help to actually engage players through a different emotional experience: collecting is the main driving force behind the model game, while Turky relies mostly on the protection instinct instead, leaving the former somewhat in the background.

CHAPTER 10

Turky on the Run
Development

D EVELOPING *TURKY ON THE Run* is going to be a bit more complicated than the two other games we have worked on so far: while
we managed to keep *Moon Wolf* and *Kitty & Katty* within the 100 events
limit so that they could be developed on the Construct 2 Free Edition, the
full version of *Turky on the Run* we can find on the Apple AppStore and
BlackBerry World counts more than 600 events!

For this reason, here we will focus on describing how to achieve the actual
gameplay only, leaving the other parts of the game, like splash screens, navigation between layouts, etc., as a simple exercise: this shouldn't be a problem
by now since these tasks would involve essentially the very same steps we did
when developing *Kitty & Katty*. The gameplay alone, though, will still need
more than 100 events overall, so, if developing on the free edition, you may
have to try different features individually in independent projects or simplify certain aspects of the game, for example by reducing content. Specific
places where this can be done will be pointed out as we progress.

Our step-by-step development will be subdivided into the following
sections:

1. **Layout and shuffling**, where we place the different tiles to form the
   grid and shuffle them around.

2. **Moving tiles**, where we are going to allow the player to move a tile
   into the empty area by clicking on it or touching it. We will also

implement a tile highlighting mechanism to point out the tiles that can actually be moved.

3. **Turky: placement and movement**, here we will define where Turky starts his adventure and how it moves.

4. **Sly, Foxy, and Otto**, in this section we will take care of Sly, Foxy, and Otto and how they should become more dangerous after each level.

5. **Timer and bonus items**, where we are going to add different bonus items as well as other elements like a timer.

10.1 LAYOUT AND SHUFFLING

Originally, *Turky on the Run* was developed with a web browser and the iPhone 3GS as target platforms, so great care was taken to keep resources as low as possible and to work on the 3GS low-resolution screen of 480 × 320 pixels, relying on the up-scaling abilities of Construct 2 to adapt to other devices. I will maintain the original 480 × 320 layout size here, but if you prefer, feel free to design for a higher resolution and scale all values accordingly.

Once our new empty project is open and the layout size set, let's rename the Layer 0 to "Action," set its background color to black, and then add a new layer named **GUI**, like we did for the other projects. We may also want to add a **Debug** layer to display helpful text while the game is running and monitoring different variables.

We saw in the game design document that our maze will consist of a grid made by four rows and five columns, making enough room for 19 tiles and one empty space. Specifically, we will have tiles of seven different types according to the paths they represent, shown in Figure 10.1.

Start by adding a new sprite for each of these and import the graphics accordingly (you can find these in the downloadable game project file or draw your own). As usual, name each sprite in a meaningful way, for example, the crossroad could be t_X, with t standing for "tile," the vertical

FIGURE 10.1 The different tiles that will make up our maze. In the game project these are named as: t_X, t_V, t_H, t_LD, t_DR, t_UR, and t_LU, respectively.

path would be t_V, the path turning from left downward t_LD, and so on. In my 480 × 320 layout, each tile was resized to a 70 × 70 square. You can use a different size if you like, but be sure all tiles are squared and have the exact same dimensions!

We also want to provide a right mix of tiles to make the construction of different paths challenging but always possible, so we should duplicate each tile wisely (don't forget we can duplicate a tile simply by pressing Ctrl, clicking on the object, and then dragging where we want the new copy to appear—the new object will share the same name as the old one). For example, we could decide for a mix including four t_X (this will clearly be the most helpful of all) and t_H, three t_V, and two copies of all remaining ones.

Let's also add a smaller black tile (e.g., 25 × 25 pixel) that will be used to check for collisions when the player makes a cat fall into the empty tile, which will act as a bottomless pit.

Once we have all the tiles in the layout, we should arrange them around to give us an idea of where the grid will be during the game (Figure 10.2). While we will shuffle and place all the tiles properly at runtime, we do need to decide now the best placement of the grid, making sure to record the offset where the first top tile on the left will be placed. In my layout, the first tile has coordinates (115,75).

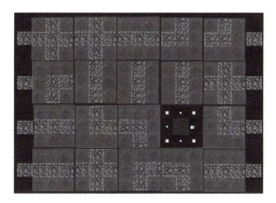

FIGURE 10.2 Placing the tiles in the layout to form the grid. Note the small black tile highlighted in the middle of the empty square: we will use this for collision detection purposes (we may want to fill it with a different color at first for debugging purposes). At this stage we can also add another small sprite to represent the four possible locations where Turky will start (on the left side) and where Picky will be waiting for him (on the right). These have to be placed accurately to match the paths of the maze tiles.

Before we can shuffle the tiles around and make a random maze, we need to define how we are actually going to represent it data-wise in the game. As you might have guessed, we are going to use an array to identify each tile position: let's add one to the project, call it "Positions," and set its size to (20,1,1).

In the event sheet, let's add a **System/On start of layout** event followed by a subevent for **Positions** to cycle through all its elements on the *x* axis and initialize them (use **Positions/For each X element** event). The simplest way to do so is to copy the current index (tracked by the **Positions.CurX** built-in variable) as its own value, i.e., slot 0 will have a value of 0, slot 1 a value of 1, and so on. Once done, we need another subevent to shuffle the array. The idea here is to switch two elements randomly several times so that we can completely reorder the array. We can do so via the **System/For** loop, with a starting index of 1 and ending at 50, for example. To perform the switch we also need to declare three local variables: two for selecting the indexes of the elements we want to switch and one for temporarily storing the first value. We can call these i, j, and temp. Then, through the **System** object, we assign i and j to a random integer number between 0 and the **Positions** array length (i.e., **Set j to *floor(Random(0, Positions.Width-1)))***), copy the value of the element having index i to temp (i.e., **Set temp to *Positions.At(i)***), and finally copy the value in j to the slot i followed by copying the value in temp to the slot j. The result is shown in Figure 10.3, where we also added two text boxes in the **Debug** layer to print out the array values before and after the shuffling to be sure everything was done properly.

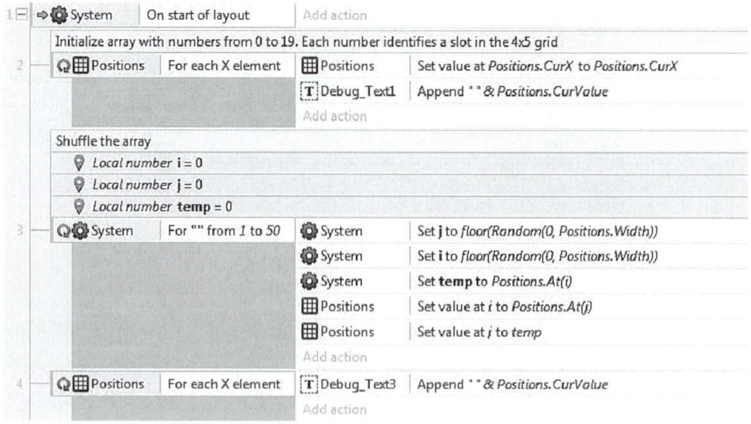

FIGURE 10.3   Initializing and shuffling the **Positions** array.

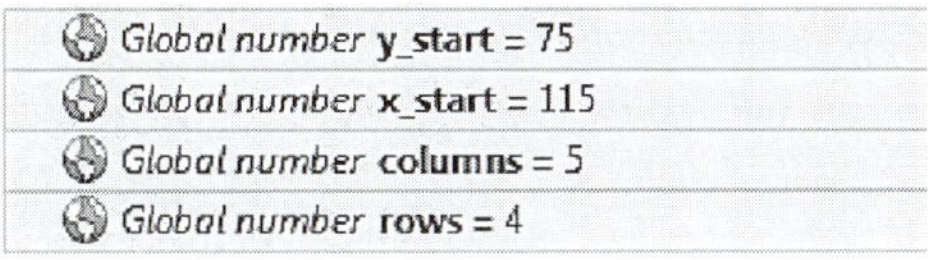

🌐 *Global number* y_start = 75	
🌐 *Global number* x_start = 115	
🌐 *Global number* columns = 5	
🌐 *Global number* rows = 4	

FIGURE 10.4 The global variables needed to handle the grid and the tile placement.

We are now almost ready to assign each tile a unique position and place them on the screen accordingly. Before doing this, though, we should first add a few more variables that we will be using throughout the game when dealing with the tiles and their positions. Specifically, we need four global variables identifying the grid size (i.e., four rows and five columns), as well as the coordinates of the first tile in the grid, which will be used as an off-set when dealing with tile positions (we marked down these values earlier when we first placed the tiles in the layout). These are shown in Figure 10.4 for my layout.

We also need to add a few instance variables to each tile so that they can be handled properly later. In particular, we need to specify a unique ID to identify the tile (from 0 to 19, for example—this will remain fixed throughout the game), its current position in the grid and, for all tiles except the small black one we use to identify the empty square, also where its exits are located (e.g., up, down, left, right—we are going to use these data when moving the characters around).

Note that we need to add a specific variable only once for each tile type (e.g., t_X, t_H, etc.) since all tiles sharing the same name (in other words, all instances of the same object) will automatically acquire the same variables, which we can then instantiate accordingly and independently (see Figure 10.5).

Once done, we can go back to the event sheet and add more subevents to **On start of layout** to place all tiles according to our previously shuffled array: the number in the array will identify the position in the grid. Referring to Figure 10.2, the top left tile will have position equal to 0, the next one on the right will have 1, the top left tile on the second row will have 5, and so on until the last one at the bottom right having a position of 19.

To achieve the correct placement, we need first to add a new local variable called **counter** and set it to 0, then we have to add subevents to scan all instances of a specific tile type to set its **grid_pos** instance variable to **Position.At(counter)** value and then determine the *x* and *y* coordinates

Object type properties	
Name	t_DR
Plugin	Sprite
UID	54
Global	No
Common	
Layer	Action
Angle	0
Opacity	100
⊞ Position	-298, 19
⊞ Size	70, 70
Instance variables	
id	4
grid_pos	0
up	false
down	true
left	false
right	true
Add / edit	Instance variables

FIGURE 10.5 Instance variables for the tile objects. We need to specify an ID, an index position in the grid, and also which exits are active. Here is one of the t_DR tiles.

accordingly. For these, we can write a formula where, starting from the position of the first tile (the global variables **x_start** and **y_start**) we add n times the size of a tile where n is equal to **Positions.At(counter)%columns** and **floor(Positions.At(counter)%columns)** for x and y, respectively. The % (called "modulus") operator returns the remainder of the division between two numbers, and we can use it to separate the tiles properly on the x axis. For example, for the very first tile, counter is 0, columns is 5, so the modulus operation returns 0, and we simply place the tile in x_start. For the second tile, counter is now 1, so the operation returns a 1. We place the new tile at an x coordinate equal to x_start plus one tile size and so on for the entire row. When counter is equal to 5, the modulus operation returns 0 again, so the tile simply has x_start coordinate on the x axis, but we change the y coordinate by checking for the integer part of the division between counter and columns: this is now 1, and we add a tile width size to the y axis coordinate, and so on. The event and actions are shown in Figure 10.6.

Once this has been done for every tile type, we can run the layout and see how the tiles are rearranged in a different way every time. Be sure to

Assigning each tile a position.				
⬤ *Local number* **counter** = 0				
⊙⚙ System	For each ▦ t_X	▦ t_X	Set **grid_pos** to *Positions.At(counter)*
		▦ t_X	Set X to *x_start + Positions.At(counter)%columns * t_X.Width*
		▦ t_X	Set Y to *y_start + floor(Positions.At(counter)/columns)* t_X.Width*
		⚙ System	Add 1 to **counter**
		Add action	
⊙⚙ System	For each ▦ t_DR	▦ t_DR	Set **grid_pos** to *Positions.At(counter)*
		▦ t_DR	Set X to *x_start + Positions.At(counter)%columns * t_X.Width*
		▦ t_DR	Set Y to *y_start + floor(Positions.At(counter)/columns)* t_X.Width*
		⚙ System	Add 1 to **counter**
		Add action	

FIGURE 10.6 The **On start of layout** subevents to place t_X and t_DR tiles according to the values in the shuffled array **Positions**. Each tile type, including the small empty tile, requires a subevent like this.

place the small path tiles, where we will be placing Turky and Picky, at the side of the grid in a way that they match eventual entries in the maze.

Before moving to the next section, I'd like to solve a problem we will face later when playtesting the game. There could be special cases where Turky starts at the top or bottom position and the tile in front of him is a t_LU or t_LD, respectively, as shown in Figure 10.7. If this happens, Turky is going to be stuck, and we force the player to use a magic wand right away to be teleported somewhere else.

This would be quite annoying, so we want to avoid it, and we should do that right now.

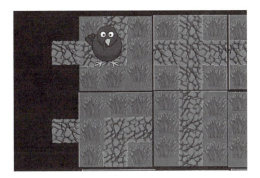

FIGURE 10.7 And now what? Turky looks puzzled and rightly so! This is a special case we want to avoid: Turky starting on the top spot and getting stuck right away on a left-up (t_LU) tile at the very beginning of the game (remember we can't move the tile that Turky is on even if there is the empty tile next to it). Same problem when starting at the bottom with a left-down (t_LD) tile.

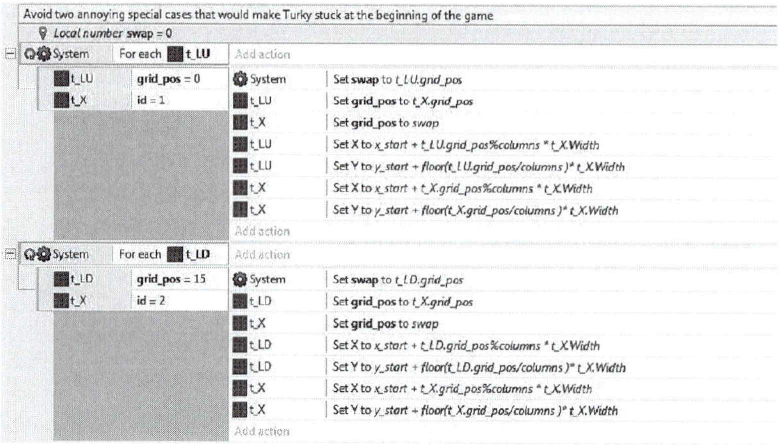

FIGURE 10.8 Avoiding the special case just discussed. We check whether the wrong tile is in place, and we also select another tile by picking up a specific type and ID to swap it with. Note we also need a local variable to swap the grid_pos values for the two tiles, and then we proceed to update their coordinates accordingly.

What we have to do to be sure this never happens is to check the position of the t_LU and t_LD tiles and see if one of them is on that critical spot (grid_pos equal to 0 means the top left corner while grid_pos equal to 15 identifies the bottom left corner). If so, we pick a specific instance of a different tile (for example, one of t_X) and swap their positions. This is done easily following the same approach we just did for placing the tiles. The corresponding events, together with all the different actions, are shown in Figure 10.8.*

10.2 MOVING TILES

Now that the grid is in place, we can code the moving tiles mechanism allowing players to shift any tile adjacent to the empty square by clicking it (or touching it, in case of a mobile device), as long as it is not the tile Turky is on or the tile he is moving to. To identify the latter cases, we should first add two instance variables to Turky himself, so add a new sprite for Turky and import the **turky.png** image you can find in the project artwork folder,† place our hero somewhere outside the layout, and add two instance

---

* There are actually a few more special cases we should consider to be sure such forced blocks don't happen, but I leave these to you to find out via playtesting as a simple quality assurance exercise.
† All artwork for this game is taken from www.clker.com.

variables: **target** and **grid_pos**, both of type **number** and with an initial value of −1 (since all values form the **Positions** array identifying a tile range from 0 to 19, we can use negative numbers to represent special cases like the character still being outside of the grid).

The next step consists in adding the **Touch** object to the game so that we can finally start programming the tile-moving process. For this, we are going to introduce a new concept: **groups**. A group acts like a self-contained subsection of events and not only helps in keeping our event structure clean and easily readable but can also be explicitly activated (i.e., called) and deactivated, making it a very useful tool somewhat similar to functions, but without the possibility of passing parameters. Indeed, in the earlier versions of Construct 2, where functions were not available yet, groups were the only option to organize a set of events together and trigger them from another event when needed.

To add a **group**, right click on the event sheet and select the appropriate command. Name this group "Move Tiles" and add its first event: **On touched object** from the **Touch** object. We can start with the t_X tile, for example. Remember we are allowed to move the tile only if Turky is not on it or moving into it. To check for this, add the necessary conditions to compare the tile's own **grid_pos** variable with Turky's **grid_pos** and **target** variables via the **Compare instance variable** event to see whether they are different. If Turky is not around, we can proceed to move the tile into the empty space and swap it with the t_empty collision tile. In doing this, we need to identify whether the empty space is above, below, in front of, or behind the tile and act accordingly.

Let's work first on the case where the empty space is above or below the tile. Here, the grid position of the tile is equal to t_empty's grid position variable plus or minus 5 (remember we have five columns, so adding 5 to the position will move us to the next row, subtracting 5 will take us to the previous row instead). If this is true, we proceed in swapping the two tiles (we need to add a local variable to handle this as we did previously).

Since the actions we need to take are the same in both cases, we can put the two events together and make an **OR event** (select the event and right click on it to choose the **Make 'OR' block** option), which is triggered when any of the two conditions is true. The event is shown in Figure 10.9.

We can now take care of the two other cases, i.e., when the tile to move is before or after the empty space. We can identify these configurations by checking whether the tile **grid_pos** is equal to **t_empty** position plus

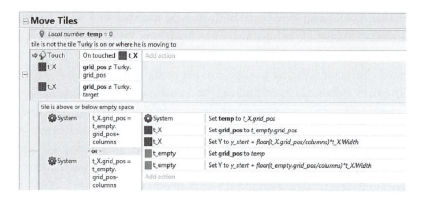

FIGURE 10.9   The **Move Tiles** group: when touching a tile, we also need to check that it is not Turky's current or targeted tile and that it is next to the empty area (identified by the t_empty tile). Here we check whether the t_X is above or below the t_empty.

or minus 1, but we need to pay a little more attention here, since we want to avoid wrapping the tile around, i.e., moving it to a different row. This could happen when, for example, the empty space has position 4 (end of the top row) and we click on the tile with position 5 (the first on the second row).

So, when the tile is before the empty space, we need to be sure its **grid_pos** is not equal to **columns-1, (columns*2)-1,** and **(columns*3)-1** before proceeding. Similarly, when the tile is after the empty space, we need to check that its grid position is not equal to **columns, columns*2,** and **columns*3**. Note that the second condition needs to be preceded by a **System/Else** statement, otherwise it will be triggered right after the first movement bringing the tile back!

The new events are shown in Figure 10.10.

This concludes the **On touched** event for one type of tile but, within the **Move Tiles** group, we also need to have such an event for all tiles. Simply copy and paste the whole event and then select it, right click, and choose the **Replace object** command to update the tile object to the correct one (Figure 10.11).

Note that handling each tile type will take a few events, so if you are using the Construct 2 free license limited to 100 events, you may prefer to implement only a specific subset of tiles (for example, add more t_X, t_H, and t_V and remove the others) to see how the other features of the game work.

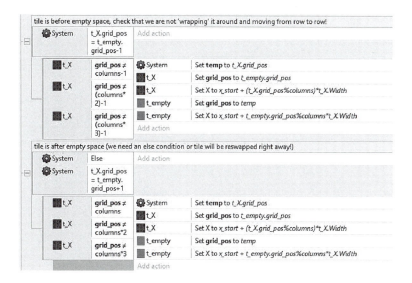

FIGURE 10.10   The last set of subevents completing the **Touch t_X** tile event in the **Move Tiles** group. Here we take care of shifting the tile back and forth avoiding the special cases where the tile is on the leftmost and rightmost columns, in which case a shift would imply the tile wrapped around the edges of the grid and moved to a different row.

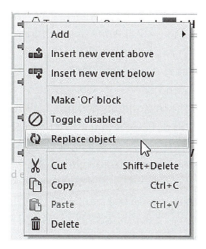

FIGURE 10.11   After copying and pasting an event, we can quickly update the object involved by replacing it automatically across all conditions and actions by selecting the **Replace object** command.

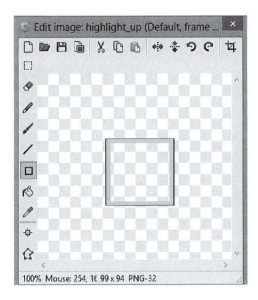

FIGURE 10.12   A possible simple frame we can use as a highlight effect to point out the tiles around the empty space, i.e., the tiles players can move in the game.

Once all tiles have been taken care of, run the layout and test that everything is working properly.

In the early testing I did for *Turky on the Run* I noticed that some players were confused and didn't know which tiles they could move, so I thought of adding some way to highlight the tiles next to the empty space. If you would like to do so as well, start by adding another sprite and calling it **highlight_up**. Draw something like a simple frame (Figure 10.12), resize it to have the same dimensions as the other tiles, add a **grid_pos** instance variable to it, and set its opacity property to about 50 (we don't want the highlight frame to stand out too much either, otherwise it can be distracting for the players). Place it outside the visible layout, right click it, and select **Clone object type** three times, renaming each instance **highlight_down**, **highlight_left**, and **highlight_right**.

We are all set to implement the highlight effect now: what we will be doing is simply to superimpose the frames to the tiles around the empty space as long as Turky is not around.* Figures 10.13 and 10.14 show the different events arranged into one new group, **TileHighlights**, where, for

---

* Note that this feature is not critical for the game, so, if you have the 100-event limitation, you may want to skip it and move forward.

TileHighlights
– Displays highlighting images on tiles

⇒ System	On start of layout	⟳ Function	Call "UpdateHighlights" ()
		Add action	
⇒⟳ Function	On "UpdateHighlights"	☐ highlight_left	Set **grid_pos** to t_empty.grid_pos-1
		☐ highlight_right	Set **grid_pos** to t_empty.grid_pos+1
		☐ highlight_down	Set **grid_pos** to t_empty.grid_pos + 5
		☐ highlight_up	Set **grid_pos** to t_empty.grid_pos - 5
		Add action	

Highlight for square above empty space but only if not on the first row and if tile is occupied or targeted by Turky

⚙ System	highlight_up. grid_pos ≠ Turky. target	☐ highlight_up	Set X to x_start+(highlight_up.grid_pos%columns)*t_X.Width
		☐ highlight_up	Set Y to 5+y_start+floor(highlight_up.grid_pos/columns)*t_X.Width
⚙ System	highlight_up. grid_pos ≠ Turky. grid_pos	Add action	
◼ t_empty	**grid_pos ≥ 5**		
⚙ System	Else	☐ highlight_up	Set position to (-200, -200)
		Add action	

Highlight for square below empty space but only if not on the last row and if tile is occupied or targeted by Turky

⚙ System	highlight_down. grid_pos ≠ Turky. target	☐ highlight_down	Set X to x_start+(highlight_down.grid_pos%columns)*t_X.Width
		☐ highlight_down	Set Y to 5+y_start+floor(highlight_down.grid_pos/columns)*t_X.Width
⚙ System	highlight_down. grid_pos ≠ Turky. grid_pos		
◼ t_empty	**grid_pos ≤ 14**		
⚙ System	Else	☐ highlight_down	Set position to (-200, -200)
		Add action	

FIGURE 10.13 The **TileHighlights** group with a function updating each tile grid_pos instance variable followed by two events to place the **highlight_up** and **highlight_down** frames. There we check that we are not highlighting Turky's own tiles and that we are in the appropriate area of the grid (i.e., t_empty's grid_pos should be equal to or greater than 5, meaning we are in the second row of tiles for **highlight_up** or less than 15 for **highlight_down**, meaning the empty space is not in the last row). If these conditions are not met, we simply move the highlight off screen. Note that adding a small offset to the coordinates may be needed according to your tile's size.

Highlight for square right of empty space but only if not on last column and if tile is occupied or targeted by Turky

⚙ System	highlight_right. grid_pos ≠ Turky. grid_pos	☐ highlight_right	Set X to x_start+(highlight_right.grid_pos%columns)*t_X.Width
		☐ highlight_right	Set Y to -5+y_start+floor(highlight_right.grid_pos/columns)*t_X.Width
⚙ System	highlight_right. grid_pos ≠ Turky. target	Add action	
⚙ System	t_empty.grid_pos%5 ≠ 4		
⚙ System	Else	☐ highlight_right	Set position to (-200, -200)
		Add action	

Highlight for square left empty space but only if not on the first row and if tile is occupied or targeted by Turky

⚙ System	highlight_left. grid_pos ≠ Turky. grid_pos	☐ highlight_left	Set X to x_start+(highlight_left.grid_pos%columns)*t_X.Width
		☐ highlight_left	Set Y to -5+y_start+floor(highlight_left.grid_pos/columns)*t_X.Width
⚙ System	highlight_left. grid_pos ≠ Turky. target	Add action	
⚙ System	t_empty.grid_pos%5 ≠ 0		
⚙ System	Else	☐ highlight_left	Set position to (-200, -200)
		Add action	

FIGURE 10.14 The events for **highlight_right** and **highlight_left** frames. Note how we use the modulo operator to identify the last and first columns, respectively.

each frame, we check whether the frame position is in the proper range of values (e.g., we should display the **highlight_up** only if the empty space is not in the first row, or **highlight_right** only if not in the last column, etc.), if not we simply move it off screen (alternatively, we could set it to invisible and set it back to visible when needed). We perform the check within a dedicated function, which is called right away as the game starts as well as anytime we move a tile (for this, we need to update the events in Figures 10.09 and 10.10 by calling the function after moving t_empty).

10.3 TURKY: PLACEMENT AND MOVEMENT

We are now ready to start writing down Turky's movement, which is also the most difficult part of the tutorial. First of all, let's look at how the movement should work: we want Turky to start in one of the four possible spots on the left, randomly. As soon as a path opens, i.e., we place a tile with an exit matching Turky's position, we mark the tile, so that it cannot be shifted as long as Turky is moving toward it, and let Turky start his journey to meet Picky. Every time we shift tiles in the grid, we need to check whether there is a path Turky can take and, if so, pick one randomly.

This can also be described via the following algorithm:

1. Identify exits of the tile Turky is on.

2. Identify exits for the tiles right above, below, before, and after Turky.

3. If there is any match, pick one at random and start moving Turky.

4. Mark the selected match so that it is clear to the player where Turky is going. That tile can't be shifted anymore as long as Turky is going toward it, even if he has not reached it yet.

5. When the targeted tile has been reached, check whether we have an exit leading to Picky. If not, repeat from step 1.

To start implementing all these steps, we need to define all the variables required for implementing this algorithm.

Luckily, we already added instance variables for each exit across the different tiles earlier (Figure 10.5), so now we only have to worry about

Turky. Currently he has only two variables (**target** and **grid_pos**), so let's add the following:*

- **startAt** is the number that will identify the beginning row for Turky.

- **direction** is the number needed to identify where Turky is going. We will be using the following values: 0 for left, 1 for up, 2 for right, and 3 for down plus two special cases: −2 to identify the beginning case when Turky is outside of the grid and −1 to identify the case where there are no exits and Turky is stuck on a tile.

- **speed** is the number defining Turky's own movement speed. By default, we can set this to 15. It will be changed according to different power-ups (or power-downs).

- **comingFrom** is the number used to identify the direction Turky is coming from. This will allow us to avoid going back unless there is no other choice.

- **possibleExits** is a counter we use to know how many options Turky has at any given time.

- **up**, **down**, **left**, and **right** are Boolean flags used to identify available exits.

- **superTurky** is a Boolean flag we will later use to identify whether Turky has acquired the super power-up.

Once done, Turky's properties will look like those shown in Figure 10.15.

To implement Turky's movement, we are going to write three big groups of events: **Turky-Begin**, where we initialize Turky at the beginning of the game as well as when he gets caught and needs to restart, **Turky-Move** to handle the actual movement, and **Turky-LookAround** to assess the situation, i.e., look for possible exits and choose one.

Let's start by adding the **Turky-Begin** group and then a **System/On start of layout** event where we call a function named **InitializeTurky**. There, we set all instance variables as shown in Figure 10.16. It is useful to have this part of code in a standalone function instead of simply adding it

---

* For simplicity, we will be adding all variables at once, also those that we will need later when discussing power-ups.

Instance variables	
direction	0
startAt	0
comingFrom	0
target	-1
speed	15
grid_pos	-1
up	false
down	false
left	false
right	false
possible_exits	0
superTurky	false
Add / edit	Instance variables

FIGURE 10.15   All the properties Turky needs in his quest for meeting Picky.

Turky-Begin

Initializing Turky and looking for entering the maze.

➡ System	On start of layout	🔁 Function	Call "InitializeTurky" ()	
		Add action		
➡ Function	On "InitializeTurky"	🐦 Turky	Set **direction** to -1	
		🐦 Turky	Set **startAt** to *floor(random(rows))*	
		🐦 Turky	Set **target** to -2	
		🐦 Turky	Set **speed** to *15*	
		🐦 Turky	Set **grid_pos** to -1	
		🐦 Turky	Set **comingFrom** to *0*	
		🐦 Turky	Set **possible_exits** to *0*	
		🐦 Turky	Set **up** to *False*	
		🐦 Turky	Set **down** to *False*	
		🐦 Turky	Set **left** to *False*	
		🐦 Turky	Set **right** to *False*	
		🐦 Turky	Set **animation** to "still" (play from beginning)	
		🐦 Turky	Set X to *x_start - (2*t_empty.Width)*	
		🐦 Turky	Set Y to *y_start -10 + (Turky.startAt * t_X.Width)*	
		🐦 Turky	Set **superTurky** to *False*	
		Add action		

FIGURE 10.16   Initializing Turky. Note that **startAt** is set to a random number identifying a specific row, and Turky's coordinates are also set accordingly to match one of the four entrances we placed previously just outside the maze. The specific numbers here have to match your particular layout. Here, I described the exact position to place Turky in terms of reference tiles like t_X and t_empty.

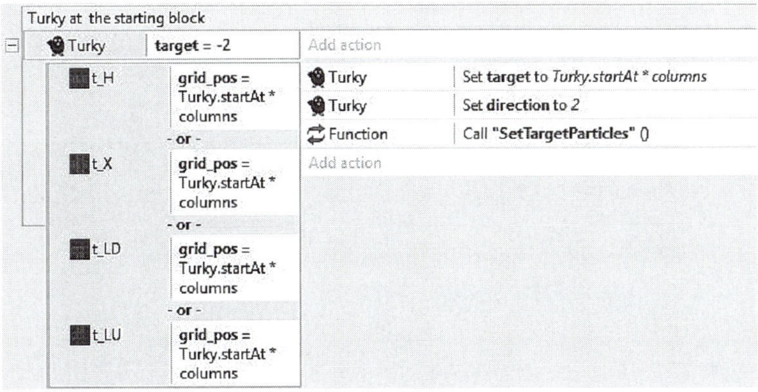

FIGURE 10.17 The other subevent in the **Turky-Begin** group. Here we check whether a tile providing an entrance in the maze is next to Turky. If so, we update Turky's relevant variables (target and direction) besides calling a function to visually mark the tile as Turky's target via some particle effect.

to the **On start of layout** event so that we can reinitialize Turky not only when the game starts but also when he gets hit by Sly, Foxy, and Otto.

In the function **InitializeTurky** we set **target** to –2. We use this value to specify the case where Turky is out of the maze. Clearly, this is the first case we have to deal with, so let's add a new subevent to the **Turky-Begin** group identified by this very condition. In it, we start another subevent where we check whether the tile next to Turky has an exit on the left, i.e., t_X, t_H, t_LU, and t_LD. All these conditions must be tied together in an **OR** block as shown in Figure 10.17, so if any of these cases happens, we can proceed by updating Turky's target variable to the specific tile while also setting the appropriate movement direction (i.e., moving right is identified by the number 2, so that's the value we will need to assign to the **direction** variable).

Before we get into the consequences of changing the **direction** variable, let's see the other function we are calling here: **SetTargetParticles**. This is where we want to mark the tile Turky is moving to, providing players with some visual feedback. We can handle this by drawing some particles trying to simulate a flower-like effect by combining yellow and red dots, for example, as shown in Figure 10.18.

The function itself, shown in Figure 10.19, is actually pretty simple: what we have to do is only to update the particle's own **grid_pos** variable to the value in Turky's **target** variable and compute the position accordingly. The

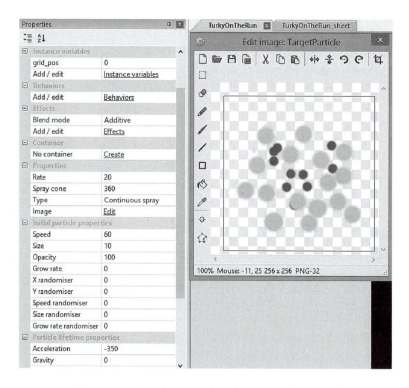

FIGURE 10.18 Properties for the particle effect as implemented in the game. Note we have grid_pos variable here too to identify the position in the maze. The image itself is a simple set of yellow and red dots that will spread to simulate little flowers.

animation will play automatically thanks to the properties we just set in Figure 10.18.

We can now proceed to add a new group, **Turky-Move**, which should be structured with a main event checking for Turky's **target** variable being greater than or equal to 0 and then a specific subevent for each moving direction. Let's not forget, though, that for this to work properly and to handle Turky's walking cycles, we should also add the **CustomMovement** behavior (do this now through Turky's **Properties** panel) besides setting

FIGURE 10.19 The **SetTargetParticles** function, taking care of positioning the particle effect on the tile Turky is moving to.

Turky-Move

⊟	Hanlding movement once a target position has been set. Direction = 0 means left, 1 means up, 2 means right and 3 means down.				
⊟	🐢 Turky	target ≥ 0	⊤ Debug_Text1	Set text to "Turky pos" & Turky.grid_pos & " " &Turky.target	
				Add action	
⊟	🐢 Turky	direction = 0	🐢 Turky	Set ✂ CustomMovement Horizontal speed to - *1*Turky.speed	
			🐢 Turky	Set animation to "**left**" (play from current frame)	
				Add action	
	🐢 Turky	X ≤ x_start + (Turky. target% columns)* t_X.Width	🐢 Turky	Stop ✂ CustomMovement	
			🐢 Turky	Set **comingFrom** to 2	
			🐢 Turky	Set **target** to -*1*	
			📍 TargetParticle	Set position to (-*200*, -*200*)	
				Add action	
⊟	🐢 Turky	direction = 1	🐢 Turky	Set ✂ CustomMovement Vertical speed to - *1*Turky.speed	
			🐢 Turky	Set animation to "**up**" (play from current frame)	
				Add action	
	🐢 Turky	Y ≤ y_start - 10 + floor(Turky.target/ columns)* t_X.Width	🐢 Turky	Stop ✂ CustomMovement	
			🐢 Turky	Set **comingFrom** to 3	
			🐢 Turky	Set **target** to -*1*	
			📍 TargetParticle	Set position to (-*200*, -*200*)	
				Add action	

FIGURE 10.20   The events handling Turky's left and up movements. Note also that we have a debug line first to point out the values of Turky's grid_pos and then target variables to check that the group is called properly and everything is working as planned.

up different walking animations. Double click on **Turky** and add all the needed animation cycles (up, down, left, right) by importing the different frames as provided in the project artwork folder.

Figure 10.20 shows the subevents triggered when Turky is moving left (direction = 0) or up (direction = 1). What we are doing there is pretty straightforward: we use the **CustomMovement** behavior to set Turky in motion with the proper speed and direction and trigger the corresponding animation. After this, we stop the movement when Turky gets in the middle of the target tile, which we identify by looking at Turky's x position when moving horizontally, or at his y coordinate when moving vertically. Once Turky stops, we update the **comingFrom** variable accordingly (e.g., if we are moving left, i.e., direction = 0, **comingFrom** will be set to right, i.e., 2) as well as setting **target** to −1, meaning we need to look for another exit. Last, we move the target particle off screen by setting its x and y coordinates to −200.

Right and down movements are handled in the exact same way, as shown in Figure 10.21.

So, what happens when **target** is set to −1? Here it is when the last group, **Turky-LookAround**, comes into play (Figure 10.22). To have the

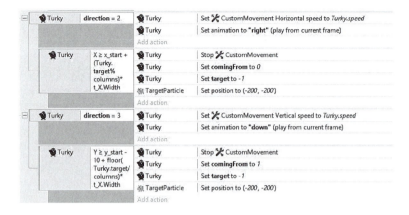

FIGURE 10.21   The events for moving Turky right or down.

group work properly, we need to set up a few local variables for the group itself:

- **Exit** is a number used to identify the direction of the exit Turky is going to take. We initialize this to −1, meaning no exit found yet.

- **Ok** is a flag we will use later to signal that an exit has been found.

- **Options** is the total number of possible exits available to choose from.

We also need an array to keep track of the various exits at any given time. Let's call it "Exits4Turky" and give it dimensions equal to (4,1,1) to cover all possible directions. Each array element represents a direction

FIGURE 10.22   The beginning of the **Turky-LookAround** group: setting up the required variables and array to keep track of available possibilities while also resetting Turky animation to its idle state as long as a new direction is not picked up.

(e.g., element 0 represents an exit available to the left, element 1 represents up, and so on as usual), and it is going to be set to 1 if an exit in that specific direction is available.

Once these variables and array have been initialized (the **clear** command for the array object resets all elements to 0), we are ready to look for possible exits. To do so, we are going to proceed as follows. First, we check which exits are available on the tile Turky is currently on, then we check for matching exits in the nearby tiles (i.e., above, below, before, and after Turky's tile), and finally we pick an available exit, if any, also making sure to avoid going back where Turky came from unless that is the only option available.

The first step is handled by the **UpdateTurky-Exits-Position** function, shown in Figure 10.23. Here we check whether Turky is on each tile type and then update Turky's corresponding variables accordingly, together with its **grid_pos** variable.

Next comes the step where we match Turky's exits with those of the nearby tiles. To do so, we define a specific event for each of Turky's directional variables (right, left, up, and down) and then check whether the next tile in that specific direction offers a matching entrance.

For example, Figure 10.24 shows the details for Turky's **right** variable and is triggered whenever this is set to true. We also have to check that it makes sense to look for another tile right ahead, i.e., Turky is not on the last column of the grid, a special case we identify once again thanks to the modulo operator (**turky.grid_pos%5** is not equal to 4). If so, we can update to 1 the

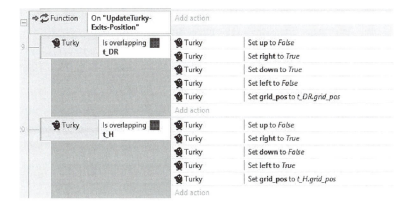

FIGURE 10.23 The **UpdateTurky-Exits-Position** function, here showing the actions for updating Turky's variables in case he is on a t_DR or t_H tile. Such events have to be replicated for all other tile types as well.

Checking for an exit on the right, as long as we are not in the last column of the grid				
Turky	Is right		Add action	
System	turky.grid_pos%5 ≠ 4			
System	For each t_X	Exits4Turky	Set value at 2 to 1
t_X	grid_pos = Turky.grid_pos + 1	Add action	
System	Else	Exits4Turky	Set value at 2 to 1
System	For each t_H	Add action	
t_H	grid_pos = Turky.grid_pos + 1		
System	Else	Exits4Turky	Set value at 2 to 1
System	For each t_LU	Add action	
t_LU	grid_pos = Turky.grid_pos + 1		
System	Else	Exits4Turky	Set value at 2 to 1
System	For each t_LD	Add action	
t_LD	grid_pos = Turky.grid_pos + 1		
Turky	Is left	Add action	
System	turky.grid_pos%5 ≠ 0		
Turky	Is up	Add action	
System	turky.grid_pos ≥ 5		
Turky	Is down	Add action	
System	turky.grid_pos ≤ 14		

FIGURE 10.24 Matching Turky's exit variables with possible entrances in adjacent tiles. If there is a match, the corresponding slot in the Exits4Turky array is updated to 1. Note also that we avoid checking for directions that would be outside the grid (e.g., checking for an up exit if we are on the top row or for a left exit if we are on the first column).

corresponding element in the **Exits4Turky** array (i.e., the one having index equal to 2, corresponding to the direction toward the right). This is repeated for all the tiles that have an opening to the left, where each block is preceded by a **System/else** condition to avoid checking them if we already found a match.

The very same approach is used for Turky's other variables, **left, up,** and **down**.

Now that we identified a set of potential exits, we need to pick one. As discussed in our one-page design document, Turky isn't very smart, so he simply chooses one option at random, as long as it is not the one he is coming from. Still, we need to develop this simple approach carefully and the whole process is outlined in Figure 10.25.

We begin by scanning the **Exits4Turky** array and count how many 1s we have in there, i.e., we check the numbers of matching exits available and save the result in the **options** variable we defined earlier. If there are no options, we do nothing and wait for the players to rearrange

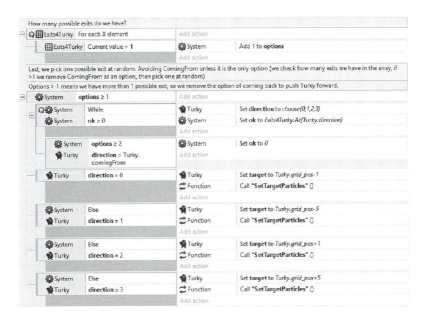

How many possible exits do we have?				
Q Exits4Turky	For each X element		Add action	
Exits4Turky	Current value = 1	System	Add 1 to options	
			Add action	

Last, we pick one possible exit at random. Avoiding ComingFrom unless it is the only option (we check how many exits we have in the array, if > 1 we remove ComingFrom as an option, then pick one at random).

Options > 1 means we have more than 1 possible exit, so we remove the option of coming back to push Turky forward.

System	options ≥ 1		Add action	
Q System	While	Turky	Set direction to choose(0,1,2,3)	
System	ok = 0	System	Set ok to Exits4Turky.At(Turky.direction)	
			Add action	
System	options ≥ 2	System	Set ok to 0	
Turky	direction = Turky. comingFrom		Add action	
Turky	direction = 0	Turky	Set target to Turky.grid_pos-1	
		Function	Call "SetTargetParticles" ()	
			Add action	
System	Else	Turky	Set target to Turky.grid_pos-5	
Turky	direction = 1	Function	Call "SetTargetParticles" ()	
			Add action	
System	Else	Turky	Set target to Turky.grid_pos+1	
Turky	direction = 2	Function	Call "SetTargetParticles" ()	
			Add action	
System	Else	Turky	Set target to Turky.grid_pos+5	
Turky	direction = 3	Function	Call "SetTargetParticles" ()	
			Add action	

FIGURE 10.25   The second part of the **Turky-LookAround** group. Here we select a specific direction based on the available options and mark the new target tile by placing the particles on it as well.

the tiles until some exit gets opened, but if **options** is at least 1, we can proceed with the selection. For this, we use the **ok** variable as a flag in a **System/while** loop: as long as **ok** is 0 we keep searching by picking up a possible direction. We do so by assigning a random number between 0 and 3 to Turky's **direction** variable and then use this as an index to look into the **Exits4Turky** array, with its returning value assigned to **ok**. If the exit is available, **ok** will be 1, otherwise it will remain 0, forcing the **while** loop to repeat the process once again until we finally pick one of the available exits.

Remember we also have to be sure Turky doesn't pick the same direction he came from, unless this is indeed the only available option. To do so, we add a subevent within the **while** loop where we check for this specific condition, i.e., Turky's **direction** variable equal to his **comingFrom** while also the number of **options** is greater than or equal to 2. If this happens, we reset **ok** to 0, forcing the **while** loop to repeat itself.

Once we finally exit the loop, the new direction is set, and all we have to do is to define a subevent for each value of the **direction** variable where we set Turky's **target** variable accordingly, activating the **Turky-Move** group, and also place the particles on the tile Turky is moving to by calling the **SetTargetPatricles** function.

Play the game: Turky should now be able to walk in the maze according to how we manipulate the tiles around him!

Now that this is settled, it's a good time to start implementing the score system.

Add a new global variable named **score**, initialized to 0, together with two new text objects. We can name one **txt_score** and set its text to Score (choose a font you like in a suitable size) while the other will be used to actually display the **score** variable, and we can name it **current_score** or whatever you like. Place these two text objects in the top left area of the screen above the first tile, as in Figure 10.26.

According to the game rules, the player's score increases as long as Turky keeps walking around, so we can simply update the **score** variable and the related text in the **Turky-Move** group when **target** is greater than or equal to 0 as shown in Figure 10.27. We should also add an action to update the **current_score** text when the game starts, for example in the **On start of layout** event we added in the **Turky-Begin** group.

Play the game and see how the score increases when Turky moves and stops whenever he gets stuck on a tile.

Each journey should have an end, and we don't want Turky to wander aimlessly in the maze forever, so taking care of Picky is a good idea now.

Add a new sprite object and import the image of Picky. Let's define a new group that takes care of anything Picky related, starting from her placement (Figure 10.28), which we handle in a **On start of layout** event,

FIGURE 10.26 Placing the score counter on top of the screen.

Turky-Move
⊟ Hanlding movement once a target position has been set. Direction = 0 means left, 1 means up, 2 means right and 3 means down.

	🦃 Turky	target ≥ 0		T Debug_Text1	Set text to "Turky.pos" & Turky.grid_pos & " " &Turky.target
				⚙ System	Add 0.1 to score
				T current_score	Set text to floor(score)
				Add action	

FIGURE 10.27 Updating the main event in the **Turky-Move** group to update Player's score and the corresponding text. The score is increased by 0.1 points per frame, and we round it to the lower integer via the **floor** instruction before displaying it in the text object. Note that here I have disabled the debug information about Turky's whereabouts, since this was checked and tested to be working as expected by now.

where we set her *x* and *y* coordinates to randomly match one of the small paths we placed at the right side of the maze.

The next event we need is the one to check whether Picky has finally been reached by Turky. When this happens, we want our Romeo to get close to his sweetheart and then restart the action at a higher difficulty level.

To achieve this, add another event to the **Picky** group where we check for the following conditions: first, Turky must be on a tile with an exit to the right (i.e., its **right** variable must be set to true), the tile must be on the last column (i.e., **turky.grid_pos%5** should be equal to 4), and the two sprites should be aligned horizontally, i.e., their *y* coordinates should be almost the same, as shown in Figure 10.29, where we check that the absolute value of the difference between the two *y* coordinates is less than 10 pixels.

When all these conditions are met, we can lead Turky toward Picky by setting the **Horizontal speed** in his **CustomMovement** behavior while switching to the **right** animation. We should also remember to remove the **TargetParticle**, by moving it off screen as usual and set Turky's **target** to a unique number to stop the process of looking for other exits and keep moving around.

Picky
⊟ A beautiful peacock and Turky's sweetheart.

	⇨ ⚙ System	On start of layout		🦚 Picky	Set X to x_start - 10 + t_X.Width*columns
				🦚 Picky	Set Y to y_start - 15 + choose(0,1,2,3)*t_X.Width
				Add action	

FIGURE 10.28 The beginning of a small group of events related to Picky, starting with her random placement to the right side of the maze by using the **choose** instruction. (Writing "choose(0,1,2,3)" is the same as writing "floor(random(0,4))".)

Going to Picky is a special case: we check Turky is on the last column, there is an exit on the right and Picky is aligned.				
🦃 Turky	Is right		🦃 Turky	Set 🏃 CustomMovement Horizontal speed to *Turky.speed*
⚙ System	turky.grid_pos%5 = 4		🦃 Turky	Set animation to "right" (play from current frame)
⚙ System	abs(Turky.Y - Picky.Y) ≤ 10		🦃 Turky	Set target to -99
			🎇 TargetParticle	Set position to (-200, -200)
				Add action
🦃 Turky	X ≥ (Picky.X - 20)		🦃 Turky	Set 🏃 CustomMovement Horizontal speed to 0
			⚙ System	Add 1000 to score
			⚙ System	Add 1 to date
			⚙ System	Go to TurkyOnTheRun
				Add action

FIGURE 10.29 The second part of the Picky group, checking whether Turky is finally nearby and moving him toward his sweetheart.

A subevent to identify when Turky reached his position next to Picky should also be added. The triggering condition for this would be, for example, when the distance between the two sprites is less than 20 pixels. When this happens, we stop Turky, add a big bonus to the current score, and increase the level by adding 1 to the **date** global variable (which we have to create now).

Once all this is done, we can reload the layout for the next challenge or design a congratulations screen for the player to enjoy, like in the iOS and BB10 version of the game.

10.4 SLY, FOXY, AND OTTO

In the previous section we implemented the core gameplay as described in the one-page game design document through the AGE framework, i.e., based around the **herding** theme, where Turky moves autonomously but we can still control him indirectly thanks to our tile shifting abilities. Now we have to add more challenges, and we will do so thanks to Sly and Foxy the cats and Otto the owl. With them chasing after Turky, we will be able to implement the **avoidance** gameplay theme and make the overall experience more exciting.

Let's start with Sly. Add a new sprite and import the main image. Also add the corresponding walking animations (all frames are provided in the artwork folder, exactly like we did with Turky). Sly will roam the maze taking a possible path at random and, if he ever catches Turky, a small fight will ensue, with Turky being sent back to the starting blocks with a time penalty, unless Turky has previously acquired the super power-up (but we will implement this feature later, so for now Turky will be helpless).

The walking algorithm will work exactly like the one we designed for Turky: we spawn Sly on a random tile, look around to find an exit on nearby tiles matching those on the tile he is on, and finally pick a choice. To set this up we need to add the **Custom Movement** behavior for Sly as well, together with a set of instance variables like **direction, target, comingFrom, grid_pos, speed** (all of type number) and **up, down, left, right** (of type Boolean to identify the exits).

We also need a few more variables specific to Sly:

- **timePenalty** is the number of seconds we want to subtract from the timer when Sly catches Turky. This is going to be level (i.e., date) dependent.

- **ko** is a Boolean flag we will use when colliding with Turky in his power state.

- **falling** is a Boolean flag to identify the case when we will be removing the ground under Sly's paws, making him fall into a never-ending pit.

All these variables have to be initialized as shown in Figure 10.30, where we added a new group **Sly-begin** including an **On start of layout** event. Note that **On start of layout** is not alone this time. Sly should get into the game only after the player clears the first level. For this reason we

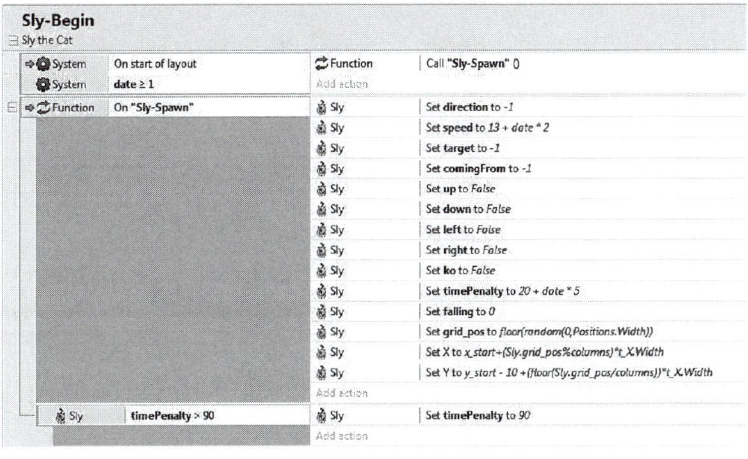

FIGURE 10.30   The **Sly-Begin** group, where we initialize all Sly's variables and decide his starting position on the grid.

also need to check out the **date** global variable, which is set to 1 when the game starts, to decide whether Sly should be in or not. Right now, though, we may prefer to check whether **date** is greater than or equal to 1 instead of 2, so that Sly appears from the very beginning, but this is done only for testing purposes so that we don't need to go past the first maze to see him in action. Don't forget to set it to 2 once the game is finished!

All discussed variables are then initialized in a dedicated function that we will be calling not only when the level starts but also when Sly needs to respawn during the game. Note also that Sly's **speed** and **timePenalty** are **date** dependent to make the game progressively more challenging but that we are capping the latter at a maximum of 90 seconds.

Following the very same approach we did for Turky, we set Sly's **target** variable to –1, triggering a **Sly-LookAround** group (see Figure 10.31), which is structured exactly like the **LookAround** group we did for Turky. To do this quickly, we can simply copy and paste the latter, select the whole group, and then use **Replace Object** substituting Turky with Sly. We also need to have an **Exits4Sly** array (working like **Exits4Turky** we used earlier) and an opportunely modified **Update-Sly-Exits-Positions** function.

Sly-Move also works exactly like **Turky-Move** (Figure 10.32), although this time we don't have to worry about placing any particle to identify where Sly is moving to.

What gets more interesting to discuss is how we are going to handle the collisions involving Sly, as shown in Figure 10.33.

Here we have two main cases to consider. First, contrary to what we decided for Turky, we know the player is free to literally move the tile under Sly's paws. This is a very useful feature, since it gives players more options for building up a path and could also help avoiding an upcoming collision whenever Turky and the cats are going toward the same tile. In addition, if the player gets angry, it gives a simple way to get some satisfying revenge against Sly, releasing some frustration, and scoring additional points. The player still has to evaluate the risk/reward balance of this action, though, since we never know where Sly is going to respawn: he might reappear right in front of Turky, making things even worse!

Collision with the small **t_tile** sprite is used to trigger a series of actions: we need to update the score and its related text, changing Sly's **target** variable to a negative number (e.g., –2) to avoid looking around for exits, stopping his movement, and setting up the **falling** variable to 1. This is used as

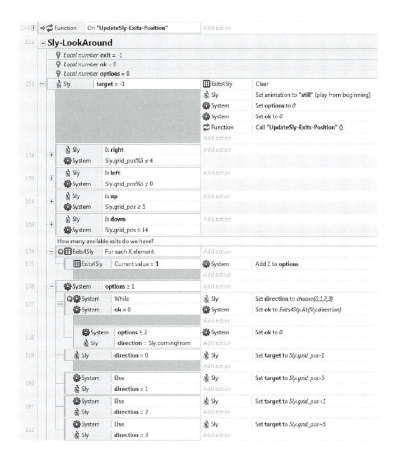

FIGURE 10.31 The **Sly-LookAround** group, simply an updated **Turky-LookAround** with relevant objects and variables changed.

a flag to simulate the fall: the empty space, as we discussed earlier, should work like a bottomless pit that Sly is falling into. To achieve this effect, we make a new event where we check, besides **falling** being set to 1, Sly's size (i.e., the width of the sprite). Frame by frame, as long as this is wider than a certain threshold (for example, five pixels), we keep shrinking both its width and height via the **Set size** action. When Sly is finally small enough, we move him off screen and resize the sprite to its original dimensions before calling the **Sly-Spawn** function and place him back into the action.*

---

* An important detail to note here: moving Sly out of the screen before respawning him is actually needed to take Sly off t_empty. If we don't do this and Sly happens to respawn on the very same tile, the **On collision** event won't register a new collision, leaving Sly floating in empty space!

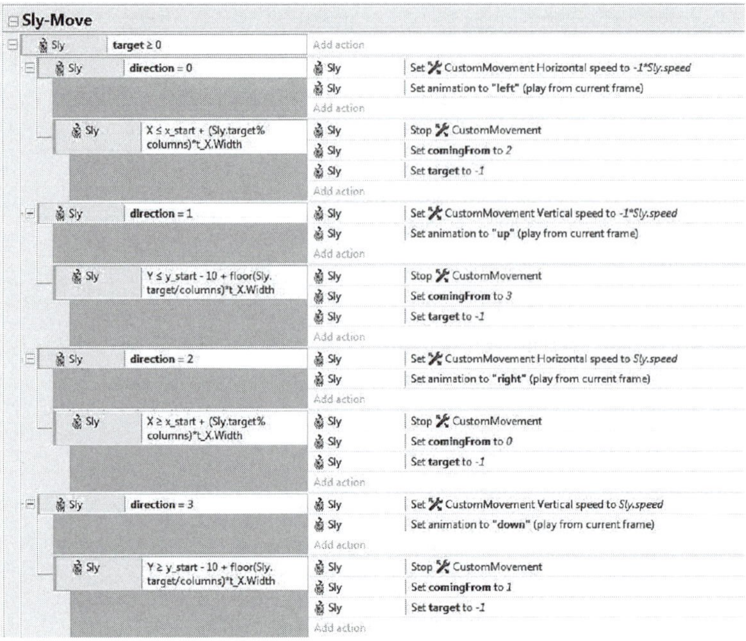

FIGURE 10.32 The **Sly-Move** group, setting Sly in motion according to the direction selected in the **Sly-LookAround** group.

The other case we need to work on is the collision with Turky himself, where we have to further discriminate between two subcases: whether Turky has acquired the **SuperPower** bonus item or not. While the actual **SuperPower** sprite will be added in the game only in the next section, we already know from the game design document how it will work and the effect it would have, so there's no need to wait: we can implement it right away. If Turky's **SuperTurky** flag is set, the idea is to kick Sly off the screen, possibly in some funny cartoonish way. To do this, start by setting Sly's **target** variable to −2 (as we just did for the collision with t_empty: this will stop the program from going through the moving or looking for exits events, which get activated only when **target** has specific values greater than or equal to −1), then we invert Sly's speed and multiply it by a factor of 10 to simulate a powerful punch by Turky. We also set Sly's **ko** flag to true. We can use this to make things a little more fun, triggering another event where, for example, we start rotating Sly by 10 degrees clockwise as long as he is flying off the screen (via the **Is on-screen** event in the **Size & Position** event group for the sprite object). When Sly is finally outside the layout,

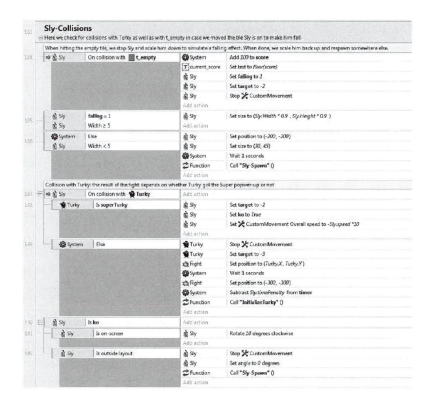

FIGURE 10.33 The **Sly-Collision** group, which handles the collisions with Turky and with t_empty, the mask identifying the empty tile.

we can stop him, restore his angle to 0 degrees, so that he won't reappear upside down, and call **Sly-Spawn** once again.

On the other hand, if **superTurky** is not set, Sly will have the upper hand. Here we can add a short fight animation to cover Turky before he gets pushed back to one of the starting spots. I added a very simple two-frame animation shown in Figure 10.34, reminiscent of old cartoons where fights used to be hidden in smoke and dust clouds, but you should definitely try to do something better!

When the fight happens, we stop Turky, set **target** to −3 to prevent him from looking or moving around, place the animation, and, after a short wait (1 second), we place the animation back outside the game layout,* apply the time penalty, and finally respawn Turky by calling the **InitializeTurky** function.

---

* Alternatively, you could use the **Visibility** property to display and hide the sprite.

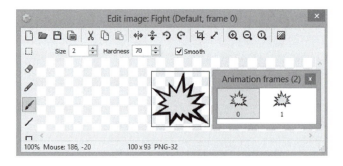

FIGURE 10.34   A very simple two-frame animation to place on Turky while in a losing fight against any of the bad guys.

To test that the **SuperPower** effect is working properly, we actually don't need to wait until we add the **SuperPower** object in the game: we just have to change Turky's **super** instance variable, launch the game, and drive Turky and Sly to hit each other!

Adding Foxy to the game implies the exact steps we just did for Sly, so once we created a new sprite and defined its animations and instance variables, we can copy and paste all four groups of events and change their names and objects accordingly. In the end, we will have a new **Foxy-Begin**, **Foxy-LookAround**, **Foxy-Move**, and **Foxy-Collision**, together with a new **UpdateFoxy-Exits-Positions** function.

Besides changing Sly with Foxy across the various groups, we also have to update some variables, since Foxy is going to be slightly more dangerous than Sly. First of all, Foxy is supposed to be in the game only when the global variable **date** is greater than or equal to 3, so we need to update this in the Foxy-Begin group. We also need to update his **speed** (for example to *15 + date * 3*) and **timePenalty** variables (e.g., *40 + date * 5*) so that they make for a more serious threat.

Once we have tested and everything is working fine (trust me, it's very easy to forget to update some variables or to rename an array like **Exits4Foxy**, resulting in puzzling and unpredictable behavior!), we can proceed to our third bad guy: Otto the owl, who will appear from Date 5 onward.

Otto is slow but keeps flying constantly around the screen, so he is a very dangerous antagonist who can catch Turky many times. The only way for Turky to defend himself is through the **SuperPower** boost. Anyway, if this is used to kick Otto off the screen, the power will disappear, and Otto will still come back after a while. This makes Otto the most troublesome of the group, and we have to balance his stats so that we don't make him

□ **Otto the owl**				
Otto flies around slowly but constantly				
⇒ ⚙ System	On start of layout		⊙	Set position to *(floor(random(100,400)) , floor(random(75,290)))*
⚙ System	date ≥ 5		⊕	Set timePenalty to 5 + *date*
			⊕	Set animation to "**fly**" (play from current frame)
			⟳	Call "**Otto-Takeoff**" ()
				Add action
⇒ ⟳ Function	On "**Otto-Takeoff**"		⊕	Set ✂ CustomMovement angle of motion to *180*
			⊕	Set speed to *10*
			⊕	Set ✂ CustomMovement Overall speed to *Otto.speed*
			⊕	Set X to *x_start - 10 + t_X.Width*columns*
			⊕	Set Y to *y_start - 15 + floor(random(rows)) * t_X.Width*
				Add action
⚙ System	Every tick		⊕	Accelerate ✂ CustomMovement 5 toward *(target.X, target.Y)*
⊕ Otto	Is on-screen			*Add action*
⊕ Otto	✂ CustomMovement Overall speed ≥ Otto.speed		⊕	Set ✂ CustomMovement Overall speed to *Otto.speed*
				Add action
⚙ System	abs(Otto.X-target.X) ≤ 10		⊙	Set position to *(floor(random(100,400)) , floor(random(75,290)))*
⚙ System	abs(Otto.y-target.y) ≤ 10			*Add action*

FIGURE 10.35   The flying related events in the **Otto the owl** group.

overly powerful and punishing for the player. We can achieve this by making his speed not only slow (for example, 10 pixels per second), but also constant, i.e., not level dependent. Also, the time penalty for being caught should be relatively small, for example 5 plus the date number (i.e., considering Otto will start at date 5, the penalty will start at 10 seconds, and then increase only 1 second per date).

The events for Otto's flying, grouped in a specific Otto the owl group, are shown in Figure 10.35.

As we can see, Otto is constantly flying toward a target position chosen randomly in an area within the maze. In the game published on iOS and BB10, the player can decide whether the target is visible or not through a dedicated **Option** screen. This can be used for fine-tuning the difficulty level of the game, since knowing in advance where Otto is going can help the player in strategizing the safest path for Turky and keep him safe. The **Otto-Takeoff** function sets the beginning speed and position on the right edge of the maze and direction of movement. Every frame, as long as Otto is on the screen, we move him toward the target while also checking that his speed doesn't exceed a maximum value.

Once he finally reaches the target position, we simply move the target to a different location and the process starts all over again automatically, thanks to the event having as conditions **System/Every tick** and **Otto/Is on-screen**.

Regarding the collision with Turky we need to discriminate between two cases once again: whether Turky got the **SuperPower** or not. For the latter case, we can simply copy the actions we added when colliding with

Sly and Foxy, where **timer** is updated by using Otto's **timePenalty** variable. The case where Turky has the upper hand instead is a bit different from the previous ones: we make Otto go much faster by increasing tenfold his **CustomMovement Overall speed** as well as his reference **speed**. We also invert his direction by multiplying **CustomMovement.Speed** by −1 and, last but not least, we set Turky's **superTurky** flag to *false* to remove the power-up effect.

Finally, when Otto is out of the layout, we wait for a short while (10 or 15 seconds, for example) before calling the **Otto-Takeoff** function and make him start roaming the maze all over again. Note that these actions should be in a **System/Trigger once** subevent, otherwise they will be called continuously as long as Otto is outside the screen! **Trigger once** is actually a very useful condition for all those events that remain true for a while but where we need to perform the corresponding set of actions only when the conditions are first triggered. All this is shown in Figure 10.36.

10.5 TIMER AND BONUS ITEMS

With the bad guys in place, the game now needs some final touches to make the whole experience more exciting. As we know from the design document, we are trying to achieve this by adding a few power-ups, like the already discussed **SuperPower** that will make Turky able to take revenge against his chasers. Before proceeding, though, let's finish some other feature we need to properly complete the game: a timer as well as a high score. The **timer** global variable is already in place (we are updating it

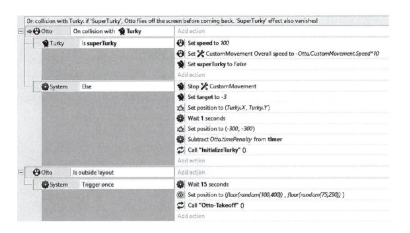

FIGURE 10.36 The collision detection part for the Otto group of events.

Score	Date #	High Score	Time Left
0	1	0	- : -

FIGURE 10.37 Completing the information to be displayed during the game. Note that the digits for the timer are split into two text objects: a **txtMinutes**, displaying - , and a **txtSeconds**, displaying **:** - (far right).

whenever Turky is hit by the other guys), but we also need to add a **high-score** variable now. We should also add the proper text objects to display this information on top of the layout, which should then look something like Figure 10.37.

When a game starts, the timer should be set, for example, to 2 minutes, and then it should be updated every second. When it reaches 0 the game is over, and we should move to a game over screen, where we eventually also update the high score value, before going back into the action. We also want the timer to change color to red and start flashing when less than 30 seconds are available to add pressure on the player. For this we need to add the **Flash** behavior to the two text objects used for displaying the time left (**txtMinutes** and **txtSeconds**). All the events and actions needed are summarized in Figure 10.38.

As we see, we start by using the **System/Every X Seconds** event, which allows us to trigger a set of actions at regular intervals. Here, every second, we deduct 1 from **timer** and then display the remaining time in terms of minutes and seconds. We also take care of adding a 0 in front of the seconds if we have less than 10 left (i.e., 1 minute and 9 seconds should display like 1 : 09).

When we get into the last 30 seconds, we change the color to red (i.e., **rgb(255, 0, 0)**) and use the **Flash** behavior to set the text visible/invisible at intervals of half a second for 5 seconds. When, eventually, time goes up, we stop flashing the text and load the **Game Over** layout.

We don't need to do anything fancy for this new layout: just add a black screen with a "Game Over" sign plus a button to start play-ing again (Figure 10.39), together with the corresponding event sheet (Figure 10.40).

The events for the **Game Over** layout are very simple: the button to play again is handled exactly like those we used in *Kitty & Katty*, with a highlight image that starts invisible and pops up whenever the button is

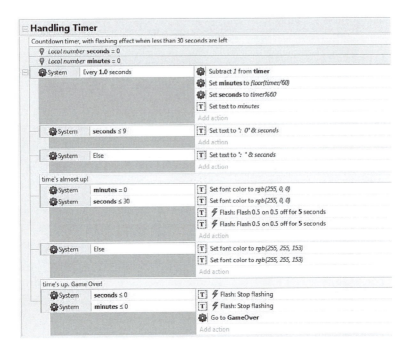

FIGURE 10.38 All the events necessary for handling the in-game timer.

touched or clicked. We also take care of checking for a high score when the layout starts and of resetting the **timer, score,** and **date** variables before leaving the layout and starting a new game.

Try the game now: getting caught by Sly, Foxy, or Otto should decrease the timer, and, once this gets to 0, the **Game Over** layout will load. Finally,

FIGURE 10.39 A simple game over screen. We don't need anything fancy here: just a sign and a button to start playing again is enough.

FIGURE 10.40 The event sheet for the **Game Over** layout, handling the play again button, checking for a high score, and resetting some important variables, like score, date, and timer.

when starting a new game, everything is reset properly, with an updated high score.

It's time now to work on the most exciting power-up in the game: Turky's Super Power!

Graphic wise, we need two versions of our asset: a big one to be displayed on the grid and a small one to pin on Turky to show his new, powerful status. The big version also needs a **grid_pos** instance variable to identify its location in the grid (Figure 10.41).

Coding wise, we should add a **SuperPower** group where we set up the big icon on a random tile when the game begins. Remember, from the game design document, this power-up should be available only from the second date onward, so we have to add a check on the date number in the **On start of layout** event. Then, when we register a collision between Turky and the icon, we destroy the latter and set Turky's **superTurky** flag to true. As long

FIGURE 10.41 The **P** icon of **SuperPower**, giving Turky enough strength to defeat Sly and Foxy for one whole level or Otto for one fight. On the left we can see a smaller replica of the image we will attach to Turky to show his new powerful status.

SuperPower: turning Turky into a super turkey!				
SuperPower				
⊟ Once acquired Turky can fight back with a vengeance! Last for whole current level unless fighting with Otto.				
⇨ 🔧 System	On start of layout		❤ SuperPower	Set grid_pos to floor(random(0,Positions.Width))
🔧 System	date ≥ 2		❤ SuperPower	Set X to x_start+(SuperPower.grid_pos%columns)*t_X.Width
			❤ SuperPower	Set Y to y_start +(floor(SuperPower.grid/columns))*t_X.Width
			Add action	
⇨ ❤ SuperPower	On collision with 🦃 Turky		❤ SuperPower	Destroy
			🦃 Turky	Set superTurky to True
			Add action	
🔧 System	Every tick		❤ SuperP	Set position to 🦃 Turky (image point 1)
🦃 Turky	Is superTurky		Add action	

FIGURE 10.42 The events in the **SuperPower** group. Note how the small icon, named **SuperP** in the game project, is referenced in the last action to set its position to a specific point on Turky. This is updated every frame to follow Turky's animations and changes in direction.

as Turky maintains his power status, we should also pin the small logo on Turky's breast, something we can achieve in the **System/Every tick** event as shown in Figure 10.42. The small icon should be destroyed on the collision event between Otto and Turky, where we also reset the **SuperTurky** status flag to false.

If we try the game now, though, we will see a big issue: the power-up is displayed correctly, but when we move the tile it is on, it doesn't follow, and this is not the kind of behavior we would expect: we want it to be carried around with the tile it belongs to.

To achieve this, we need to define a new function (**Check4Items**, shown in Figure 10.43), which we have to call from every event in the **Move Tiles** group right after the **UpdateHighlights** function as shown in Figure 10.44.

Check4Items takes two parameters. The first one is the location in the grid of the tile being moved. We use this to identify the specific power-up we are shifting, since their respective **grid_pos** variables have matching numbers. The second parameter instead identifies the new location of the tile that the power-up has to follow.

⇨ ♻ Function	On "Check4Items"	Add action	
♻ Function	Parameter 0 = SuperPower.grid_pos	❤ SuperPower	Set grid_pos to Function.Param(1)
		❤ SuperPower	Set X to x_start+(SuperPower.grid_pos%columns)*t_X.Width
		❤ SuperPower	Set Y to y_start +(floor(SuperPower.grid_pos/columns))*t_X.Width
		Add action	

FIGURE 10.43 The **Check4Items** function we use to update power-ups position when the underlying tile is moved. Here we have only the **SuperPower** object. **Param 0** is original position of the tile being moved; **Param 1** is the new position in the grid. This function is called from the **Move Tiles** group.

Move Tiles

Local number **temp** = 0				
tile is not the tile Turky is on or where he is moving to				
⇨ 🖑 Touch	On touched ▦ t_X		Add action	
▦ t_X	**grid_pos** ≠ Turky.grid_pos			
▦ t_X	**grid_pos** ≠ Turky.target			
tile is above or below empty space				
⚙ System	t_X.grid_pos = t_empty.grid_pos+ columns	⚙ System	Set **temp** to t_X.grid_pos	
	- or -	▦ t_X	Set **grid_pos** to t_empty.grid_pos	
⚙ System	t_X.grid_pos = t_empty.grid_pos- columns	▦ t_X	Set Y to y_start + floor(t_X.grid_pos/columns)*t_X.Width	
		▦ t_empty	Set **grid_pos** to temp	
		▦ t_empty	Set Y to y_start + floor(t_empty.grid_pos/columns)*t_X.Width	
		⮂ Function	Call "UpdateHighlights" ()	
		⮂ Function	Call "Check4Items" (temp, t_X.grid_pos)	
		Add action		

FIGURE 10.44 The first event in the **Move Tiles** group for the t_X tile, updated to call the **Check4Items** function. Note the parameters being passed: the old and new position of the tile.

When picking a power-up, it would be nice to display some information about its effect. For example we'd have a short message appear above the item and then slowly fade away. To do so, let's first add a new text object to the game, which we can call **txtBonus**: select a nice looking font, make it a bright color, add a Boolean instance variable named **fading** (false by default), and finally, place it off screen.

Now, whenever we pick a power-up like **SuperPower**, we add two simple actions before removing the sprite from the game: we move **txtBonus** on top of the power-up, and then we call a new function named **BonusText** passing as parameter the message we would like to display.

The updated **On collision** event between **SuperPower** and **Turky** is shown in Figure 10.45.

We define the **BonusText** function in a **BonusText** group as shown in Figure 10.46: here we update the text in **txtBonus** to the word we passed as parameter, set its opacity to 100 (i.e., fully opaque), and then set the **fading** flag to true.

⇨ 🐦 SuperPower	On collision with 🐦 Turky	🐦 Turky	Set **superTurky** to True
		[T] txtBonus	Set position to (SuperPower.X, SuperPower.Y - 20)
		⮂ Function	Call "BonusText" ('Power!')
		🐦 SuperPower	Destroy
		Add action	

FIGURE 10.45 The revised collision event between the **SuperPower** power-up and Turky, now displaying a text object to be updated with a specific word that is passed as a parameter in a related function.

BonusText
⊟ events in this group handle a text to be displayed when Turky picks some power up while roaming the maze.

⇒ ⟳ Function	On "BonusText"	[T] txtBonus	Set text to Function.Param(0)
		[T] txtBonus	Set opacity to 100
		[T] txtBonus	Set fading to True
		Add action	
⚙ System	Every tick	[T] txtBonus	Set opacity to txtBonus.Opacity – 0.75
[T] txtBonus	Is fading	Add action	
[T] txtBonus	Opacity ≤ 10	[T] txtBonus	Set fading to False
		[T] txtBonus	Set position to (-200, -200)
		Add action	

FIGURE 10.46 The **BonusText** group handling the events related to the fading message displayed when picking up a power-up. Note that the **BonusText** function is going to be called by all power-up related events, each with a specific text.

Setting the flag allows us to activate a **System/Every tick** event where, every frame, we reduce the current opacity level of **txtBonus** little by little to produce the desired fading-out effect. Once the opacity gets below a specific threshold, e.g., 10, we can reset the **fading** flag to false and remove the text from the screen.

It is now very straightforward to define the other power-ups and bonus items. For example, let's work on the **Ring** bonus: when collected we award 500 extra points to the player and **BonusText** would be called with something like 500 points! The different events are set up exactly like for **SuperPower** and are displayed in Figure 10.47. Note that also the **Check4Items** function needs to be updated accordingly to cover this new bonus as well.

Groups for the other planned items are structured in the exact same way and are shown in Figures 10.48 (hourglass), 10.49 (diamond), 10.50 (winged shoes), and 10.51 (snail). Don't forget to add a **grid_pos** instance variable to each sprite we add to the game!

Bonus-Ring
⊟ 500 Points

⇒ ⚙ System	On start of layout	⊙ Ring	Set grid_pos to floor(random(0,Positions.Width))
		⊙ Ring	Set X to x_start+(ring.grid_pos%columns)*t_X.Width
		⊙ Ring	Set Y to y_start +(floor(ring.grid_pos/columns))*t_X.Width
		Add action	
⇒ ⊙ Ring	On collision with 🐢 Turky	⚙ System	Add 500 to score
		[T] current_score	Set text to floor(score)
		[T] txtBonus	Set position to (ring.X, ring.Y - 20)
		⟳ Function	Call "BonusText" ("500 Points!")
		⊙ Ring	Destroy
		Add action	

FIGURE 10.47 The group of events for the bonus ring (500 extra points).

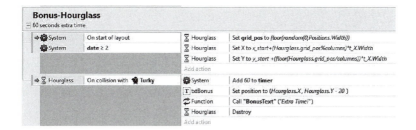

FIGURE 10.48   The Hourglass group. Getting the hourglass gives Turky an extra 60 seconds to play. This item will be available from date 2 onward.

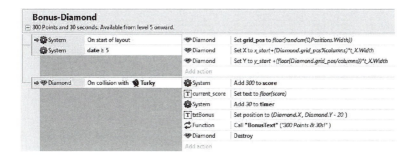

FIGURE 10.49   The Diamond group: 300 points and 30 extra seconds! Available only from date 5 onward.

FIGURE 10.50   The Wingedshoes. These set Turky's speed to 30 pixels per second. These are readily available from the first date.

The final **Check4Items** function is shown in Figure 10.52.

Our game is almost finished now. We only need one more thing: the magic wand to transport Turky to a random tile, a very useful action to help Turky when he gets stuck or needs to escape from an otherwise unavoidable clash with Sly and friends.

Malus-Snail				
⊟ Halves Turky speed (8 pixel/second)				
⇒⚙ System	On start of layout	🐌 Snail	Set grid_pos to *floor(random(0,Positions.Width))*
⚙ System	date ≥ 3	🐌 Snail	Set X to *x_start+(Snail.grid_pos%columns)*t_X.Width*
		🐌 Snail	Set Y to *y_start +(floor(Snail.grid_pos/columns))*t_X.Width*
		Add action	
⇒🐌 Snail	On collision with 🦃 Turky	🦃 Turky	Set speed to **8**
		[T] txtBonus	Set position to *(Snail.X, Snail.Y - 20)*
		♻ Function	Call **"BonusText"** *("Half Speed...")*
		🐌 Snail	Destroy
		Add action	

FIGURE 10.51 The Snail. This slows down Turky, setting his speed to 8 pixels/second. It will appear from date 3 onward.

Start by adding a global variable named **magicleft**, with a starting value of 3, and then place a button on the bottom left corner of the screen, like in Figure 10.53.

The button is made by three layers: an off image, a highlight image to be made visible when the button is clicked or touched, and, last, an image of the wand itself on top of them all. We should also add a text object below the button to show how many uses we still have (**txtMagic**). This will display the value of the **magicleft** variable.

Function to update any item position if the underlying tile is moved. Param 0 is original position, param 1 is new position in the grid. This function is called from the MoveTiles group			
⊟ ⇒♻ Function	On "Check4Items"	Add action	
♻ Function	Parameter 0 = SuperPower.grid_pos	🏆 SuperPower	Set grid_pos to *Function.Param(1)*
		🏆 SuperPower	Set X to *x_start+(SuperPower.grid_pos%columns)*t_X.Width*
		🏆 SuperPower	Set Y to *y_start +(floor(SuperPower.grid_pos/columns))*t_X.Width*
		Add action	
♻ Function	Parameter 0 = Ring.grid_pos	💍 Ring	Set grid_pos to *Function.Param(1)*
		💍 Ring	Set X to *x_start+(ring.grid_pos%columns)*t_X.Width*
		💍 Ring	Set Y to *y_start +(floor(ring.grid_pos/columns))*t_X.Width*
		Add action	
♻ Function	Parameter 0 = Hourglass.grid_pos	⧗ Hourglass	Set grid_pos to *Function.Param(1)*
		⧗ Hourglass	Set X to *x_start+(Hourglass.grid_pos%columns)*t_X.Width*
		⧗ Hourglass	Set Y to *y_start +(floor(Hourglass.grid_pos/columns))*t_X.Width*
		Add action	
♻ Function	Parameter 0 = Diamond.grid_pos	💎 Diamond	Set grid_pos to *Function.Param(1)*
		💎 Diamond	Set X to *x_start+(Diamond.grid_pos%columns)*t_X.Width*
		💎 Diamond	Set Y to *y_start +(floor(Diamond.grid_pos/columns))*t_X.Width*
		Add action	
♻ Function	Parameter 0 = Wingshoes.grid_pos	👟 Wingshoes	Set grid_pos to *Function.Param(1)*
		👟 Wingshoes	Set X to *x_start+(Wingshoes.grid_pos%columns)*t_X.Width*
		👟 Wingshoes	Set Y to *y_start +(floor(Wingshoes.grid_pos/columns))*(_X.Width*
		Add action	
♻ Function	Parameter 0 = Snail.grid_pos	🐌 Snail	Set grid_pos to *Function.Param(1)*
		🐌 Snail	Set X to *x_start+(Snail.grid_pos%columns)*t_X.Width*
		🐌 Snail	Set Y to *y_start +(floor(Snail.grid_pos/columns))*t_X.Width*
		Add action	

FIGURE 10.52 The updated **Check4Items** function, covering all available objects Turky can pick up.

FIGURE 10.53 The magic wand button.

The events related to the button are to be grouped in a **Button-MagicWand** group and are shown in Figure 10.54.

As we see, we start by setting **txtMagic** text in the **On start of layout** event, and then we take care of displaying the button properly, i.e., if there are no touches, we set the highlight image to off. On the other hand, this becomes visible whenever a touch is registered. When the touch event ends and we still have magic uses available (i.e., **magicleft > 0**), we update the variable and text, remove the target particle from the screen, and move Turky to

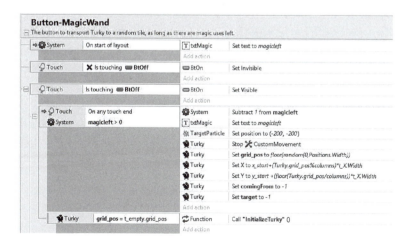

FIGURE 10.54 The group of events taking care of the magic wand button. Press it to teleport Turky to a different tile in the maze!

FIGURE 10.55 The group handling the **Wand** bonus item, giving Turky an extra magic shot.

a random location, making sure to also reset the **comingFrom** and **target** variables to −1 so that our program can start searching for a new path.

The unlucky case where the new location is the empty space has to be considered as well, and it is handled by a dedicated subevent where we simply call the **initializeTurky** function and have Turky restart anew.

The magic wand itself is a bonus item we have to add in the maze. Add a new sprite object to the game, call it **Wand**, and define a new group of events as usual (Figure 10.55). Once again, don't forget to update the **Check4Items** function with a corresponding wand event!

Well done! You can now enjoy *Turky on the Run*!

TAKE AWAY

Turky on the Run was our most complex game by far: different enemies, bonus items, and shifting tiles on the grid presented unique challenges that required us to perfect all the elements we saw previously, including an effective use of groups, to keep our code easily readable and accessible, and to name our functions with different parameters.

EXERCISES

- We didn't add any sound! List all the sound effects that you think are needed, find suitable ones (you may check the resources listed in Appendix A), and add them to the project.

- Add a splash screen and an option screen, where players can decide, for example, which date to start in, how much time they have (e.g., 1, 2, or even 3 minutes), and whether Otto's target should be visible or not.

- Think of new power-ups or new enemies to add in the game!

CHAPTER 11

The Journey Ahead

B Y COMPLETING OUR THIRD game, *Turky on the Run*, we built a solid foundation on Construct 2 upon which you should be able to expand and add additional skills and knowledge on your own. As you have probably realized by now, despite its designer friendliness, Construct is a very flexible and powerful engine, and there is really much more to explore and try out than what we saw so far. Always be curious, and start exploring the different objects and behaviors we didn't have time to cover: you will surely get lots of promising ideas to work on!

To conclude the development section of the book, I want to introduce a few more topics that may help in your upcoming projects, namely, pathfinding, sprite fonts, shaders, and source control, plus some basic performance-related tips.

11.1 PATHFINDING

Pathfinding is a very important feature in many games to make nonplaying characters (NPCs) behave naturally: poor pathfinding, where characters get stuck around every corner, is often enough to break players' immersion to the extent that they might dismiss an otherwise fine game as amateurish and poorly done. It shouldn't be a surprise then that several algorithms have been devised to accomplish this in a variety of ways. One of the best and most CPU-efficient techniques adopted in game development is called A* (A star) and, luckily for us, it is also implemented in Construct right out of the box.

In a nutshell, A* works by first subdividing the game area into tiles and then identifying the starting tiles, the target tiles, and those presenting obstacles. The algorithm then starts looking around the starting position tile by tile, using some predefined scoring methods to evaluate the cost of movement across each tile. Once the destination is reached, the algorithm backtracks the tiles forming the path having the lower overall cost. That is the path characters will take.

To see how to use this in Construct, let's start a new project with a layout of 640 × 640 pixels.

We don't have to draw the tiles in the layout. For an efficient use of the algorithm as well as for a more natural looking path, it is useful to think of tiles sized to perfectly cover the area, e.g., in our case it would be good to choose tiles measuring 32 × 32 or 64 × 64 pixels. In Figure 11.1 we have the layout showing a 32 × 32 tiled background, making apparent how the area would be divided by the A* algorithm.

Let's add some walls to define a maze seen from a top-down perspective, for example, by using a simple filled rectangle in a **Tiled Background** object. While not strictly required, we should make the barriers match the dimension of the tiles exactly or, eventually, be a little bit smaller. In fact, even if an obstacle gets into a tile only partially, the whole tile will be considered inaccessible by the algorithm, even though it would still look like there's some room for the character to move around.

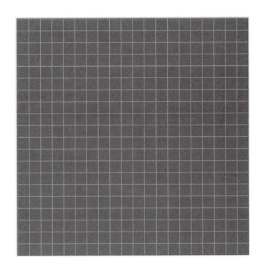

FIGURE 11.1 The layout for our pathfinding experiment. The tiled background is simply there to help us visualize the area and understand how A* is going to subdivide the playfield.

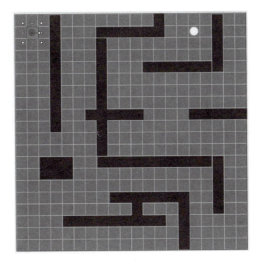

FIGURE 11.2   A simple maze layout made by adding a Tiled Background object named **Wall,** which we replicated and stretched around as needed. Can the sprite on the upper left corner find its way to the white sprite on the right?

A possible maze-like structure is shown in Figure 11.2, where we also added two small sprites, one named "Target" and placed in the upper right area of the layout and one named "NPC" starting in the upper left corner instead.

To add pathfinding capabilities to a sprite, we need to add the corresponding behavior to it first, which we find in the Movement section (Figure 11.3).

Once added, we will have a new set of pathfinding properties added to our sprite, as shown in Figure 11.4.

It is here we actually define the tile size for the A* algorithm to break down the layout and start looking for paths. We can also set the sprite speed and acceleration properties, including whether it can move diagonally or not. Most importantly, we have an option for identifying the obstacles: either anything marked with the **Solid** behavior in the game or something **Custom** we define in the event sheet. For this example I opted for the latter choice.

Defining the search space by specifying the obstacles is indeed the first thing we should take care of, so in the event sheet, start by adding an **On start of layout** event. Once done, you will see several pathfinding related actions for the NPC sprite: pick **Add Obstacle** and specify the **Wall** object (the tiled background we used to build the maze walls).

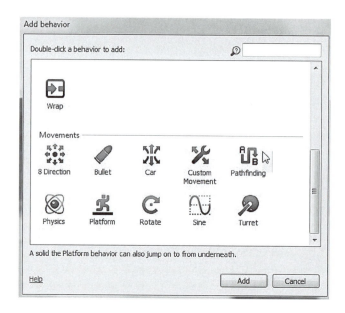

FIGURE 11.3   Adding the pathfinding behavior to a sprite.

Then call the **Regenerate obstacle map** action. This will update the system tile-based representation of the layout by including any obstacles so that computed paths can circumnavigate them. Last, we should use the **Find path** action where we have to specify the final position, i.e., the x and y

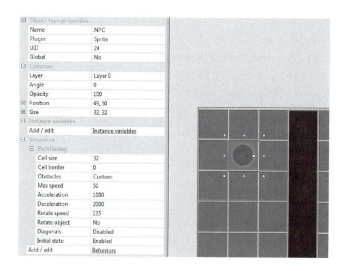

FIGURE 11.4   The properties for the pathfinding behavior. From tile (cell) size to speed, the most important parameters are set here.

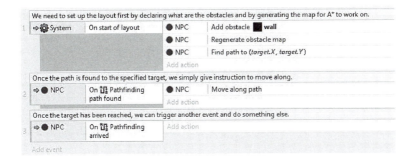

We need to set up the layout first by declaring what are the obstacles and by generating the map for A* to work on.					
1	⇨ ⚙ System	On start of layout	● NPC	Add obstacle ▪ **wall**	
			● NPC	Regenerate obstacle map	
			● NPC	Find path to (*target.X*, *target.Y*)	
			Add action		
Once the path is found to the specified target, we simply give instruction to move along.					
2	⇨ ● NPC	On ⛭ Pathfinding path found	● NPC	Move along path	
			Add action		
Once the target has been reached, we can trigger another event and do something else.					
3	⇨ ● NPC	On ⛭ Pathfinding arrived	Add action		
Add event					

FIGURE 11.5 The events and actions for defining the map, including obstacle position, and start the path search.

coordinates of the target sprite, as shown in Figure 11.5. Once the path has been found, a corresponding event gets triggered for the NPC sprite (**On Pathfinding path found**) where we can issue the action to move along said path. Reaching the target triggers another event, **On Pathfinding arrived**, where we can issue any action related to the specific game we are developing.

Run the demo and see how the NPC starts moving toward the target and stops when reaching its position, waiting for further instructions.

11.2 SPRITE FONTS

When distributing games on a variety of different computers and devices, it may happen that specific fonts we are using are not supported. In this case the system will most likely revert to a default font that would probably mess up the whole screen layout or break any style consistency we carefully planned beforehand. To avoid these pitfalls and to be 100% sure the font displayed is exactly the one we want, we may decide to opt for the so-called **sprite fonts** instead. As the name implies, we will be using a sprite map containing all needed characters. This would give us much more freedom and enable us to display even multicolored sprites, for example, something impossible when using traditional fonts. The drawback, though, is that the new sprite will have only one size and no bold or italic versions, unless we explicitly build them as well.

Adding sprite fonts in Construct is very easy: simply select it as a new object in your project. By default, we will be presented with an 8-bit like font, as shown in Figure 11.6.

The sprite font properties allow us to define the characters' width and height, their exact sequence in the sprite (with the first character starting

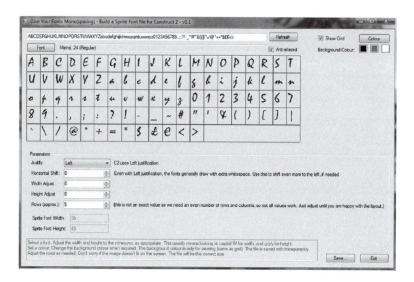

FIGURE 11.6 The default sprite font, having 128 × 256 dimension where each character taxes 16 × 16 pixels. Having dimensions which are a power of 2, while not strictly required, is recommended for performance reasons. Note also that the **Character set** property must be set to match the character sequence in the sprite: only by combining this with the width and height of each character will Construct know where to pick each letter to build our text correctly.

in the upper left corner of the image), and a scale factor, to roughly approximate different font sizes, among other things.

To edit a sprite font, simply click on the **Sprite Font Edit** link in the properties tab, then either draw your own or import a premade image.

Plenty of free fonts are available from websites such as dafont.com or fonts101.com. If you downloaded a new true type font (ttf), you can install* it first and then use **Give Your Fonts Mono(spacing)**,† a very handy sprite font generator tool made freely available by Scirra's friendly community, to convert it into a suitable image to be imported into Construct 2 (Figure 11.7).

---

* The exact procedure for installing a font can vary with the specific version of Windows you are using. In general, you can try one of the following: double click the font and then select the **Install** option, move the font in the **Windows/Fonts** directory or access **Appearances and Personalization/Fonts** via the Control Panel and install from there.
† http://www.scirra.com/forum/sprite-font-generator_topic72160.html

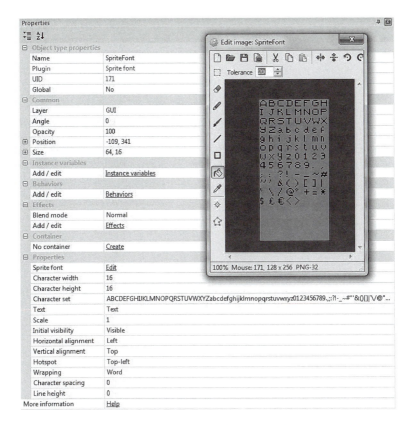

FIGURE 11.7 Using the **Give Your Fonts Mono(spacing)** utility to convert an installed font to an image ready to be imported in Construct 2 as a sprite font.

11.3 SHADERS (EFFECTS)

With more and more browsers supporting Web graphics libraries (WebGL), we can likely expect graphical quality of HTML5 games to improve significantly in the near future. Shaders, simply named Effects in Construct, are an important feature in enhancing graphics, thanks to their ability to alter a texture pixel by pixel in real time according to some predefined algorithm.

Construct comes with 70+ predefined shaders that can be used individually or mixed together to create complex effects. For example, let's start a new project and add a sprite. Fill it with a blue color: we are going to use a shader to simulate a water effect.

Click on the **Effects** link in the **Properties** panel as shown in Figure 11.8 and then choose to add an effect. Scroll down the list of available effects till you find the one for water (Figure 11.9) and add it.

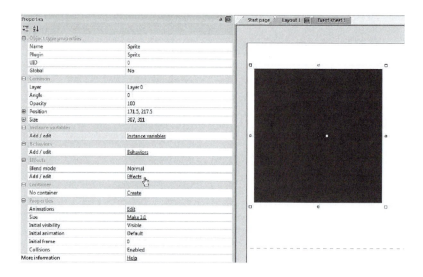

FIGURE 11.8   To start adding effects to a sprite, select the **Effects** line in the **Object Properties Panel.**

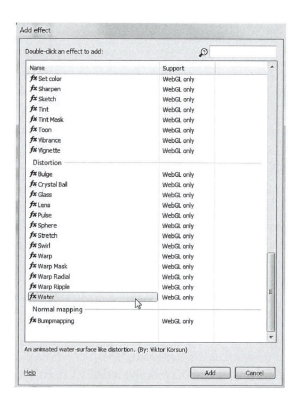

FIGURE 11.9   Selecting the **Water** shader among all the different effects.

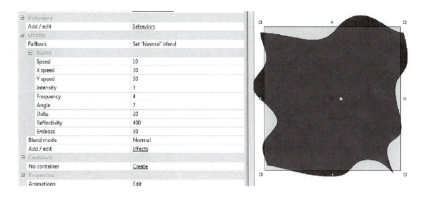

FIGURE 11.10 After adding the water effect to our blue sprite, different parameters get exposed to fine-tune the shader, giving us full control on how it should behave at run time.

Our sprite will look distorted now, and a new set of properties related to the specific effect will be displayed in the left panel, like in Figure 11.10.

Play with the different parameters related to the speed and intensity of the waves and try it out. Don't forget that WebGL must be enabled in the project properties for shaders to work!

11.4 SOURCE CONTROL

One aspect of game development often overlooked by inexperienced developers is that of source control. Source control tools allow a team to organize all files efficiently and keep track of all different versions of each in an orderly manner. Source control makes it possible, even easy, to merge changes done by different developers on the same files, check between differences across versions, and, eventually, roll back to previous releases to recover from some sudden breaking bugs.

One of the most popular source control tools is Apache Subversion (abbreviated SVN). This, like all similar software, works by storing a master copy (repository) of the project on a server machine, which can also be one of the developers' computers, and then allows individual developers to commit (i.e., upload) their files to the repository. Each developer works with a client installed on his own machine to manage a local copy of the repository to download to and to modify and then to commit again to the server any file they work on. That way everyone on the team will then see the different versions and the changes that have been made, so that everyone can keep working on the latest files.

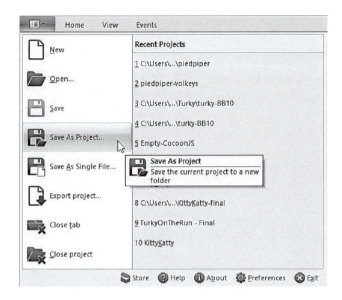

FIGURE 11.11   So far we saved our project as a single, big file. This may be handy when working alone, but when part of a team, we should definitely save our work in a folder and commit each file to the central repository for easy source control.

SVN is a general tool and is not explicitly integrated with Construct 2, so we need to install and set it up independently. Fear not, though, since Construct developer Ashley Gullen has written a very detailed and easy-to-follow tutorial exactly for this, which we can find on Scirra's website.[*]

Thanks to their flexibility and sharing functionalities, it's no surprise that source control software like SVN is among the most fundamental tools used by all professional teams. If you and your team want to act like pros as well, start saving your Construct files individually in a project folder (Figure 11.11) and start committing each of them to your team's central repository!

11.5 PERFORMANCE TIPS

If you plan on deploying your games on a variety of mobile devices, you will soon realize that, despite mobile devices getting more and more powerful by the day, they are still far from matching the raw power of the computer you develop on, especially when your game has to run through

---

[*] https://www.scirra.com/tutorials/537/how-to-collaborate-on-projects-with-svn

a browser and not as a native code executable program. This means that keeping the same, or similar, performance in terms of frames per second (FPS, which, in Construct, we can easily display by using the **fps** keyword in a text object) may be challenging, and it is something we should consider already at the design stage of our games.

In particular, we should be careful about these features that require considerable processing power:

- **Physics:** if too many objects on-screen are using the physics engine, this will definitely slow down the game.

- **Particles:** each particle is actually a small sprite, so you can imagine how having several hundreds of them on the screen at the same time may overload a not so powerful device.

- **Shaders:** effects require additional real-time processing so they should be used only when necessary and not overused. Whenever we have several objects that should be processed by the same shader, it is much better, performance-wise, to move them in a dedicated layer and then apply the effect to the whole layer itself instead of having it work on each object individually.

CHAPTER 12

Deployment and Monetization

I N THIS CHAPTER WE are going to introduce several platforms we can deploy our HTML5 games to, together with different monetization strategies. Note, though, that the aim here is only to give an overview of the different options and point you in the right direction, which you will then have to investigate on your own: since most of the discussed platforms and tools are constantly evolving, trying to get into the details would not only be too advanced and off topic for a foundational book like this one, but it would also be pointless since any extensive step-by-step description would very likely be outdated and not applicable anymore as soon as an update is released. For such detailed information, I recommend that you check each tool, vendor, or portal website for the latest documentation and ad hoc tutorials.

By selecting **Export project** from the main drop down menu, we get several options, including web, mobile, and desktop platforms. Construct being an HTML5 engine, the first option we should talk about is to simply export our projects as HTML5 games to be added to our own websites. If so, we will first be asked a set of options (Figure 12.1), common also to the other platforms, where we can specify folders and whether to "minify" our script. Selecting this option will make our exported code much more difficult to read, and it is usually recommended for games to be delivered online if we don't want other people to easily peek into our code base. Note, though, that this option may conflict with some target platforms,

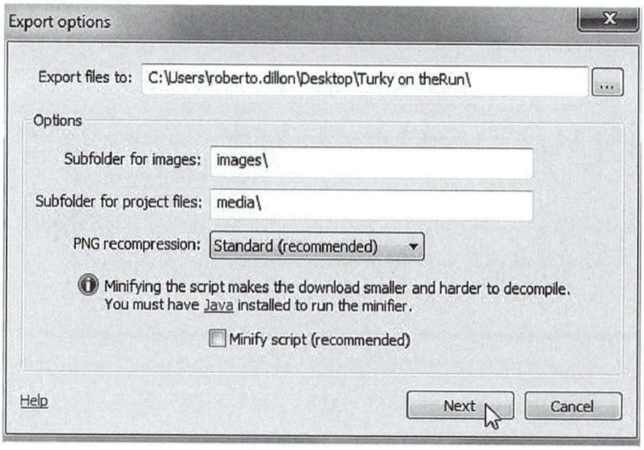

FIGURE 12.1　The first set of export options, common to all target platforms.

so be sure to check whether there could be any issue, or try leaving this unchecked if the exported game doesn't run.

Once you click **Next**, we move to a platform-specific set of options. In case of a straightforward HTML5 game export, we can choose between three different templates (shown in Figure 12.2): a standard page, a page

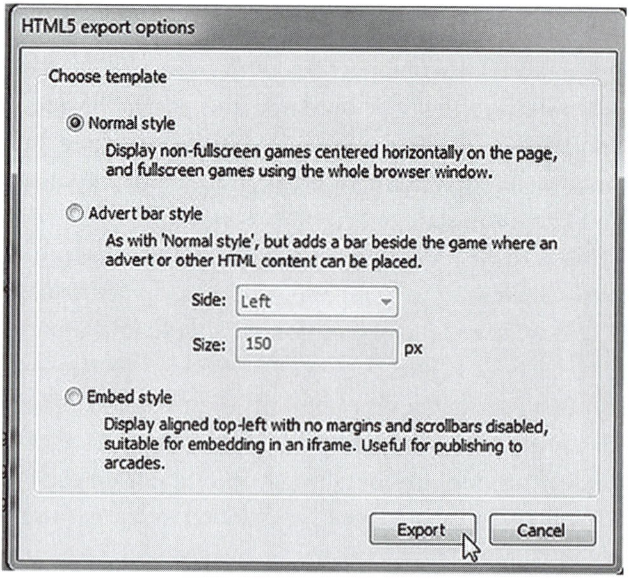

FIGURE 12.2　The second set of options. This is platform specific: when doing a straight HTML5 export, we can choose among different templates for the page containing our HTML5 game.

with some built-in empty space to easily add advertisements, and an embed template with no margins and disabled scrollbars, suitable for specific arcade-like web portals.

Try any template, export, open the game folder, and launch the resulting index.html webpage in the web browser of your choice. Your game is ready to be uploaded to your server!

12.1 WEB PORTALS

Uploading to our own website is only one of the many choices we have: with HTML5 growing in popularity, more and more web-based gaming portals are being launched, offering increased exposure and driving thousand of players straight to our games.

One of such portals is Scirra's own Arcade* (Figure 12.3).

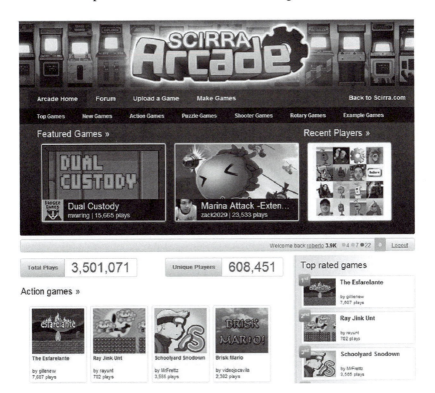

FIGURE 12.3   Scirra's Arcade home page: we can see games are grouped in different categories (Action, Puzzle, Shooter, etc.) as well as featured and top-rated games.

---

* http://www.scirra.com/arcade

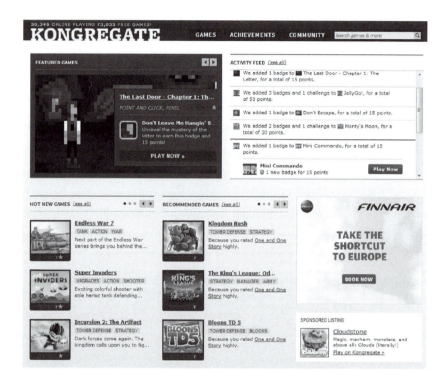

FIGURE 12.4   Kongregate home page, sporting an impressive amount of players (tens of thousands online at any given time) and available games.

Submitting to Scirra's Arcade is a very simple process: by choosing the corresponding export option our game is zipped and ready to be uploaded right after the exporting process has been completed. Note that Scirra's Arcade also offers leaderboard functionalities. To access these we need to add the **Scirra Arcade** object to our project first and use its related events and actions to submit and retrieve scores: once the first few scores get submitted, a high score table will be automatically displayed on the game page for all to see!

One of the most well-known web-based game portals is, without doubt, Kongregate* (Figure 12.4).

This portal hosts a huge variety of games (more than 70,000 games freely playable developed in Flash, Unity, and HTML5) and managed to build a very active community thanks to its many ways of engaging players through challenges, badges, and leveling systems.

---

* http://www.kongregate.com/

FIGURE 12.5   Uploading new games on Kongregate is a very simple process that can be started right away from a link at the bottom of the home page.

Registering as a developer is a simple process: basically, we just have to register as players and then we can submit our games from a link provided in the **Developer Center** section (Figure 12.5).

Once the submission process starts, we need to fill out some basic information about the game, including description and simple playing instructions (Figure 12.6).

Then, in the next form (Figure 12.7), select the **Iframe** radio button and fill the resulting fields accordingly. In the **Iframe URL** field, we have to specify a link to the index.html file we get when exporting our game in Construct targeting Kongregate. This file, together with the whole

Upload your game to share with the world!

STEP: ☐ 1 Game Info   ☐ 2 Upload   ☐ 3 Preview

Title	
Game Description *Tell the world why they should play your game. Read our formatting guide.*	
Game Instructions *Example: Arrows to move, space bar to shoot.*	
Category	Please select ▼
Collaborators *Add up to three users who collaborated with you on this game.*	
API Callback URL	

Continue

FIGURE 12.6   The first step in adding a new game to Kongregate. Note that Construct 2 developers may leave the **API Callback URL** blank.

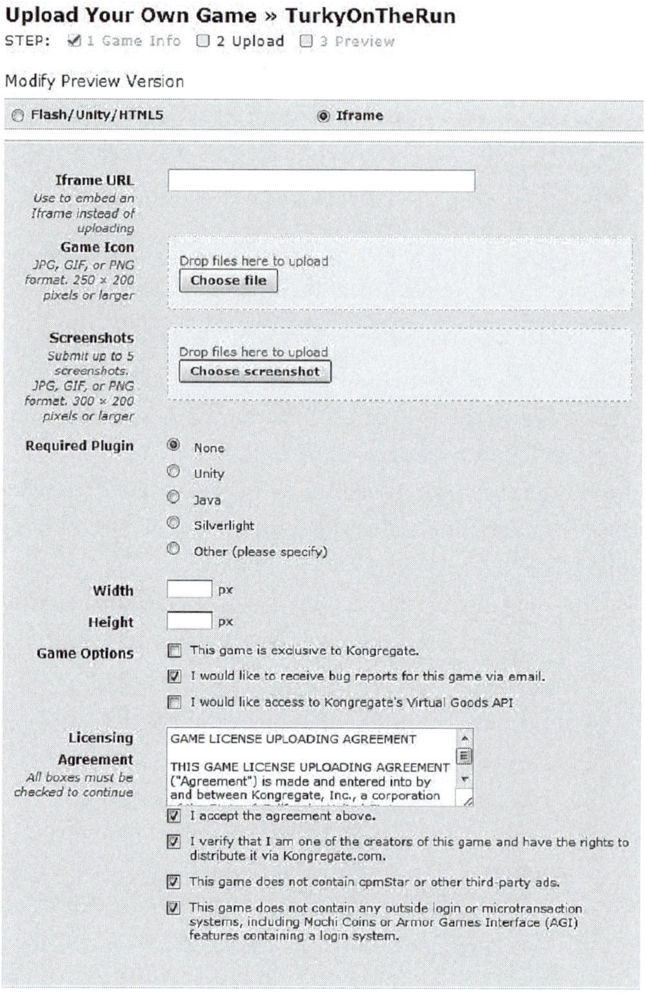

Upload Your Own Game » TurkyOnTheRun

STEP: ☑ 1 Game Info ☐ 2 Upload ☐ 3 Preview

Modify Preview Version

◯ Flash/Unity/HTML5   ◉ Iframe

Iframe URL
Use to embed an
Iframe instead of
uploading

Game Icon
JPG, GIF, or PNG   Drop files here to upload
format. 250 × 200   **Choose file**
pixels or larger

Screenshots
Submit up to 5   Drop files here to upload
screenshots.   **Choose screenshot**
JPG, GIF, or PNG
format. 300 × 200
pixels or larger

Required Plugin   ◉ None
                       ◯ Unity
                       ◯ Java
                       ◯ Silverlight
                       ◯ Other (please specify)

Width   [   ] px

Height   [   ] px

Game Options   ☐ This game is exclusive to Kongregate.
                   ☑ I would like to receive bug reports for this game via email.
                   ☐ I would like access to Kongregate's Virtual Goods API

Licensing   GAME LICENSE UPLOADING AGREEMENT
Agreement
All boxes must be   THIS GAME LICENSE UPLOADING AGREEMENT
checked to continue   ("Agreement") is made and entered into by
                         and between Kongregate, Inc., a corporation
                 ☑ I accept the agreement above.
                 ☑ I verify that I am one of the creators of this game and have the rights to
                   distribute it via Kongregate.com.
                 ☑ This game does not contain cpmStar or other third-party ads.
                 ☑ This game does not contain any outside login or microtransaction
                   systems, including Mochi Coins or Armor Games Interface (AGI)
                   features containing a login system.

FIGURE 12.7 The second submission step requires more details, including a game icon, screenshots, and game width/height. Most importantly, a link to our game iframe page is required. For this, we can use DropBox's public folder and export the link to the file from there.

exported folder, must be available online, for example in a public folder provided by a cloud storage service like DropBox.*

At the bottom of the page we will also notice a section named **Statistics** (Figure 12.8). This is where we can define a score-based leaderboard or keep track of some variable to award different achievements. Once defined,

---

* www.dropbox.com

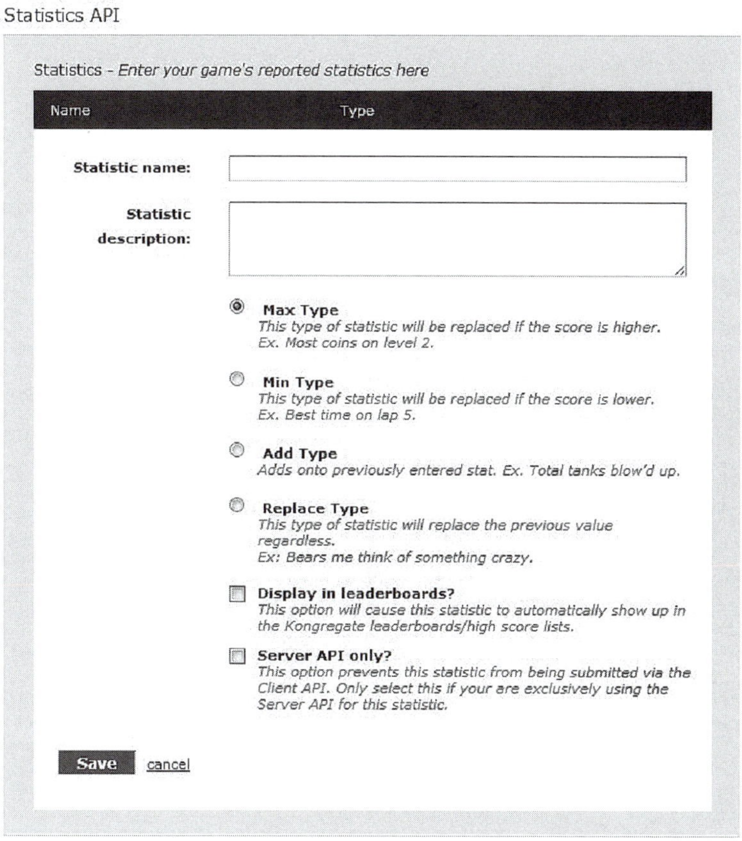

Statistics API

Statistics - *Enter your game's reported statistics here*

Name	Type

Statistic name:

Statistic description:

○ **Max Type**
This type of statistic will be replaced if the score is higher.
Ex. Most coins on level 2.

○ **Min Type**
This type of statistic will be replaced if the score is lower.
Ex. Best time on lap 5.

○ **Add Type**
Adds onto previously entered stat. Ex. Total tanks blow'd up.

○ **Replace Type**
This type of statistic will replace the previous value
regardless.
Ex: Bears me think of something crazy.

☐ **Display in leaderboards?**
This option will cause this statistic to automatically show up in
the Kongregate leaderboards/high score lists.

☐ **Server API only?**
This option prevents this statistic from being submitted via the
Client API. Only select this if your are exclusively using the
Server API for this statistic.

Save cancel

FIGURE 12.8 Via the **Statistics** section we can define a high score table or different achievements, like obtaining a specific item or shooting with a certain degree of accuracy.

statistics can be sent from the game to Kongregate via a specific action accessible through the **Kongregate** object we need to add to our game.

After this step we can preview the game and finalize the submission. Once done, the game will need to be approved by an admin before going live.

Note that using Statistics is also relevant in terms of our prospective revenue. On Kongregate, in fact, games generate income mostly by displaying ads[*] whose revenue is then split between Kongregate itself and the developers. By default, developers receive 25% of the ad revenue generated from the pages showcasing their games but, by using the Statistics API,

---

[*] In-app purchases via Kongregate's own currency, named Kreds, are currently being tested and available to selected developers.

FIGURE 12.9 The main panel in Clay.io from where we can add new games and access many different features.

the developers' share gets increased by another 10%. Games that are exclusive to Kongregate receive an additional 15% in revenue, bringing the total possible share to 50%.

Besides Kongregate, there are many other portals suitable to HTML5 games, and we can expect even more in the near future. Gamesgames.com* and ToonGoggles,† a portal dedicated to young children and very suitable for games targeting this particular audience, may be good choices for your games as well. One of the most exciting new portals and overall tool for HTML5 developers in general and Construct 2 in particular is, without doubt, Clay.io.

In fact, Clay.io is not only a portal we can publish to and monetize our games in, but it is a sort of Swiss army knife, including many different features like leaderboards, achievements, in-app purchases (IAPs), integration with social networks, and much, much more.

Start by registering at http://clay.io/join and, once logged in, head over to the developers' page (http://clay.io/developers), where you can upgrade your status from standard user to developer and input some more information about your indie game business.

From now on, when you log in, you will be greeted by a panel similar to Figure 12.9.

The first thing we should do to enable all the different Clay.io features in our Construct 2 games is to download and install two plugins. To do so, click on API and scroll down the page until we get to the **Plugins** section (Figure 12.10). Click on the Construct 2 link and download the plugin named scirra.zip. Also download the advertisement-related plugin (scirra-ads.zip) found in the next page.

---

* Check www.spilgames.com/developers for information on how to submit a game.
† www.toongogglesinc.com/games

FIGURE 12.10   In the API page, scroll down till you see the dedicated **Plugins** section. Click on **Construct 2** and its related **Advertisements Plugin** page to download the latest version of the plugins.

Installing plugins in Construct is a very straightforward process: simply unzip the files we just downloaded in your **Construct 2/exporters/ html5/plugins/** folder, and the plugins will be ready next time you launch the program. You will find them available when adding new objects to your projects (Figure 12.11).

Once the Clay.io object has been added to the game, we can start preparing for its inclusion to the Clay.io portal: on the website (Figure 12.9) select the **Add new game** option and fill in the required details, such as name, description, etc. You don't need to upload the game at this stage, but take note of the different icons and images you will need and, most importantly, check out the **API key** for your game. This key, which is the same as the subdomain we just specified when adding the game, needs to be pasted in the Clay.io object properties within the game itself (Figure 12.12).

Once the game is finished, we can proceed by exporting it as a straight HTML5 project or use the Chrome Web Store exporter. The resulting files

FIGURE 12.11   After installation, the Clay.io plugins will show up among the web-based objects, ready to be imported in our game.

⊟ Object type properties	
Name	Clayio
Plugin	Clay.io
⊟ Properties	
API Key	
Debug Mode	Disabled
Use Clay.io Styles	Enabled
Use Clay.io Loader	Disabled
More information	Help

FIGURE 12.12   The Clay.io object properties. Here we have to specify the unique game key we got when adding the game on the portal. This is the same as the game subdomain. Debug mode allows for testing high scores and other functions without these being actually published on the Clay.io stream. Remember to turn this off before uploading the game!

should be zipped together, and the zip file is what we have to upload on the Clay.io game details page (Figure 12.13).

Monetization in Clay.io can be implemented in many different ways: games can be free or paid, can have IAPs or can be supported by ads. Needless to say, the two last options are the most interesting ones.

To work, IAPs have to be set up first on Clay.io back end: access your game developer page and click on the **Items** link (Figure 12.14).

Click on the **Add Item** button, and then you will be able to define the item name and price. A unique ID will be assigned to each item created,

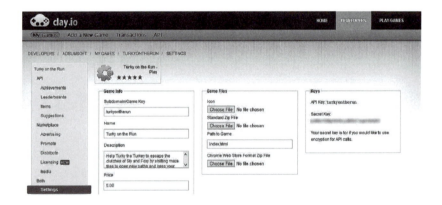

FIGURE 12.13   Back on the Clay.io website, on the page where we specify all the details needed for our game. The exported, zipped game has to be uploaded here from the **Game Files** section.

FIGURE 12.14   By selecting the **Items** link for our games in the Clay.io developer's page, we can define as many IAPs as we want.

and these are the reference numbers we will have to use in Construct 2 when adding items to a shopping cart. As an example, let's say we want to sell magic wands in *Turky on the Run:* when the player touches a "Buy Magic" button, we first check that Clay.io is ready, and then we add the specific item before proceeding to the checkout (Figure 12.15).

During the checkout players can review their shopping cart before proceeding to the payment page (Figure 12.16). Once there, they can choose among all the options we made available in the **Payment Processor** group of the game **Settings** page (Figure 12.17).

For each transaction using Clay.io, API developers will get a share of 80%.

The Clay.io object in Construct 2 also provides us with several other events to give us full control of what's happening, including events for checking that the payment has been successful and that items have been properly retrieved.

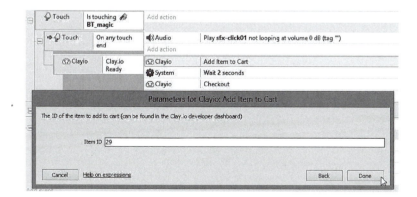

FIGURE 12.15   An example of in game purchase for *Turky on the Run*. The specific item is identified by its ID, assigned automatically when we created it through Clay.io developer's page.

FIGURE 12.16 Thanks to Clay.io we can give our players plenty of options for IAPs: from credit cards and Paypal to Google wallet and more.

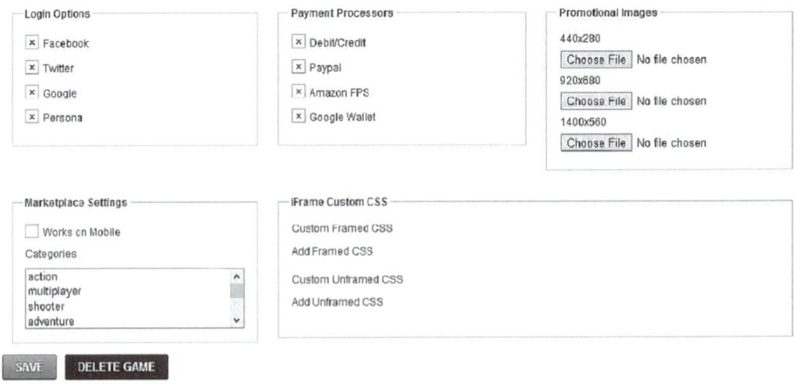

FIGURE 12.17 A part of the game **Settings** page showing the **Payment Processors** section. This is where we specify which payment options we want to make available to our players.

FIGURE 12.18   A section of the game settings page on Clay.io where we can set up advertisements to be displayed on our game's own page within the Clay.io portal. Note that we can also have a preroll ad to be displayed before the game is launched.

Moving on to advertisements, these can be added in the game's own Clay.io page (Figure 12.18) or embedded in the game itself via the advertising plugin (Figure 12.19).

The revenue share we can expect by integrating ads in our games varies between 50% to 70%, depending on the different publishers pushing their content on the Clay.io network of games.

For more detailed information on how to set up IAPs, ads, and other features, such as achievements and high scores, refer to the official documentation available at the following addresses: http://clay.io/docs/construct2, for the main plugin; http://clay.io/docs/advertising and http://clay.io/docs/construct2ads, for the advertising plugin.

To conclude this section on web portals, it is important to know that many are actually actively looking for fresh content to keep attracting visitors. To do so, they are willing to license HTML5 games, especially if these take advantage of the portability such games can

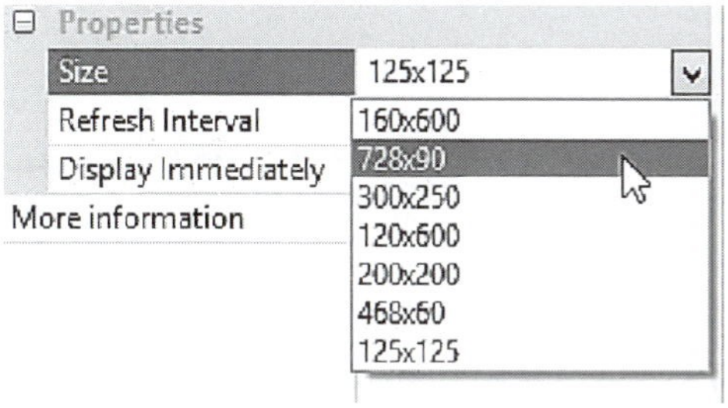

FIGURE 12.19   The properties of the Clay.io advertisement plugin: here we can set the size of the ad within the game layout and its refresh interval in seconds.

offer and can be played on both desktop and mobile browsers. A good HTML5 game should be able to get between $500 to $1000 (or even more) for a nonexclusive license, although the game might have to be customized a little bit by adding the publisher's logo or integrating a specific API.

Clay.io can work as a bridge to connect you with potential publishers and other vendors as well. To take advantage of this feature, we have to select the **Licensing** link (under the **Marketplace** section of our game, see Figure 12.14), check the box stating the game is available for publisher licensing, and decide the licensing fee and whether you are willing to customize the game (e.g., integrating an additional API).

Besides Clay.io, a good website where we can look for publishing partners is **MarketJS** (www.marketjs.com). Once registered, you can add the game details and decide which type of license you are interested in: exclusive, nonexclusive, or revenue share are possible and common options. After the game is set up, it will be up to the interested publishers to knock on your door and discuss things further.

Apptopia (www.apptopia.com) is also another portal that is quickly growing in importance and shows a steadily increasing number of users. Currently, it is focused on iOS and Android apps only (see Section 12.8 for directions on how to turn your HTML5 games into native looking apps for such devices), and it is surely an interesting option to check if we want to monetize our games by selling them to other companies.

12.2 CHROME WEB STORE AND MOZILLA MARKETPLACE

Following the success of mobile-based app stores, big players in the Web spaces decided to also move in this direction and offer similar marketplaces.

Two of the most well-known examples are the Chrome Web Store and the Mozilla Marketplace,

The former, working in synergy with the Chrome web browser, is steadily growing in importance and many famous, high-quality indie games like *From Dust, Bastion, Cut the Rope, Angry Birds, Bejeweled*, etc., can be found there. Publishing involves a one-time registration fee of $5, after which developers will be allowed to upload and publish their games. To publish on the Chrome Web Store, we can either use

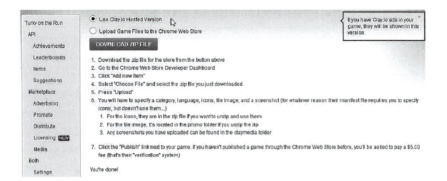

FIGURE 12.20   The instructions for pushing a game from Clay.io to the Chrome Web Store.

the dedicated export function in Construct 2, take care of the required assets (icons, banner, screen shots, etc.) and proceed as described in the detailed tutorial available on Scirra's website* or, if the game is already published on Clay.io, take a small shortcut from there. In this case, start by clicking on the **Distribute** link in the game's **Marketplace** section (Figure 12.14) and then pick the Chrome Web Store icon. In the next form (Figure 12.20) we can simply download a zipped file containing all the game assets, which can then be pushed on the web store by following simple instructions.

Following Chrome's success, Mozilla also started developing its own HTML5-based marketplace, accessible by Firefox operating system (OS) or Firefox for Android on supported phones and 7 inch devices. Games to be submitted can be either packaged or hosted (more information can be gathered from https://marketplace.firefox.com/developers/), and Clay.io makes things very simple for us by using the latter approach. All we have to do, in fact, is go to the submission app page,[†] agree to the terms, and specify the Clay.io-based URL http://yourgame.clay.io/firefox.webapp for the app manifest (needless to say, "yourgame" is our own game subdomain!). Last, we will be asked to add a few more details about the game and whether we plan to release it for free or with an upfront payment. When done, the game enters the review queue and will be available once approved.

---

* https://www.scirra.com/tutorials/68/publishing-to-the-chrome-web-store/
† https://marketplace.firefox.com/developers/submit/

12.3 FACEBOOK

Being able to distribute our games on Facebook is a great opportunity and a testimony to HTML5 and Construct 2's flexibility.

Construct 2 provides its own Facebook object, allowing us to log in, share links, post wall messages, and more, and we can integrate our games as Facebook developers ourselves by hosting the games on our server and following one of the official Scirra's tutorials.[*] Tackling things completely by ourselves also exposes us to what many developers jokingly call "Facebook developer love": Facebook has a great engineering team that updates the different APIs very often, and, unfortunately, a few things here and there can get broken in the process. This has led to many frustrated developers. Well-known professor and game designer Ian Bogost stated in his blog that "the Facebook Platform is a shape-shifting, chimeric shadow of suffering and despair."[†]

In other words, this means features that were working perfectly until a moment ago may suddenly change at short or even no notice, forcing affected developers to understand the changes and fix their games in a hurry.

To reduce these risks, it would be great if there were somebody who would take care of the low-level work for us while, maybe, also hosting the games on our behalf. Luckily, there is someone who helps in doing just that: Clay.io!

Once the game is published on Clay.io, move to the Facebook Developers Page[‡] and click on the **Create New App** button. The creation process requires us to input a few simple data, like **app name** and **namespace**. The latter is going to be used for accessing the app's actual URL (e.g., http://apps.facebook.com/namespace) as well as for more advanced tasks like **Open Graph** actions. There is no need to check the **web hosting** box because Clay.io is already taking care of it for us.

Once Facebook generates a specific **App ID** and **Secret Key** unique to our game, we need to input these back to Clay.io either in the **Settings** page of our game (look for the **Social Settings** section) or in the corresponding fields in the **Push to Facebook** page (accessible through the **Marketplace/Distribute** links in the developers' panel on the left of the screen).

---

[*] https://www.scirra.com/tutorials/58/how-to-make-a-facebook-game/page-1
[†] http://m.bogost.com/blog/oauth_of_fealty.shtml
[‡] https://developers.facebook.com/apps

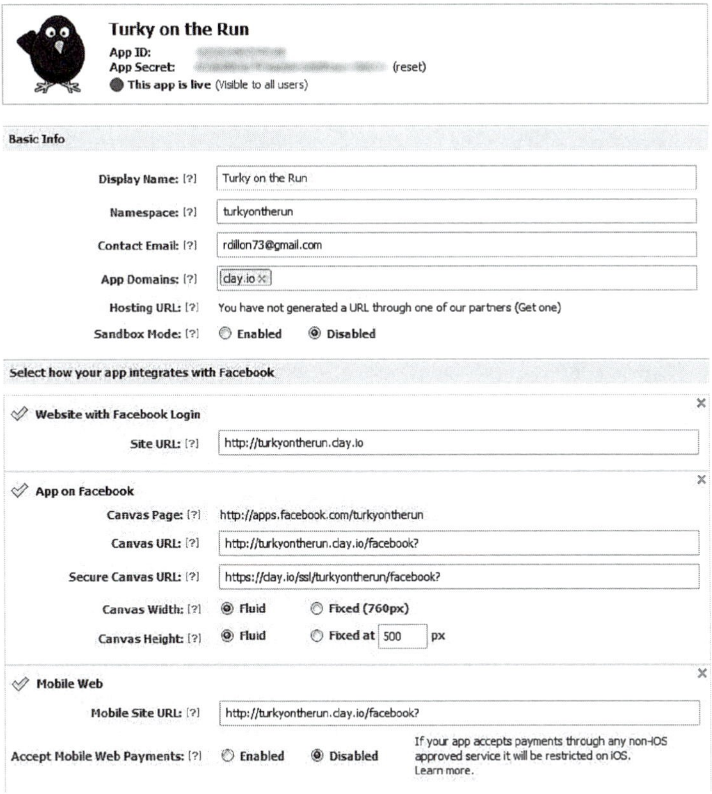

FIGURE 12.21   The Facebook settings page for *Turky on the Run*.

Back on the Facebook developers' page, we have to specify the app domain as Clay.io and all the corresponding URLs as follows (see also Figure 12.21 for an actual example using *Turky on the Run*):

- **Site URL:** http://namespace.clay.io
- **Canvas URL:** http://namespace.clay.io/facebook?
- **Secure Canvas URL:** https://clay.io/ssl/namespace/facebook?
- **Mobile Site URL:** http://namespace.clay.io/facebook?

Save the changes, and your game should be available on Facebook for all your friends to play: congratulations!

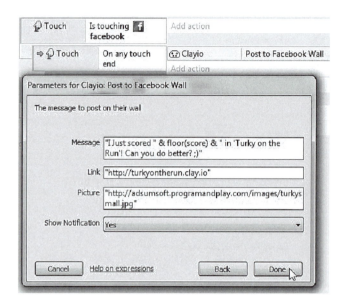

FIGURE 12.22 When touching a Facebook button in the game, the corresponding Clay.io action is called to specify the message we want to post on the player's wall, for example, we'd want to emphasize the score, together with a link to the game and a picture.

Now that we have a game on a social platform, we shouldn't forget to take advantage of the social features the Clay.io object offers us: letting players log in and then invite their friends, post on their wall, and more (Figure 12.22). All this can be done easily via the Clay.io object in Construct 2: check the API documentation on Clay.io for further details.

12.4 WINDOWS 8 METRO

As with Facebook, we have two options for deploying our games as Metro Apps, suitable for the newest Windows 8 interface that aims at offering a seamless experience between PCs, tablets, and mobiles: straight from Construct 2 or, again, via Clay.io.

Regardless of our approach, we need to download and install Visual Studio 2012 Express* (or the latest available version), and, if we want to actually distribute and sell our games on the Windows Store, we also

---

* http://www.microsoft.com/visualstudio/eng/downloads

This layout includes a hidden 'Paused' layer which will become visible, and
pause the game, when the view state is 'Snapped'. To view this layer,
enable it in the Layers bar.

| Share | Share the text 'Hello world'. You can also share links and HTML. |

Purchase status is:

| Purchase |

Note: you must publish this project to Windows 8 before any of the above
features will work.

FIGURE 12.23 After selecting **New Project,** choose **New Windows 8 Project**
from the available templates. This layout, already taking care of a **Paused** layer as
well as of a possible game purchase after a trial period, will be displayed and will
be an effective starting point for your game.

need to register for a developer account.[*] Currently, Microsoft requires
two different licenses for publishing on the Windows Store for PC and for
Mobile because the two are kept separate: the latter requires a $99 annual
fee, while the former requires a $49 fee for individual developers. If you
are a student joining the DreamSpark program,[†] registering as a Microsoft
Developer is completely free.

A good idea to have a head start in developing a Windows 8 game in
Construct is by using the corresponding template offered in Construct 2,
which already takes care of a couple of features required for our game to
be approved during the review process (Figure 12.23).

We can then follow the detailed tutorials offered on Scirra's website,
such as "How to Make a Windows 8 App,"[‡] if we are targeting a desktop
application, or "How to Make a Windows Phone 8 Application,"[§] if we are
making a mobile game.

If, on the other hand, we also have the game on Clay.io, we can find all
relevant and up-to-date instructions in the Windows 8 section of the API

[*] https://appdev.microsoft.com/StorePortals/EN-US/Account/signup/Start
[†] https://www.dreamspark.com/
[‡] https://www.scirra.com/tutorials/272/how-to-make-a-windows-8-app
[§] https://www.scirra.com/tutorials/429/how-to-make-a-windows-phone-8-app

documentation* as well as on the Scirra published tutorial "Windows 8 and Clay.io Integration."†

Regarding monetization, Microsoft allows developers many options: games can be free with ads, be sold upfront, offer a free trial period after which players have to pay to continue playing, or include IAPs. If you are using Clay.io, API things are to be set up as usual, but if you are deploying straight from Construct, you may like to check another tutorial on Scirra's website, "Adding In-App Purchases to your Windows 8 Game."‡

Whatever the monetization strategy, Microsoft takes 30% of the sale price of Windows Store apps until sales reach $25,000. The cut is then reduced to 20% after this earning milestone is reached.

12.5 WINDOWS, OSX, AND LINUX

Good, old-fashioned games to be downloaded and run as executable files still have a significant market share that shouldn't be ignored. Our HTML5 games can target this market as well by using the Node-WebKit exporter.

Basically, Node-WebKit is a standalone version of Google Chrome but without all those browser identifying elements (like address bar, navigation buttons, etc.) so that it looks like any other standard application.

Exporting this option will allow us to run our games as executable files, where, in fact, what we do is actually launch a dedicated browser app embedding the game.

After the exporting process is completed, we will find folders for Windows, OSX,§ and Linux (both 32 and 64 bits) containing all the relevant files.

Note also that Construct includes a Node-WebKit object that can be included in a game to allow for proper file access.¶

Regarding monetization for downloadable PC/Mac games, the old-fashioned business model of asking players to pay upfront or offering a trial period before requesting the actual full payment is still a very viable approach. While this model doesn't seem to work anymore on mobile

---

* http://clay.io/docs/windows8

† https://www.scirra.com/tutorials/483/windows-8-and-clayio-integration

‡ https://www.scirra.com/tutorials/596/adding-in-app-purchases-to-your-windows-8-game

§ For having a proper XCode based project to work on, Mac developers may also consider MacGap, available here: https://github.com/maccman/macgap.

¶ Refer to Construct 2 manual for detailed documentation on events and actions available: https://www.scirra.com/manual/162/node-webkit.

FIGURE 12.24   Desura, one of the biggest indie friendly game portals currently available.

games, several dedicated PC portals do employ it and manage to be successful, offering excellent opportunities to aspiring indie developers.

Most PC gamers know about Steam (www.steampowered.com), which is the portal that offers the most exposure to developers by far. Its greenlight process, currently the only way for self-published indies to add their games, has been subject to much criticism lately,* and aspiring developers may also want to consider other venues.

A few popular choices I'd recommend to check out are, in no particular order, the following:

- **Desura (www.desura.com):** This is a steadily growing portal featuring games from all different genres and showing more than 13,000 daily visitors. Once registered, games can be submitted via an online form (http://www.desura.com/games/add). Revenue is split 70/30 and developers are paid monthly via PayPal (see Figure 12.24).

- **Big Fish Games (www.bigfishgames.com):** This is the biggest portal for casual games. Definitely the place to submit well-polished hidden object games and many more. Games can be submitted in any stage

---

* gamasutra.com/view/news/176887/Discoverability_on_Steam_Greenlight_Its_nonexistent.php and gamasutra.com/view/feature/177100/steam_greenlight_developers_speak_php.

FIGURE 12.25 Big Fish Games, while casual PC/Mac downloadable games are still the bulk of the catalog, the portal is also expanding to mobile and web-based games, making for a very comprehensive offering.

of production. New games and sales are offered every day to keep the community engaged (see Figure 12.25).

- **Wild Tangent Games (www.wildtangent.com):** This is another portal very popular with casual gamers. They offer games on many platforms and formats through a dedicated gaming client, which also uses a proprietary coin system, named WildCoins, for IAPs as well as for granting access to different games, like in an arcade (see Figure 12.26).

- **GamersGate (www.gamersgate.com):** This is a big portal featuring both more mainstream games as well as indie productions. To submit a game, you need to get in touch first with the site administrators, writing to publisher@gamersgate.com and including game details like a short description, URLs with screenshots and videos, etc. (see Figure 12.27).

- **Get Games Go (www.getgamesgo.com):** This is the PC/Mac download service offered by Eurogamer and showcases both AAA and indie content. Indie developers willing to distribute their

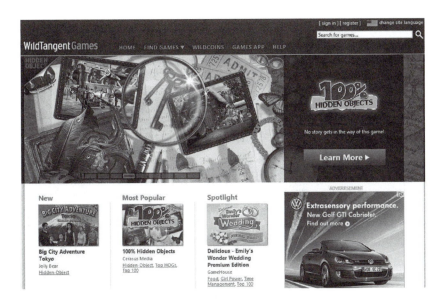

FIGURE 12.26   Wild Tangent Games. With more than 20,000 daily visitors, it is surely going to offer some good exposure to your games!

FIGURE 12.27   GamersGate, a portal mixing both AAA and indie games. It has more than 18,000 daily visitors.

FIGURE 12.28   Get Games Go, a portal brought to you by Eurogamer.

games have to contact the website administrators via the standard "contact us" form. Revenue from sales is generally split 70/30 (see Figure 12.28).

- **Indievania (www.indievania.com):** This is a very indie-friendly marketplace where, as explained on the website, developers can sell their digital rights management free games and keep 100% of the revenue, paid via PayPal. It has more than 1000 daily visitors (see Figure 12.29).

- **IndieCity (www.indiecity.com):** This is a comprehensive portal for indie developers, offering personalized pages, analytics, and the possibility of showcasing in-progress games (see Figure 12.30).

12.6 BLACKBERRY 10

With its new BB10 OS, Blackberry is proposing itself as a serious alternative to the dominant iOS and Android platforms. Interestingly, Blackberry has also identified games as a central component in its strategy to attract a new, younger audience to its latest breed of devices such as the Z10 model. To incentivize game developers, the company has set up a very indie-friendly procedure for deploying games made by using a huge variety of tools, HTML5 included.

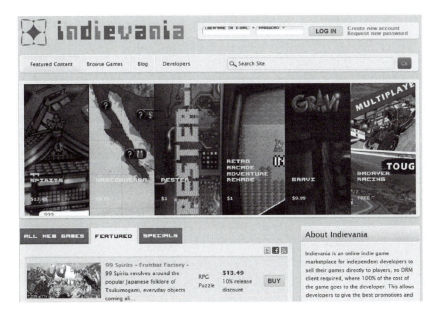

FIGURE 12.29   Indievania, a marketplace leaving all the sales revenue to game developers.

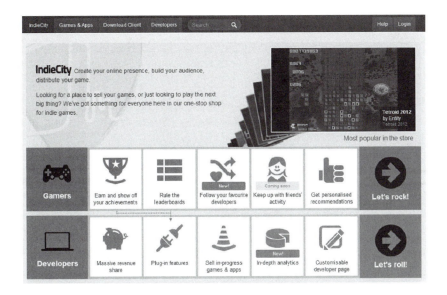

FIGURE 12.30   IndieCity. Revenue is split 75/25 and games are peer approved.

Head to https://developer.blackberry.com/html5/ to have a general overview of how HTML5 games are handled. Detailed tutorials and documentation are available at https://developer.blackberry.com/html5/documentation/.

In any case, the first step would be to start downloading the WebWorks software development kit (SDK) and the BlackBerry 10 Simulator we can find at https://developer.blackberry.com/html5/download/ and then register as a BlackBerry Developer which, in line with the indie-friendly approach adopted, is completely free. Currently, in fact, there are no annual fees required to publish apps and games on BlackBerry World!

The process to publish a game on a BB10 device can be summarized in three main phases:

1. Have all the needed HTML5 files zipped together with a config.xml file.

2. Package, sign, and test the app.

3. Publish it on BlackBerry World.

To start we can either export our project as a standard HTML5 game (and then follow BlackBerry instructions) or use Construct BlackBerry export feature, which will allow us to take a couple of shortcuts, though we will still have to fine-tune a few files.

If we opt for the latter, Construct will ask us for the path to WebWorks SDK as well as for other information (Figure 12.31), including the signing keys we have to request at https://www.blackberry.com/SignedKeys/codesigning.html. This pair of keys will be sent via e-mail. They are tied to our developer account and, needless to say, are very important. Be sure to back them up and don't misplace them!

Construct will also build a simple config.xml file for us, but you may want to see how to customize it to suit your specific needs and requirements by checking the relevant documentation.*

Once this is done, zip all the files in your game's folder, including the config.xml. It is now time to test our game and then deploy it. As explained by BlackBerry official documentation, testing can be done in a few different ways. Here I will briefly discuss only the command line approach, since it usually looks intimidating to beginners but, in reality, there is nothing to worry about.

---

* https://developer.blackberry.com/html5/documentation/config_doc_elements.html

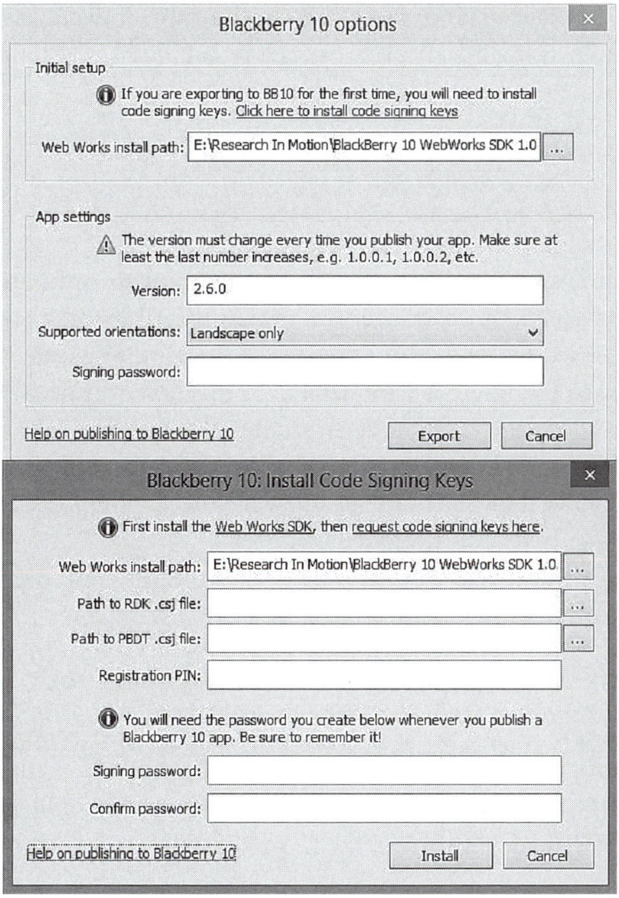

FIGURE 12.31   When exporting for BlackBerry, Construct will ask us for the path to the WebWorks SDK and the signing password. If we didn't install the two signing keys yet, we can do so here by clicking on the link (in the above window), which will open an **Install Code Signing Keys** pop-up where we can look for the two specific .csj files we received by e-mail and saved somewhere safe.

You might have noticed that Construct also built two additional batch (.bat) files: package_bb10_app and deploy_bb10_app. These are the files we need to run to package the game, making it ready for distribution (as a .bar file), and then deploy it to the simulator, our BB10 device, or upload it to BlackBerry marketplace for distribution.

I had some issues when testing these, so let's see exactly what should go into these files and how to make our own versions if the ready-made ones don't work as expected.

To package and sign the game, making it ready for deployment on our device as well as the marketplace, we need a bat file like the following:

```
"C:\Research In Motion\BlackBerry 10 WebWorks SDK 1.0.4.11\bbwp"
"C:\Users\robert\Desktop\Turky on the Run-BB10\turky.zip"
-g <YOUR SIGNING PASSWORD> --buildId 5 -o "C:\Users\robert\
Desktop\Turky on the Run-BB10\signed"
```

The first line specifies the path and the program to run (bbwp is the BlackBerry WebWorks Packager we have in the WebWorks SDK folder). This is followed by the path to the zip file we want to package, which is then followed by different parameters.* In this case we specify our signing password via the -g parameter, a unique, progressive ID for our current build via --buildId (note the double hyphen) and then -o (output), which is followed by the output path (which was, in my case, a project-specific folder in C:\Users\robert\Desktop\).

To deploy the signed game to our device, the bat file should have the following commands:

```
"C:\Research In Motion\BlackBerry 10 WebWorks SDK 1.0.4.11\
dependencies\tools\bin\blackberry-deploy"
-installApp -password <YOUR DEVICE PASSWORD> -device
169.254.0.1
-package "C:\Users\robert\Desktop\Turky on the Run-BB10\
signed\device\turky.bar"
```

Here we are calling the blackberry-deploy program with the -installApp parameter followed by the device password, its internet protocol address on our network, and then the path to the specific bar package we want to install.

If, instead, we want to simply deploy to the simulator or to test a development build on a device, we don't need to specify a build ID or even the signing password in the package file, but on the other hand, we need to generate and install a debug token as explained in the official documentation.†

Finally, to upload the game, log in at https://blackberryid.blackberry.com/bbid/login, then click on **Managing Products** and then on **Add**

---

* Full reference for parameters can be found here: https://developer.blackberry.com/html5/documentation/command_line_packaging_parameters_1873323_11.html.
† https://developer.blackberry.com/html5/documentation/running_your_bb10_app_2008471_11.html

Product. You will be taken to a series of forms to fill out with all relevant data before being able to add a release and ultimately upload your game for approval.

12.7 TIZEN

Tizen is a new mobile OS developed by Intel and Samsung with the very ambitious aim of taking away a significant market share from Android. HTML5 is being built in the system from the start: Tizen's browser, in fact, has been designed to support most of HTML5 advanced features, including also the WebAudio API as well as WebGL. In addition, HTML5-based games can be included in the marketplace side by side with native apps.

We can start our Tizen development process by registering and downloading the SDK at https://developer.tizen.org.

Once the SDK is installed, we can try our games on the Tizen simulator following a few simple steps.

1. Export the game in Construct by using the **Tizen** option.

2. Launch the Tizen integrated development environment (IDE) and create a New Tizen Web Project selecting the **Basic Application** template (Figure 12.32).

3. If this is your first time running the IDE, you should also add an **Active Secure Profile** that will be used later to sign your games. You can do so via the **Window/Preferences/Tizen SDK/Security Profiles** menu.

4. Copy all contents (files and folders) exported by Construct into your Tizen project folder, overwriting existing files in the process. Pay attention to the config.xml file, though. There may be differences between the fields and values that the latest version of the Tizen SDK expects and those actually generated by Construct 2; my recommendation is to open the two in a text editor and merge them manually. In any case, the one generated by Tizen has a line specifying a unique Application ID and package name, which we are going to lose if we copy over Construct 2 files blindly. If lost, we will have to generate a new one by opening config.xml in the IDE, selecting the **Tizen** tab, and then clicking on the **Generate** button.

5. Click on Run to build and test your game in the web simulator!

FIGURE 12.32 To import a Construct 2 game in Tizen start by creating a new basic web project from the Tizen IDE.

Assuming everything works properly, we can now proceed to testing the game further on the SDK device emulator or on an actual device. When ready, we can package and publish the game to the Tizen app store, following the instructions provided in the SDK documentation itself* or in Scirra's specific Tizen tutorial.†

12.8 IOS AND ANDROID

Last, but certainly not least, are the platforms that made indie mobile game publishing not only popular but possible in the first place: iOS and Android.

---

* Check for the **Application Development Process** group within the **Tizen Web App Programming** section of the documentation.
† https://www.scirra.com/tutorials/669/how-to-export-to-tizen/page-1

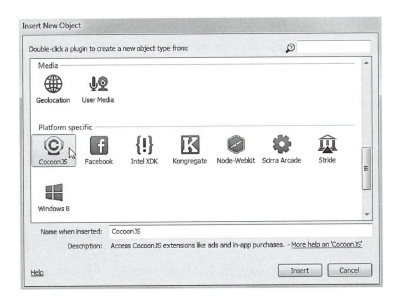

FIGURE 12.33   To export for iOS or Android we need to use a third-party tool: CocoonJS by Ludei.

While HTML5 games can be played on these devices and even installed on the home screen via the devices' own browsers, performance can be a real issue. Besides, a game distributed in this way would completely lack all the promotion and discoverability features of the official marketplaces reserved to native apps. Luckily, a few options exist to wrap HTML5 games and turn them into apps that look, feel, and perform exactly like native apps. CocoonJS by Ludei is one of these tools, able to transform a Construct 2 game into a native app to be published on the Apple App Store or Google Play.

Before proceeding further, though, remember that to publish on these marketplaces, you need to register with them first: developing for Apple App Store requires a $99 per year fee, and apps have to be built and signed via XCode on a Mac computer,* while Google Play requires a one-time $25 registration fee.†

CocoonJS works by taking an HTML5 game and then compiling it via its cloud-based services to provide a native project file that can be used to proceed in the publication process.

In Construct, while not strictly necessary to export the game, we may want to start by adding the CocoonJS object to our project (Figure 12.33).

---

* https://developer.apple.com/programs/ios/
† http://developer.android.com/index.html

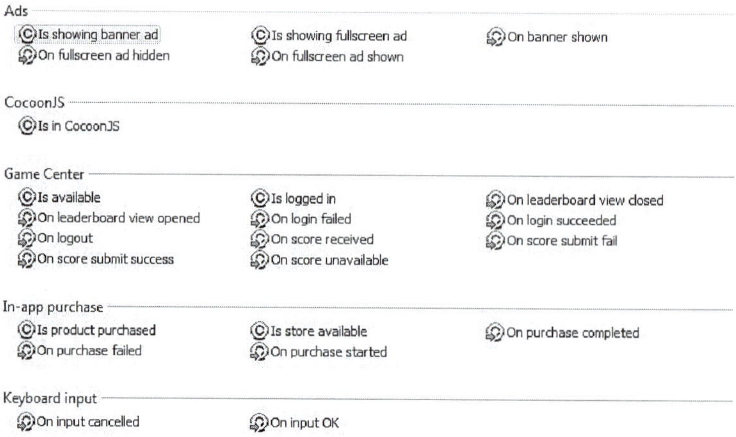

FIGURE 12.34   List of CocoonJS available conditions for triggering new events related to ads, game center, IAP, and keyboard input.

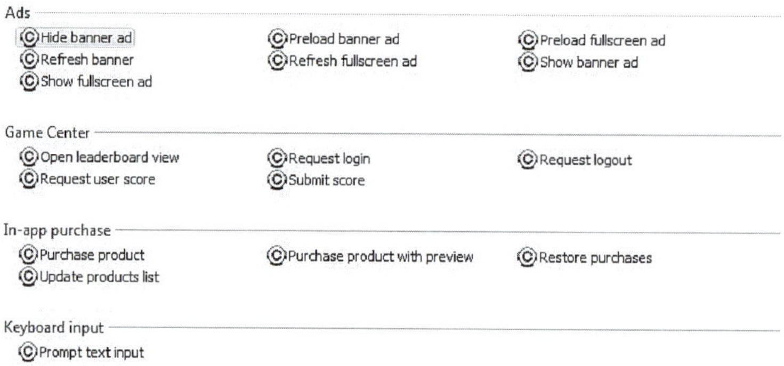

FIGURE 12.35   An overview of CocoonJS actions for handling ads, game center, IAP, and keyboard input.

This will enable us to access several important features that CocoonJS offers via specific extensions, which are discussed in detail on Ludei's official documentation.*

Once the object is added, we will have a new set of events and actions at our disposal to manage things like in-app purchases, ads, and the Apple Game Center, as shown in Figures 12.34 and 12.35.

---

* The latest CocoonJS documentation can be found here: http://wiki.ludei.com/cocoonjs:extensions.

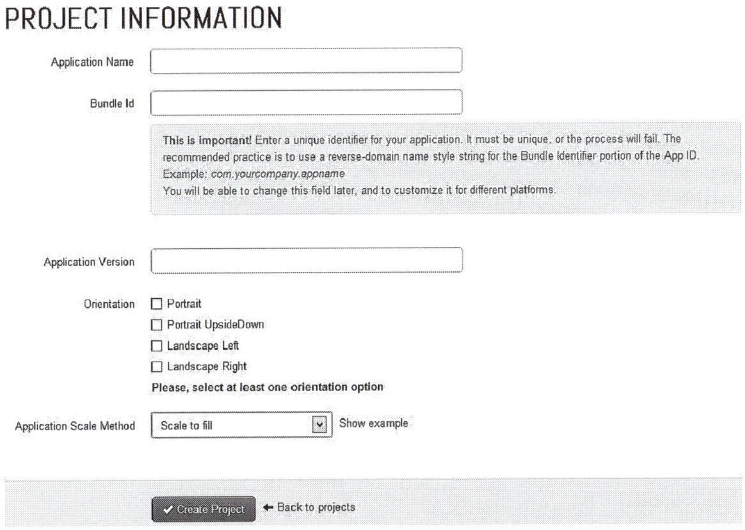

PROJECT INFORMATION

Application Name

Bundle Id

This is important! Enter a unique identifier for your application. It must be unique, or the process will fail. The recommended practice is to use a reverse-domain name style string for the Bundle Identifier portion of the App ID.
Example: com.yourcompany.appname
You will be able to change this field later, and to customize it for different platforms.

Application Version

Orientation
☐ Portrait
☐ Portrait UpsideDown
☐ Landscape Left
☐ Landscape Right
Please, select at least one orientation option

Application Scale Method   Scale to fill ⌄   Show example

✔ Create Project   ← Back to projects

FIGURE 12.36   The first screen in the new project creation process.

One of the most useful features Ludei is offering to developers is a CocoonJS app we can find on both the Apple App Store and Google Play to test our games before submitting them for compilation. To do so, download the app, register for a developer account, and then export the game via Construct 2 CocoonJS option. This creates a zip file that we can then easily test on our devices: for example, if using DropBox, place it in your public folder and then write the link in the CocoonJS app to start downloading and launching it.

Once we have confirmed the game works as expected, we can proceed to the actual cloud-based compilation,* which will result in either an apk file for Android or an XCode project for iOS.

Head to **https://cocoonjsservice.ludei.com/cloud/login** and log in (or register if you haven't done so already). We can then add a new project to our account by specifying information like the application name, a bundle ID (usually in the reverse domain format, e.g., com.yourcompany.yourgame), a version number, the supported orientation, and how the game should eventually scale to accommodate devices with different resolutions (Figure 12.36).

Once done, we will be able to access a main menu for setting up the project: we will only discuss iOS and Android here, but more and more

---

* http://support.ludei.com/hc/en-us/articles/201048503-How-to-use

options are getting added as the platform matures, so don't be surprised to find several other possibilities you can take advantage of!

Clicking on iOS will display a form where we need to specify and upload a series of icons at different sizes, ranging from 320 × 480 to 2048 × 1496 pixels, while, when selecting Android, we will have only a few required small icons to upload, plus, possibly, specify the minimum and maximum Android versions supported. If using extensions for supporting ads, game center, or IAPs, we also need to specify these under the **Services/Configuration** link.

Finally, we can click on the **Compile Project** link, where we have to upload our zip file (the same we got when exporting the game from Construct 2) and check the specific marketplace of choice.

Once the compilation starts, relax and wait: when done, you will be notified by e-mail!

For building and publishing the resulting iOS XCode project or apk file, besides referring to the official Apple and Android documentation available in the respective developers' websites, Ludei has also provided two very helpful tutorials we should definitely check and study carefully: "Using the XCode Project"* and "Creating an Installable Android .apk."†

On a final note, it is worth remembering once again that we are breaking new ground here, and all these technologies and platforms are very new and are evolving very fast, adding and fine-tuning different features all the time.‡ This means they are prone to constant changes and, to remain up to date, it is important to play an active role on the different community forums, like Scirra, Ludei, Clay.io, etc., to be aware of any eventual issues and corresponding fixes as soon as they happen.

---

* http://support.ludei.com/hc/en-us/articles/200924196-Using-the-XCode-Project
† http://support.ludei.com/hc/en-us/articles/200767258-Creating-an-installable-Android-APK
‡ For example, support for the OUYA console and its controller via CocoonJS is currently under development as well.

Appendix A: Resources for Indies

THE FOLLOWING IS A short compendium of resources including graphics, audio, and tools that would be helpful to individual developers and small indie teams to head start their projects (listed in alphabetical order).

A.1 ASSETS: GRAPHICS

- **Clker** (clker.com) contains a huge collection of public domain clip art. Most of the assets for *Turky on the Run* are from this site.

- **HasGraphics** (hasgraphics.com) includes some very nice tile sets and sprite sheets.

- **Mayang's Free Textures** (mayang.com/textures) offers a huge collection of more than 4300 high-quality textures.

- **Open Game Art** (opengameart.org) is an excellent website featuring free sprites and textures suitable for many game genres. It also has a section for music and sound effects.

- **PV Games** (pioneervalleygames.com/free-resources.html) has tiles and sprite sheets suitable for role-playing games and adventure games.

A.2 ASSETS: SOUND EFFECTS AND MUSIC

- **Free Music Archive** (freemusicarchive.org) has free downloads under Creative Commons and other licenses of music across many genres.

- **Free Sound Project** (freesound.org) includes a huge database of Creative Commons licensed sounds.

- **Open Music Archive** (openmusicarchive.org) is a collaborative project to source, digitize, and distribute out-of-copyright sound recordings.

- **Partners in Rhyme** (partnersinrhyme.com) is a well-known collection of royalty-free music and sounds effects.

- **PD Sounds** (pdsounds.org) is a free sound library made of public domain sounds.

- **SFX Source** (sfxsource.com) is a great collection of professional quality special effects; it also includes royalty-free music.

- **Sound Jay** (soundjay.com) is a neat collection of many free and useful sounds; it also includes a few music tracks.

A.3 TOOLS: GRAPHICS

- **Gimp** (gimp.org) is the best free image processing tool. A must have!

- **PFXR** (headchant.com/pfxr/) is a simple random sprite generator, suitable for (very) retro and abstract style games.

- **Pyxel Edit** (pyxeledit.com) is a very useful pixel art and tileset creation tool (free).

- **Spine** (esotericsoftware.com) is a great two-dimensional skeletal animation tool for games. It provides a JavaScript runtime for integration with HTML5 tools like Construct 2 (free trial).

- **Spriter** (brashmonkey.com) is another excellent all-around tool for two-dimensional animation (available in free and pro versions). There is also a Construct 2 plugin.[*]

---

[*] http://www.scirra.com/forum/topic59694.html

A.4 TOOLS: AUDIO

- **Audacity** (audacity.sourceforge.net) is a relatively simple but fully functional digital audio workstation (DAW) for recording and editing sounds and music. Files can be exported in a multitude of formats (free).

- **LMMS** (lmms.sourceforge.net), the "Linux Multi Media Studio" (a version for Windows is also available), is an advanced tool for music production. Create melodies and beats, synthesize and mix sounds, and arrange samples. LMMS supports MIDI keyboards and much more (free).

- **Reaper** (cockos.com/reaper/) is one of the most advanced DAW available (shareware).

- **SFXR** (drpetter.se/project_sfxr.html) is a small, free tool that is worth its bytes in gold. Designing 8-bit style sound effects has never been so easy and fun!

Appendix B: Selected Bibliography for Further Study

THE GAME DESIGN AND development literature has grown significantly during the last few years, and, among the many good books available today, I recommend the following to the serious student who wants to gain an in-depth knowledge of all the different facets of game design.

Books are listed in alphabetical order by author.

Adams, Ernest, *Fundamentals of Game Design*, New Raiders (2009, second edition).
> A step-by-step approach written in a very clear style that covers all important areas, from storytelling and character development to balancing and user interfaces.

Adams, Ernest, *Game Mechanics: Advanced Game Design*, New Raiders (2012).
> A more advanced text introducing design patterns and detailing aspects such as game balancing, economies, and progression.

Brathwaite, Brenda and Ian Schreiber, *Challenges for Game Designers*, Cengage Learning (2008).
> An excellent collection of exercises to build up (board) game prototypes aimed at understanding the core concepts and constraints of game making.

Csikszentmihalyi, Mihaly, *Flow: The Psychology of Optimal Experience*, Harper Perennial Modern Classics (2008).
> The concept of "flow" is central to many discussions in game design circles. This book explains flow and its broad implications in terms accessible to the layman.

Dillon, Roberto, *On the Way to Fun: An Emotion-Based Approach to Successful Game Design*, A K Peters/CRC Press (2010).
> This is the book that introduced the 6-11 framework. Besides a detailed analysis of the theoretical model, it also includes several case studies you can use to practice your analytical skills.

Dillon, Roberto, *The Golden Age of Video Games: The Birthplace of a Multibillion Dollar Industry*, A K Peters/CRC Press (2011).

If you want to know more about how it all began and which games were the most groundbreaking and inspirational in the 8 and 16 bits era, this is a good starting point.

Fullerton, Tracy, *Game Design Workshop: A Playcentric Approach to Creating Innovative Games*, Morgan Kaufmann/CRC Press (2008, second edition).

A comprehensive introduction to all the different phases needed to build up a game, from conceptualization to playtesting and much more. The book stresses the importance of adopting a proper iterative process through the teaching of design fundamentals and hands-on exercises.

Knizia, Reiner, *Dice Games Properly Explained*, Blue Terrier Press (2010).

Understanding how to use dice effectively to establish and manipulate the probability of different events and outcomes is a fundamental aspect in countless games. This book clearly explains many dice-based games whose study would greatly benefit the skills of any game designer.

Koster, Raph, *A Theory of Fun for Game Design*, Paraglyph Press (2004).

A simple but delightful read to remind us all about what really matters for making games fun.

Kremers, Rudolf, *Level Design: Concept, Theory, and Practice*, A K Peters/CRC Press (2009).

Level design is an often overlooked area in game design, so, by explaining good level design practices in general terms and not bound to any specific development tool, this book fills an important void.

Loguidice, Bill and Matt Barton, *Vintage Games: An Insider Look at the History of Grand Theft Auto, Super Mario, and the Most Influential Games of All Time*, Focal Press (2009).

A great read that analyzes several classic games and how they affected the evolution of different genres. Lots of insights and inspirational material here!

Moore, Michael, *Basics of Game Design*, A K Peters/CRC Press (2011).

A comprehensive introduction carefully explaining different genres and the underlying data-driven structures that make them work.

Salen, Katie and Eric Zimmerman, *Rules of Play: Game Design Fundamentals*, MIT Press (2003).

A slightly more scholarly book dissecting games in terms of three fundamental concepts, namely, rules, play, and culture.

Schell, Jesse, *The Art of Game Design: A Book of Lenses*, Morgan Kaufmann/CRC Press (2008).

A modern classic outlining a set of "lenses" to look through for an in-depth understanding of games.

Swink, Steve, *Game Feel: A Game Designer's Guide to Virtual Sensation*, Morgan Kaufmann/CRC Press (2008).

An extremely fascinating discussion of the game feel model of interactivity, a very helpful perspective for creating more engaging and immersive experiences in our games.

Index